CHILDREN

OF THE

FIFTH WORLD

"If you believe that major changes are coming and the children coming into the world are harbingers of those changes—and this has antecedents reaching back thousands of years—then once you pick up this book you won't put it down. I suggest you be careful when you pick it up, because your thinking, and your world, will never be the same. And this will be good, very good, for you and for your—our—world."

ERVIN LASZLO, FOUNDER OF THE CLUB OF BUDAPEST THINK TANK,
TWO-TIME NOMINEE FOR THE NOBEL PEACE PRIZE,
AND AUTHOR OF MORE THAN 80 BOOKS

"In *Children of the Fifth World,* P. M. H. Atwater has contributed a brilliant consideration of fast-forward human evolution. This is the most thorough treatment of the subject of our new children to date! If you are a parent, caregiver, advisor, or working with the Children of Now in any capacity, read this book. It will tell you what is happening, and why it is happening. In a frank no-nonsense way, she challenges every reader to dig a little deeper, try a little harder, and soar beyond social challenges and into collaboration with the children who will ultimately change our world indelibly. How they change it is up to us, and this book will tell you how."

MEG BLACKBURN LOSEY, PH.D., AUTHOR OF
TOUCHING THE LIGHT, THE SECRET HISTORY OF CONSCIOUSNESS,
AND *THE CHILDREN OF NOW*

"Packed with mind-boggling insights, this book is a must-read for parents, educators, and all humans as we ponder how to navigate our fast-changing life on Earth and to respond to the needs of our children. Combining tough talk with uplifting messages, Atwater covers a vast array of challenges and choices with stunning creativity, very much like the new children she is describing."

VIRGINIA COLLIER, PH.D., PROFESSOR EMERITA OF BILINGUAL/
MULTICULTURAL/ESL EDUCATION AT GEORGE MASON UNIVERSITY

"P. M. H. Atwater delivers another brilliant work! Filled with great social commentary on our times, it will give anyone outside this genre food for thought. She details with precision and clarity what we must comprehend about this long-prophesized evolutionary leap humans are now making. This is a must-read guide for the shift into the New World that we have been waiting for!"

JOHN J. OLIVER, PSYCHIC MEDIUM,
STAR OF COURT TV'S AND TRU TV'S *HAUNTING EVIDENCE*

"P.M.H. does not lie when she says there's a youth-quake going on. Today's kids have capabilities and understandings that are way beyond many parents' understanding. These kids have much to teach us if we will only watch, learn, and listen. Finally, we are seeing the evidence of what humanity is *really* capable of. P.M.H.'s 'new kids' books should be required reading for *all* who profess to care about where humanity is heading."

SANDIE SEDGBEER, RADIO HOST AND PUBLISHER OF
CHILDREN OF THE NEW EARTH AND *INSPIRED PARENTING* MAGAZINES

"In this new book Atwater focuses on new children as she describes an increasingly rapid rate of consciousness evolution. With a compendium of behavioral documentation that supports her thesis, she integrates tangible evidence of out-of-body and past-life legacies with esoteric sources to explain this phenomenon. Aware of the needs of these new children, she sagely advises adults to help children balance new technologies with the natural world to support their self-development."

PAUL VON WARD, INTERDISCIPLINARY COSMOLOGIST
AND AUTHOR OF *WE'VE NEVER BEEN ALONE* AND *THE SOUL GENOME*

"Atwater offers solutions for families of why their children are so "different" from her well-researched and disparate facts, which she has synthesized into actionable processes. Modern neuroscience continues to confirm the ancients' innate knowledge regarding 'sound body, sound mind,' and Atwater brings to light the cutting-edge issues in health, environment, and education that the mainstream media tend to ignore. Atwater shows that what looks like a perfect 'pardon our mess' scenario is in reality an entire overhaul of our whole culture."

NANCY K. BAUMGARTEN, MLA, DIRECTOR OF PROFOUND
AWARENESS INSTITUTE AND AUTHOR OF *THE AWARE HUMAN*

CHILDREN
OF THE
FIFTH WORLD

A Guide to the Coming Changes
in Human Consciousness

P. M. H. ATWATER, L.H.D.

Bear & Company
Rochester, Vermont • Toronto, Canada

Bear & Company
One Park Street
Rochester, Vermont 05767
www.BearandCompanyBooks.com

Bear & Company is a division of Inner Traditions International

Library of Congress Cataloging-in-Publication Data
Atwater, P. M. H.
  Children of the fifth world : a guide to the coming changes in human consciousness / P. M. H. Atwater.
    p. cm.
  Includes bibliographical references and index.
  Summary: "Explores how our species is evolving in preparation for the new world on the horizon"—Provided by publisher.
  ISBN 978-1-59143-153-4 (pbk.) — ISBN 978-1-59143-800-7 (e-book)
  1. Children. 2. Consciousness. 3. Human evolution. I. Title.
  HQ767.9.A893 2012
  305.23—dc23
                                                                                    2012016273

Printed and bound in the United States by Versa Press, Inc.

10 9 8 7 6 5 4 3

Text design by Priscilla Baker and layout by Brian Boynton
This book was typeset in Garamond Premier Pro and Legacy Sans with Gill Sans and Golden Cockrel used as display typefaces

To send correspondence to the author of this book, mail a first-class letter to the author c/o Inner Traditions • Bear & Company, One Park Street, Rochester, VT 05767, and we will forward the communication, or contact the author directly at **www.pmhatwater.com**.

***To children everywhere:** Thank you for being here. No matter how long you stay, we are glad you were born and we are grateful for your energy, your thoughts, your breath.*

***To my own children and grandchildren:** You are each a special blessing and a warm heart of love, hugs, and kisses. I am so grateful to be a part of your life and to have you be in mine.*

***Extra thanks to the following, without whose help this book would never have happened:** Terry Atwater, Stephanie Wiltse, Art Yensen, William G. Reimer, Roger Pile, Joseph Chilton Pearce, Linda Silverman, Betty Maxwell, Robert Silverstein*

No one has captured life's truth about children better than Kahlil Gibran in his masterpiece *The Prophet:*

> *Your children are not your children.*
> *They are the sons and daughters of Life's longing for itself.*
> *They come through you but not from you.*

CONTENTS

PREFACE

The subject of our newer generations and our changing world snuck up on me. For the past thirty-three years I have been busily pursuing a deeper and clearer understanding of the near-death phenomenon, what it is, how it affects the people who experience it, and the changes that result—in both adults and children. I have written ten books on my findings, including the latest, and I feel my best, *Near-Death Experiences: The Rest of the Story*.[1]

I quickly noticed in my work a similarity in altered behaviors and character traits between children who were near-death experiencers and kids who were naturally born with the same distinctive patterning. Why, I wondered, were near-death kids so much like our newest generation of children—especially those born since around 1982?

The New Children and Near-Death Experiences (the book that replaced *Children of the New Millennium*) was not only the first book to examine children's cases from the eyes of the child; it was also my initial attempt to find a link between the behavior differences I kept seeing and the possibility of evolution, that the human race was changing as a species . . . right under our very noses.[2] This was global and, I felt, important.

Beyond the Indigo Children was an exposé of sorts, my way of showing the utter uselessness of labels like *indigo, crystal, starseed, cosmic, rainbow,* and *psychic*.[3] Whether from channeling, visions, or dreamwork, most of these label claims do not hold up to careful research. Toss the labels, I advised in the book; then I promptly turned around and invented another one—*ascended blues*—to make a point. I apologize for that. It was a silly thing to do.

This time, for the third in what has become a series of books, I intend to cut to the chase and tackle the fuller story of what is happening to our children, our species, our world. Yes, we really are witnessing evolution at work. Yes, it is stressful and exciting and frightening. And it's absolutely necessary that we look at the *whole picture,* not just the parts we prefer or were channeled by angels. I respect all forms of information, but consider of value only those that can be verified and tested through multiple sources over time.

If you have read any of my books on near-death research, you know that my protocol is that of police investigative techniques. I'm a cop's kid, raised in a police station, where I saw the value of field-work firsthand and absorbed my father's teaching of how to utilize such information. I was also raised by the Spirit Keepers of Idaho's deserts and canyons and grew up able to merge into rock walls—as if passing through the rock itself—as easily as I could bake bread. What we regard today as the polarity between left- and right-brain functions was nowhere to be seen in my world. Let's just say I had an unusual childhood, made even more unusual by my determination to become an objective, logical adult who "lost it" when I died three times in three months in 1977 and experienced a different near-death state each time. Know, then, that information sources in this book will be as varied as my life has been . . . and always was.

I said I intend to tackle the fuller story of what is happening to our children, our species, our world. Count on it. I am a woman of my word.

P. M. H.

Introduction

Setting the Stage

In my end is my beginning.
T. S. Eliot

Priest and scientist Teilhard de Chardin predicted the emergence of a new species (or type of human), one that is more elevated in consciousness, more aware of the innate divine nature, at this turning of the Great Cycles. So did sage Sri Aurobindo and psychic Edgar Cayce and every notable visionary and seer going back as far as we have records for. Mayan peoples, as well as the Hopi, Zulu, Hindu, Inca, Aztec, Dogon, Pueblo, Cherokee, Algonquin, Tibetan, Egyptian, Babylonian, Eastern Indian, Aborigine, and others have creation myths and calendar renderings that map out evolutionary changes in the human species, climate and environment, and social and living structures that correspond—with little or no cross influence—in a kind of precision unknown today.

We are fixed on one of these, the Mayan calendar (long count), without realizing that this so-called calendar is actually a tracking device to show how consciousness develops in the earth plane overtime. This sundial artifact places our current passage as the Fifth Sun or Fifth World (not Sixth, as some claim), and does not indicate what's next, except to suggest that this sundial's cosmology eventually wraps back or folds back to its beginning—a sweep in an upward energy spiral—as do most ancient calendar maps. Interestingly, the majority of other creation/calendar myth maps also refer to our current time as the fifth turning of the Cosmic Wheel (similar to that of the Mayan).

No matter what you read now, be it the *New York Times* or *Newsweek* or the latest predictions from best-known psychics and mediums, you encounter the same themes: kids today are different and they are driving their parents nuts, education has failed us, climate upheavals are nothing short of biblical, every country and every government and every religion and every culture and all peoples are either panicking from austerity changes necessary to survive or from cultural and behavioral switches that occur quicker than services and industries can support. Privacy is no more, as people and countries are quickly becoming transparent. Communication is instantaneous. What we thought was true yesterday changed today. Why, then, am I even bothering to write this book? Tim O'Reilly of O'Reilly Media flat-out states that many of our existing publishers will go out of business. "People don't care about books (or other packaging). They care about ideas."[1]

O'Reilly is right on. And that's why I bother: ideas.

Tucked into every page of every chapter ahead of you are ideas and challenges presented primer style. Pared down for fast, easy reading are such subjects as the new kids, root races, evolutionary aspects, birth and growing up, the brain, the pattern of characteristics, education, health issues, sex, entertainment, digital worlds, creativity/intuition, humanitarians, the environment, communities, jobs, politics/governments, religion/spirituality, social revolutions, terrorism, the march of generations, a biological imperative, the Great Shifting, datelines, life as movement through a grand plan.

It is fair to say that the material gathered for the ideas that follow came from sources both broad and far-flung, as research based as they are centered in mass mind (the confluence of mind energy said to surround Earth and all living things). Many bits of information can be traced back to the morning news we hear on TV as we prepare for the day, on the radio on our commute to work, or the daily e-mail newsletters we subscribe to. We are all affected by this bombardment of information, even if we don't recall the original source. As a result, endnotes might be a little sparse in some areas, but this doesn't diminish their accuracy.

Clearly, evolution is "stacking the deck," forcing us to find ways of living beyond the struggle and crush of polarities. Our children, in league with the situation at hand, are arriving with their DNA encoded as if they were mirrors reflecting back to us every nuance of feeling and relationship imaginable—every aspect of business, culture, politics, religion, entertainment, invention—so we don't miss a single thing. The *end of things* we are now witnessing, the ultimate battle between good and evil, is an awakening to what we see in the mirrors our children provide. We have come to this . . . a chance to start over, to repair and rewrite history.

1   Tossing Labels

God does not call the qualified; God qualifies the called.

Author unknown

Specifics on how children in the human family are changing actually went viral in the public's mind nearly two hundred years ago. But it wasn't until the 1960s and '70s that people took such alerts seriously. Then, as the twenty-first century rolled in, channelings from famous psychics along with best-selling authors announced, "The indigos are here." The color indigo (a deep blue) did appear in the aura (energy field) of a number of children in California. An indigo aura, in esoteric traditions, is said to be indicative of an individual who is wiser and more spiritual than others, someone who is highly intuitive, creative, possessed of knowing, and able to see beyond the "veil" into the invisible worlds of spirit. Should the energy of indigo manifest in a negative manner, it is the sign of a sociopath or one who is amoral.

In a flash, these kids were everywhere, along with the description of other colors and related types variously named *crystal, starseed, rainbow, psychic,* and *cosmic children*. Parents pulled their hair. Educators blinked. Scientists shook their heads—as most of the medical claims supporting their differences either could not be replicated in peer-reviewed studies or were found faulty to begin with—especially stories of how these wunderkinds born with HIV/AIDS cured themselves. As of this writing, all such claims have been proven false.

I mean it when I said folks went nuts. Married women left their husbands and went chasing after teenage indigo boys. Crowds started to hang on every word the kids spoke, almost worshipping these new paragons from God Almighty. Cottage industries sprang up: indigo music, indigo clothing, indigo books, indigo jewelry. Indigo anything became a cash cow. A female star from a movie about them kept insisting, even years later, that she was no indigo, but her mother would just smile and say, "She's so humble." Claims were topped off with "proof" of how evolved these kids were: wildlife would come to them; nature would bend to them; the sick were healed by them; miracles spiraled out from their every word, deed, and wave of the hand; they knew the future and could see right through you. Few listened when I said, "These kids are just like children who have had a near-death experience. No difference."

I want to take a moment to thank the originators of the indigo movement—all the psychics, mediums, ministers, and parents, even the media who bought into the whole thing. You caught our attention. You showed us that something profound was happening right under our noses: our children were beginning to change, alter, and evolve. Our kids were as if new—maybe not a new race, but a new version of what the human species is and can be. Truly like near-death kids, only these youngsters were born that way. . . . And the phenomenon is global.

Where the early prognosticators messed up was in the labeling. Once we categorize kids like that, we force them into exclusive "boxes" of specialness or handicap; we deny them the incredible quirkiness they display as a collective. We hurt, not help, who and what they are. Take the labels—indigo, crystal, starseed, rainbow, cosmic, psychic—and toss them, every one of them. And so too those additional labels of indigo adults and indigo grandparents/golden indigos. Even the ascended blue concoction I invented for *Beyond the Indigo Children*. Really silly of me.

Now take all the characteristics each category was said to describe, bunch them together, and you have a profile of what is really happening to the human family. We are evolving. We are becoming new.

2 THE NEW CHILDREN

Everyone has been made for some particular work, and the desire for that work has been put in our hearts.

RUMI

Now that I've got your attention, let's get to it.

PUTTING THINGS IN PERSPECTIVE

Let's linger briefly on this stuff about auras and energy colors, just for a little perspective. The color of one's aura (energy field) changes during a lifetime. That's why identifying someone accordingly can be a mistake. Although one main background color usually stays the same (matching the basic energy factors of individual personality, attitudes, and sense of purpose), even that can morph as one's choices and life experiences take him or her in different directions. Even a momentary switch of emotions—how we feel—can shift an aura's coloring for a while. And there are levels to the energy of one's aura, like sheaths or transparencies of varying hues, blends, and imagery said to emanate from the four fields that make up the self: *physical*—temperature, odor, density factors, and electromagnetics (all of which are measurable scientifically); *emotional*—feelings, sensations, attachments, expressions (all of which are automatically sensed or felt organically); *mental*—thoughts, ideas, perception, memory (all of which are analyzed and processed intellectually); and *spiritual*—insight, wisdom, knowing, creativity (all of which transcend avenues of definability).

By having an appreciation of our biofield of electromagnetic energy, we can have a better sense of self and the world around us. We can also become more sensitive to the sweep of history and the various "road maps" that our forebearers left us. In this book, *devolution* describes the descent of spirit from "Central Authority" to human (rolling down), while *involution* covers the trip of spirit from humankind back to Central Authority (rolling up). *Evolution*, our topic, addresses spirit formation on the earth plane (development over time).

Humankind has changed quite considerably in each evolutionary phase we have record of. And that is happening again now. The new pattern—a basic profile of characteristics the vast majority of our children are manifesting worldwide—looks like this, on both the plus and minus sides.

BASIC PROFILE ON THE PLUS SIDE

Intelligent (even if flunking in school and can't spell)
About one-third are geniuses, even if "learning disabled"
Music oriented; very rhythmic
Clever innovators and inventors
Unusually creative; spiritually minded
Intuitive, psychic; many can remember past lives
Excellent with math (don't let them fool you about this)
Natural healers
Ready-to-go entrepreneurs
Irreverent, quirky ideas and unique beliefs
Visionary problem solvers; knowing
Volunteer minded, humanitarians
Groupies who move as if part of a collective
Often attend night "school," not a dream but a school on another
    plane where kids go to learn, in addition to dreaming
Abstract at very young ages; spatial learners

Fusion of sexes and gender mixing

Multisensory multichannelers who live in a multiverse

BASIC PROFILE ON THE MINUS SIDE

Impulsive and impatient—quick-click kids

Feel entitled, overconfident

Ultimate consumers

Underlying anger; little tolerance for deceit and manipulation

Prefer astral and synthetic worlds

Highly sensitive to drugs, snack and processed foods, metals

Highly sensitive to electromagnetic fields, toxic and incoherent energy (from electronic devices such as computers and cell phones)

Do not assimilate nutrition well

No concept of authority; need mentors, not bosses

Appear wiser than they are; self-deception an issue

Sensitive to "trickster" energy, possession, energy attachments (whatever energies, good or bad, that are present)

Do not understand the effort necessary to process or refine

Expect things to come to them

Do not recognize boundaries, even that of skin

Clothes are more important than language skills

Their greatest fear: silence

WHERE THEY FIT IN HISTORY

The "new" kids really are not new. You can trace the previous basic profile to certain peoples from around the time when Jesus walked the Earth, and some even earlier in history. Every renaissance the world has ever known saw clusters of them. (Where should we suppose the mysterious energy, vision, and drive for each renaissance came from in the first place?) In the 1800s, however, larger groupings were noted, especially from around 1840 to about 1921. This time period saw the rise of the New Thought movement (a response to restrictive religions, strongly based on the individual right to self-healing and direct revelation), Theosophy (an intuitive view of hidden truths and higher orders of spirit involvement), and metaphysics or First Cause (with an emphasis on the *perennial philosophy* of one God, one people, one family, one existence: *oneness*—the underlying unity of all things, as true in mathematics as in spirituality).

You can always recognize when this particular profile of characteristics infuses the newly born and overshadows their maturity. Not only do they challenge the norm; they transform entire social, political, and financial structures in ways not seen before, always pushing for more inclusive, open, and freer lifestyles. And they are decidedly reckless and provocative. If you're thinking that waves of them entered the earth plane during the 1960s and '70s, you're right: these were the flower children opposed to war and singing loudly about the Age of Aquarius and showers of "diamonds" (drugs).

Floodgates didn't open wide, though, until around 1982, when surge after surge of these children were born. That surge has not abated, nor will it. The new children are here to stay. They are the quantum leap in evolution that we have been promised. As their numbers increase, the world as we know it will disappear.

3 THE FIFTH ROOT RACE

Many prophesies in the indigenous world speak of this time in human history as a period of great transformation. Through this great transformation, a new human is emerging on the earth. I call this new human "homo luminous."

ALBERTO VILLOLDO, PH.D.[1]

There's no getting around it: this sense of destiny permeates the young adults, teenagers, and children of our world. And there's no culture or society devoid of sacred stories that predicted this Fifth Root Race.

ROOT RACES

The term *root races* refers to the gene pool of the human family. In older, esoteric literature and in legend, terms like *life streams, life waves, new people,* or even *advanced beings* were used to describe groups of folks who were decidedly different from their parents and grandparents. The larger the group, the more assuredly they bore the mark of evolution—physiological and psychological traits characteristic of gene mutation. DNA changes over time as a result of how people respond to the needs and stressors of their environment; these changes can be accelerated if transformative events, such as near-death experiences, jumpstart the evolutionary process. When DNA changes overspread land masses, a genetic "makeover"—a species-wide alteration—can occur. That shift is now happening. Think of it as an update within the human family.

In the late 1800s, during the early days of Theosophy, people like Helena Petrovna Blavatsky, C. W. Leadbeater, and Lieutenant Colonel Arthur E. Powell rocked the world with visions, channelings, and revelations about spiritual hierarchy, soul advancement, intricacies of manifestation, and how God's great plan for us actually worked. Theosophy, as a society devoted to spiritual teachings about a higher order of ensoulment, still flourishes today.[2]

THE SEVEN ROOT RACE EVOLUTIONARY PROGRESSIONS

All early cultures and indigenous groups told stories and had prophesies about times of radical earth changes and the emergence of a more intelligent, capable human. These cycles of destruction and upliftment were progressive and followed a general pattern everywhere they were present—as if such teachings were part of a grand plan. The seven progressions described in Theosophy are similar to this ancient library of information, so we'll start with them.[3]

+ *First Root Race*—Etheric, began about eighteen million years ago as the entry of spirit into matter.
+ *Second Root Race*—Hyperborean, began about eight million years ago, with early physical forms and gender differences, centered in what is today the Arctic and northern climes.
+ *Third Root Race*—Lemurian and Mu, began about 1 million years ago; full flowering of genders and racial groupings with the introduction of darker skins, movement to southern regions and the Indian and Pacific oceans.
+ *Fourth Root Race*—Atlantean, began about 85,000 BCE in the

Azores and the lands now lying beneath the Atlantic Ocean; progenitor of modern body types (including what supposedly became the first Adam).

+ *Fifth Root Race*—Aryan, began 10,000 BCE to 3000 BCE with right-brained megalithic cultures and from 3000 BCE to 2400 CE with left-brained modern cultures (consciousness that separated into two hemispheres—East and West—now fusing back together; a global leap in species refinement).

+ *Sixth Root Race*—Originally unnamed but now called Aurorean, begins around 2400 to 3000 CE, centered in North America and Europe (fuses all global patterns into one planetary consciousness).

+ *Seventh Root Race*—Unnamed, begins 7000 to 8000 CE and centered in South America; graduated from any necessity for earth-plane schools; perhaps etheric in nature, with a different means of reproduction and growth.

FROM THE PSYCHIC READINGS OF EDGAR CAYCE

In addition to Theosophy's version of the Root Race concept, there are others that have some timetable variations. This one is from the psychic readings of the late Edgar Cayce, one of the most documented and studied of all psychics.[4] Although he never went in-depth about the subject, he did sketch a general evolutionary model that goes something like this:

+ First Root Race (*initial creation of humans*)—began about 4.5 billion years ago as spiritual, free-will companions of God, who projected themselves into the denser world of matter because of a curiosity about how things worked.

+ Second Root Race (*fluid, ethereal beings*)—began about 12 million years ago. Created and came to embody humanoid life forms of a lower vibration. Androgynous; could move in and out of form. Began to gather in communities around the Pacific Ocean.

+ Third Root Race (*retained some spiritual power*)—began 200,000 years ago. Still androgynous but no longer able to come and go at will. Lived long lives. Created hybrid beings—half animal/half human, part plant/part human. Became the Atlanteans. About 108,000 BCE genders developed and a new physical body evolved. Hybrids disappear. Communities became more common.

+ Fourth Root Race (*the origin of the five races/five senses*)—began between 90,000 and 12,000 BCE. Red race developed in Atlantis (specialized in feeling/touch); white race around Ararat, the Carpathians, Iran (associated with vision/sight); yellow race in the Gobi area of China (associated with hearing); black race in African Sudan and Egypt (associated with taste); brown race in the Andes area of South America (associated with smell). Progenitor of the history and culture known today.

+ Fifth Root Race (*lighter bodies, cosmic-conscious minds*)—began during the closing years of the Mayan calendar, between 1998 and 2015 CE. Described in the Book of Revelation as a time when "Satan will be bound" for a thousand years. The indication here is that the human species will flower as never before and achieve great heights of knowledge, invention, and spiritual growth.

In none of Cayce's voluminous readings did he ever mention anything about a Sixth or Seventh Root Race. Nobody knows why. Statements he made about the Fifth Root Race—beginning now, during our current time frame—were specific about how intelligent and intuitive we would become.

SUMMARY: ESOTERIC TEACHINGS OF SOUL EVOLUTION

An amalgam follows of what can be gleaned from the ancient library of oral history, relics, symbols, legends, stories, and the kinds of memories we often label visions or knowings. The concept of something like Root Races in the evolutionary development of the human species is so old there is no way to trace its beginnings. Traditionally, colors were used to show how energy altered from one progression to the next, indicating changes in vibratory frequency and the aura's stage.

Think of each of these as a particular life stream/Root Race. Each life stream/Root Race builds on the last one, strengthening the basic components of what can be accomplished in and through form. The

Root Race/Color	Awareness	Focus
Red	Physical world	The earth plane and survival issues; individual power
Orange	Astral world	The invisible "blueprints" of spirit; heightened senses; inner guidance
Yellow	Mental/Reasoning	Intellect and decision making; personal will
Green	Mental/Abstract	Awakening to spirit, initial enlightenment/innovation; enlarged worldview
Blue	Higher intuition	Creativity, knowing, and wisdom; self as individual
Indigo	Inspiration	Collective, indivisible whole; self-contained, fully individuated
Violet	Spiritual	Alignment with soul power, surrender to the Divine/God's will

understanding has always been that the universe has a plan for the race's existence, and that plan is the manifestation of consciousness as an ever-present, expanding reality.

I am especially mindful of what the theosophical rendering pointed out for the Fifth Root Race: *consciousness separated into two hemispheres—East and West—now fusing back together; a global leap in species refinement.* This is exactly what I have discovered in my research. The Fifth Root Race is not just another step up some kind of cosmic ladder. It is a pivotal shift in who and what we are as human beings. The success or failure of human ensoulment is said to occur at this level of evolutionary growth.

Already the unique characteristics of the new kids have produced exceptional geniuses, psychotic killers, gifted artists, enraged bullies, spirit-led cripples . . . each possessing *the same overall pattern of traits.* We tend to forget that "when the tide comes in, *all* boats rise."

4

BIRTH BUMPS

A new light is coming into the world. We are on the borderland of a new experience.

ERNEST HOLMES

The topic of evolution in our time is so new, we have yet to grasp what the early models are indicating. Evidence is one thing; meaning is another. For the remainder of this book, I'll jump, hopscotch style, from topic to topic, laying the groundwork for reexamining who we are as humans, how we are changing, and where we are headed within what is called the Great Shifting.

This chapter wraps around beginnings, the here and now of womb issues and an array of birth bumps (jarring surprises) that require the kind of wake-up call no pediatrician or priest will ever give you. Specifics of what follows come from research findings on the near-death phenomenon and similar states,[1] along with results of studies conducted on babies and small children.

YES, YOU HAVE A SOUL

That driving spirit that animates us is our soul. Invisible to most, the soul's essence is light and its power comes from that spark of divinity infused by the fire of its creation, or the creative force of God/Allah/ The Divine (same Source, regardless of name). Physicians in the early

1900s weighed some patients before and immediately after death and found an inexplicable weight loss of about one ounce. Compare that to what today's computer chips can hold—almost limitless data at a small fraction of that size—and then ask yourself, How much more could an ounce carry? The realm of the soul and how it functions will become a research priority in the years to come.

IN THE WOMB

Tradition tells us that the soul enters the baby's body at birth. Well, not always. The soul can hover around soon-to-be parents for months on end, can participate at conception in choosing needed genes for what it wants to accomplish in this life, and appear in what the psychological community calls the announcing dreams of mothers. The fetus at between six and seven months in utero can not only experience REM-state dream episodes and feel pain; it is also aware of happenings outside its womb cradle, as well as parental thoughts and feelings. It can respond to threats (like parental upset, fights, abortion plans) as if *fully aware*. Language centers open up during this same time frame, enabling the audible vibration of the "mother tongue" to affect the formation of brain structures, brain functions, the nervous system, and body rhythms throughout the rest of the gestation period.

The temporal lobes of the brain (located on either side of the head near the temples) activate *before* birth. These "libraries" of the basic patterning for shapes, forms, feelings, smells, and sounds enable the newly born to be far more aware and prepared for the world around them than presently believed. From birth to not quite six, kids match this basic template with actualities in the physical world they have entered. Sometimes the patterning matches (which leads to early expressions of confidence and courage), and sometimes it doesn't (leading to some confusion, maybe fear). I believe these libraries account for why so many near-death experiencers who were born blind have full vision during their episodes and recognize colors and details of shape as if they had once been sighted.

Traits acquired in one generation *from what was learned during that individual's life* can be passed on to the generations who follow. Today's findings suggest that even illnesses like diabetes, obesity, cardiovascular disease, and breast cancer can have their roots *before* birth and not be tagged solely to lifestyle issues.[2] Might this somehow reflect soul memory? Or a life at odds or in alignment with its purpose? Will these findings alter the way we regard handicaps? Since an unusually high number of the new children are either being born with or later developing serious health problems, questions like these are all-important. There is always another side to what seems obvious.

Fact: every child born today carries a body burden of at least forty-three chemicals, some toxic. Because of dust storms, depleted uranium has spread worldwide, adding strontium 90 to every cell and bone. Some chemicals in our environment are estrogenlike, disrupting the development of the male reproductive system. Common products known to consist of chemicals that can directly affect the unborn include non-stick cookware, processed foods, personal-care products (such as certain soaps, toiletries, sprays, fragrant sanitizers), epoxy resins used to line the inside of metal food and beverage cans, pesticides, and certain plastics. It's time to get fussy about food, air, water, soil. Go organic if possible. Eat local produce/meats or grow them yourself. Use common sense instead of coupons. Being able to meet our basic needs will become vital in the years to come in *every* country because of weather, volcanism, oil prices, and political unrest.

MESSING WITH BIRTH

One woman still dies of childbirth each minute of every day. The plagues of poverty, HIV/AIDS, malaria, and tuberculosis, as well as where you live and what religion you believe in make even being pregnant, much less the actual birth, dangerous. The shame of these preventable deaths will force major changes in birthing measures. Don't be smug if you live in a richer nation. Birth has always been, still is, and will always be death for women in the sense that the old version of self gives way to a new version (more mature, more giving). Between 70 and 75 percent of the near-death episodes that happen to women occur during childbirth or hysterectomies. The significance of womb issues as a rite of passage applies to women who adopt or use surrogates, as well.

An unhealthy trend: choosing the best day and time for a baby's birth with astrology, or electing the date and time according to the doctor's convenience or the family's wishes. The resulting Cesarean delivery can cause fetal distress and birth defects. And it messes with karma (the law of cause and effect) and the will of the soul. Planned births usually occur between 8:00 a.m. and 5:00 p.m., skewing the random placement of planets in a person's chart. French researchers and statisticians Michel and Françoise Gauquelin found in a study of more than sixty thousand births that certain planetary placements were inherited and that *these planetary effects disappeared in children whose births did not occur naturally.*[3]

Stop for a moment. Look at that again. When you mess around with a child's birth, you risk interfering with the spiritual plan for the child, his or her growth and purpose in life. Plus, the child could be removed from the family's karmic line. Admitted or not, family groupings are no accident. Slanting life trajectories in this manner could backfire and wind up affecting society in ways we cannot fathom. Sometimes C-sections are necessary to save lives. But to plan them based solely on convenience or desired outcome runs counter to wisdom.

FETAL ABUSE

We don't use the term *fetal abuse*—but we should. The unborn are at risk in ways we prefer to ignore, giving rise to birth defects and preemies. In reality, the leading causes of fetal abuse are:

+ Infertility treatments used in older mothers (generally, over age thirty-five)

+ Either parent being hooked on drugs (Did you know that a male who takes cocaine ejaculates toxins from the drug along with his sperm during intercourse?)
+ Mothers who smoke or drink alcoholic beverages
+ Infectious diseases, mostly in Africa and Asia; this has a direct bearing on a baby's intelligence
+ Religious sects that make little or no provision to feed, educate, or employ their populations (About half the population in countries dominated by Islam are under the age of twenty-five; this baby boom is proving to be a problem.)

A bright spot: the majority of the new children have a strong sense of social responsibility. They couple easily but are far less likely to rush having children of their own. Many expect to be childless. They are more inclined than previous generations to form extended families in the sense of supportive community. Even if they had a typical birth in a typical family, they tend to view their family's lineage differently, as if it has little meaning for them, is somehow objectionable, or doesn't apply.

MAYBE IT'S IN THE GENES, AND MAYBE IT'S NOT

Claims of "pink brain" (girls) and "blue brain" (boys) are falling apart. We are not born with strong tendencies toward either maleness or femaleness. Children settle into sex-based play preferences at around age one, when they grasp what sex they are and identify with others like them. How we treat our children and what we expect of them is proving to be stronger than DNA. The idea that the larger band of connecting fibers between the left and right brain hemispheres of women means that they are better at holistic thinking than men has also been overturned. Concepts of masculine and feminine are proving to be more pliable than physical "plumbing." The new children know this is true; parents still do not.

The link between DNA and altruism is true. The desire to be charitable, cooperative, and help each other is inborn. We start out that way at first breath; exceptions are rare (unless the parents are drug abusers, which, unfortunately, is a widespread issue—whether it's Prozac or heroin). Watch how this altruism trait soars dramatically in the decades to come. Our new children operate as if a collective. They think in terms of we, not I.

GLITCHES IN STARTING OUT

Here are some shockers:

+ Children as young as twelve months emulate behavior they see on television. (*Never* put either a television set or a computer in a child's bedroom.)
+ Television as a "background noise" in the home retards the mental development of toddlers; they do not engage the mental muscles they need to concentrate and solve problems.
+ Chronic depression is now found in children as young as three. Even in grade school, depression and lack of sleep are major factors in learning.
+ Obesity in three-year-olds, particularly a problem in Hispanic and black poplulations, is beginning to spike in other racial and ethnic groups too.
+ Toddlers should *never* walk around with a cup of juice in their hands. When they do, they drink way too much. Too much juice can physically change their taste buds to prefer excessive sweets.
+ Language skills are established by the age of three. Read to your kids!
+ Baby DVDs created for infants between eight and sixteen months, to enhance their cognitive abilities, actually lower intelligence and the ability to understand words. This is the boomerang effect of too much too soon.
+ *Never* allow your child to be implanted with an under-the-skin

identity microchip. This can subject them to unwanted microwave frequencies with unknown consequences.

+ Make changes in the home or try natural remedies before you try to change the child with drugs like psychotropics (be they antidepressants or stimulants).

+ You can legally avoid all unwanted immunizations you and your doctor don't believe are necessary. (See www.mercola.com/ article/vaccines/legally_avoid_shots.htm for more details.)

+ Many toys today are X-rated, teaching sexiness to the very young. Images and behaviors like this increase the risk for a child to be a victim of a pedophile. Children do not know the difference between the signals they are encouraged to exhibit and the danger this exposes them to.

+ Preschool curricula for two- and three-year-olds are not as important as helping the child to feel safe and well cared for. Preschool should teach how to engage with teachers and other kids, and little else.

Our new children and their parents face a stacked deck of challenges never encountered before in recorded history. This is new territory, so let's dissect the general patterning of these challenges and see what we can discover and which solutions we can create.

5 OFF AND RUNNING

*If we love a child, and the child senses from our
relationships with others that we love them, he (she) will
get a concept of love that all the subsequent hatred in the
world will never be quite able to destroy.*

HOWARD THURMAN

Meet today's family: gay men with adopted children, lesbian women with
children fathered by a sperm donor or by gay men who are willing to have
blended families, children with one parent (divorced, separated, or never
married), mixed-race and -religion groupings, children raised by grandparents, an adopted child with a single parent, fathers much younger than
mothers, military parents absent from their children's lives for months at
a time, adopted kids of multiple ethnicities/countries/health needs in a
single family, test tube and surrogate children "arranged for" by one or
more parents, couples taking on the care of foster kids by the dozens.

Today, the ideas of a married dad who is male and a mother who is
female and who have children, or children who are biologically related
to a given family are not only fast becoming a rarity, but also no longer
apply to the majority of households.

Love, not genetics or inheritance, is now the single unifying factor
in families. Is love enough? It does not stave off hunger: according to a
study reported in the November 2009 issue of *Archives of Pediatrics and
Adolescent Medicine,* nearly half the children in the United States will

be on food stamps at some point during childhood (with blacks, it's 90 percent).[1] It does not provide basic needs: record numbers of children have been abandoned, many of their homes are in foreclosure, essential services and social programs are being cut. Poverty has achieved "middle-class" status here, the richest nation on earth.

Dare we admit it? Large numbers of our new children are being born into extreme hardships, abusive families, and painful life-shattering situations. Is their cup half-empty or half-full? Both.

Every child in every country has been lifted by the tide of change. One-third are so exceptional in their intelligence and their abilities that they defy how we categorize and educate the young. The rest are equally unique. All of this irrespective of environments and parentage. Give them the right kind of food (avoid too much fat, sugar, and processed foods) before the age of three, and give them a safe home, friends, playtime, puzzles to think through, and the type of love they can understand and respond to, and they will grow up miracle kids. Deep within them, encoded in their very DNA, is a driving energy that will either help them re-create and remodel the world or drive them to explode with anger governmental bodies are not prepared to handle. Make no mistake. These children are willing to die to get what they want: freedom.

No other generation except theirs views the world first through a screen. Cell phones, smart phones, iPads, computers, television . . . all screens. Hence, their mind-set is global and they think in multiples or grids. Imagery, virtual realities, and digital worlds are their comfort zone; nature is a foreign object. Because they are so capable, so quick, we cram more into their young lives than is healthy or appreciated.

David Elkind, Ph.D., a professor of child development at Tufts University and author of *The Hurried Child,* noted that "children have lost twelve hours of free time a week, including eight hours of unstructured play and outdoor activities. The health impact of the disappearance of play is already apparent: 13% of our children are obese. But equally troubling is the way this lack of play stunts children's emotional, behavioral, and even their intellectual growth."[2]

What toys do our children have? Since so many of them are X-rated, the "old stuff," like activities that promote the fun of free thinking and free play, creativity, and storytelling, are now superimportant. They become even more significant when you realize that the greatest truths throughout history have been preserved by the symbolism in children's stories and games. Hopscotch, for instance, is a representation of the ancient Kabbalah (book devoted to Jewish mystical teachings). The layout of the game with its circles and lines resembles the Kabbalistic Tree of Life. As children hop between doubles and singles, to the top and back down again, they are connected to ancient wisdom. Great truths such as these are the backbone to spirituality and the "bread and butter" of childhood. Pull kids away from play that is natural for them and you separate them from their very spirit.

Get the book *Awakening the Hidden Storyteller: How to Build a Storytelling Tradition in Your Family* by Robin Moore.[3] If you learn the mechanics behind the magic of storytelling, you can use stories as a parenting tool and as a way to hold families together. Stories preserve history; the telling of them is an act of faith and of love. But there's a whole lot more to this art form. Moore clues us in with this astute observation: "Storytelling is a technique that was developed 50,000 years ago to allow humans to enter the dreaming state while they're awake." Being awake in a dream gives one the ability to recognize and then own authentic power, and to develop on a conscious level the ability to know and to participate in that knowing with clarity and courage.

See what I mean about the importance of play and storytelling? Engage children in both and you automatically reassure them that it's okay to share their reality. Do this, create a space in your family for spontaneity, feelings, creativity, and imagination (the products of play and storytelling), and you will unleash a knowing in your children that will apply as much to mathematics as to healing. Our new children do not understand what boundaries are, nor do they understand limits. Teaching them this will require creative reasoning—on the part of adults.

Let's eavesdrop on Jessica. She is seven years old and her mother is recording what she says. Both have given me permission to share this with you.

> *I told my friend Andrea to sit down, put her feet flat on the ground, and to close her eyes, and so she did it. I told her to feel all of the love from her friends and family . . . breathe deeply. I told her to let everything that was bad out her toes, fingers, or anything, and so she did it. Then she opened her eyes and all her tightness and bad stuff was out, and she felt better. Andrea said that it works for her and she is going to try it when she is tense. Plus the colors . . . I just look at the top of heads . . . my friends and mom and dad. I see colored halos. Right now my mom has blue-green-purple and purple colors, and it means that she is tired and happy. I know that because that is how those colors make me feel. I think I remember Andrea's, and hers was purple, green, blue, and pink—and that means she is super happy. They all go together to make a puzzle of emotions. My dad's first three colors were red, red, red, but I can't remember the last one. They kind of mean sort of happy and stressed and tired. Also I'm listening to your song . . . my mom's CD of your soul. It makes me feel better when I am sad or angry. It lets all my bad stuff go out my head or toes.*

Children are attuned to the reality of Creation. They think in images as well as words and use their whole bodies, all their sensory/ motor skills, to connect with and explore nonverbally. They must dance around, taste, touch, smell, hear, focus on, and study each aspect of what is around them. And that includes the electromagnetic spectrum—the energy world that eludes most adults. Jessica could see auras and knew inside her deepest self what each color meant and how to use that knowledge to help others. With her mother's encouragement, she has learned to trust her knowing and to respect what others might call dreamy nonsense.

A teenager has this to say:

My name is Cecelia Stebbins. I am fourteen years old and homeschooled. I am very different. When my mom started reading [the second book you wrote about the new kids], it was scary how everything you talked about matched up to me. I'm very mature for my age (as you can probably tell), and I want to know what I can do to find more out about myself, like maybe seeking a spiritual advisor, or ????

Here's a few of my experiences. When I was three years old my great-grandmother was very sick. So one day I went into my bedroom and started to pray (I didn't know why; I just had the urge). My mom walked in and asked, "Honey, what are you doing?" I replied "I'm praying for Grandma. She's going to die." About thirty minutes later we got a phone call and my great-grandma had just passed away. Note: nobody had ever talked to me about praying or God prior to that. I swear I can also remember when I was three days old, I had an upper GI done because I had sensitive reflux. My mom also asked me if I could remember being in the womb, and I swear I can remember it was dark and warm, and I can also remember being born. I didn't cry. I was just curious . . . just wanted to see everybody.

Cecelia is typical of our new children. If you talk with them before they get involved with school, most are very open about what it was like in the womb and being born. Few I've spoken with enjoyed their birth; most complained about how cramped things were and how tough it was squeezing through that long tunnel to get out. Once out, they're off and running. Bodies are fun for these kids, and they love poking at things. This is so true of youngsters that I wrote a series of small books featuring animal babies talking about womb life and what it was like to be born or miscarried or develop handicaps. Kids loved hearing these stories so much, they started babbling about their own memories of what it was like for them "in mama's tummy." This unsettled parents so much that I shelved the project.[4] I mention this because our new children *remember* what we don't want them to.

To get a better sense of how different today's kids are, Susan Stebbins, Cecelia's mother, has a few stories of her own:

When I was pregnant with her, I knew there was something special about this baby (not knowing she was a girl). I just felt loved. I was always talking to her, rubbing my belly, and truly wanted to hurry to see her. I was so happy when labor started and was calm as the whole birth progressed. Upon her delivery, she didn't cry. She just opened her eyes and wanted to look around. The doctors kept flicking her feet and finally she let out a yell, kind of letting them know "Okay, I'll just give a little yell," but was quiet from then on. When she was just twenty-four hours old, I woke up to nurse her at 3:00 a.m. I looked at her as I laid her down to change her, and said, "Hi, pretty girl." She smiled the biggest smile, as if she were a child around the age of nine months. I thought to myself, No way, so I did it again, with the same beautiful results. I knew then she was a special gift. A couple days later, she was diagnosed with having sensitive reflux and had to have an upper GI done. This was very scary for us, as you could imagine. We survived by sleeping upright for three months straight. When she was three she asked me about the big machine she was under, and I asked her, "You remember that?" She said she did. I asked her if she remembered being in my tummy. Well, we know the answer to that silly question. I asked her to tell me about it. She told me it was dark and warm. It felt good.

When my mother-in-law saw her for the first time, something told her that this was my baby, and she surely has been. We are the best of friends. I have never heard of a stronger mother-daughter relationship. We both finish each other's sentences and laugh all the time.

I have had to homeschool her because she was reading at three years old. Was chosen as a peer mediator in preschool, and always in independent study in grade school. With her being a child of knowing, friends at school just didn't understand her. She was so much further than them. I pulled her out of public school in the middle of fifth grade, when she came down with mono and missed a month of school. Cecelia made up all her missed school work in three days and was beyond the class on the fourth day. It was obviously not a challenge for her, and we felt the school was actually holding her back. So we decided to homeschool. The best thing we could've ever done.

Cecelia is now fourteen years old and planning on becoming a tanker pilot as soon as she finishes getting her GED. The only negative part of her having to be homeschooled is that she'd really like to have friends. It breaks my heart that the other kids at school couldn't understand or respect her level of maturity. On the other hand, I have an incredibly beautiful daughter (inside and out) that her dad and I get to share with only each other. I know when the time comes for her to have friends or even the "dreaded" boyfriend, I really won't have much to worry about. Her self-respect and respect for others is way beyond my imagination. She told me, "It's going to be hard to find somebody who loves me more than me!" How cool is that?

Despite being homeschooled, Cecelia fits the same pattern as millions of kids worldwide. They are exceptionally self-aware, remember being in the womb and the birth experience, begin to read and know things when very young, abstract (conceptualize) on a regular basis, are highly intuitive and psychic, impatient, have limitless points of view, are almost brazen in making choices, have a strong sense of confidence, are highly intelligent, can *see through* excuses as if the people making them were transparent, and have formulated an idea of how they want to live their life.

Past generations do not define our new crop. Any parent, teacher, employer, or politician can affirm that. So can dictators throughout the Middle East, who have no idea how to control the "youth quake" that is engulfing their countries. The old way of handling a situation like this was: kill 'em off. The new way is: negotiate. Be honest here. How are the entrenched going to negotiate with young people who are smarter than they are and who can *see through* a con?

6 PIVOT

Change breaks down our boundaries, links us to all else,
providing the grounds of our interconnectedness, our
interdependency.

THOMAS BUCKLEY

What we know about children: 95 percent of all decisions and attitudes they form about themselves and their lives—their belief systems—are arrived at by the age of six. If they do not receive the attention, guidance, and encouragement they need by the age of ten, they drift away from any moorings they might have had.

What we have discovered about the new ones: being the shift generation in the age of shift, they fit neither stereotypical labels nor the scholarship of child experts. Thus they mark a significant pivot in evolutionary patterning.

Fourteen-year-old Katie Snodgras has this to say about herself:

I know I am different. Even as a small child, I felt different, and somewhat superior to everyone else. My mind does not work the same way as others'. I don't have a conscience as such. I cannot think specifically, and when I do it is not in words but in pictures, emotions, intentions. It is often difficult for me because when people speak, I have to translate what they are saying into my way of speech. I seem born with knowledge. I know many things that I never learned. If someone asks me a question, before I can register what they are saying, my mouth opens and answers it for them. I am superaware of the energy around me. I learned to sense moods by the energy signature and can manipulate and change it to suit me. I used to loathe myself for doing that to people, and try to avoid it as much as possible by eating or taking energy from plant life. I don't see but rather feel colors and feelings surrounding people. I also have a few other abilities, such as being able to fall instantly into and out of a trance. When I am in these trances, my mind can leave my body and I can communicate with other people if they are doing so at the same time, no matter where they are in the world, like a shared dream. I call this mind wandering. Sleep is not necessary for me. I can never sleep on a full moon. In some objects when there has been a strong emotion or sudden change in energy to it or near it, this leaves an imprint. I can access these imprints and get a vision of sorts about the time when this happened.

I feel as if I have lived for many years. I like to believe that I follow my own rules and that no one controls me. I never forget anything, yet I cannot recall memories at will. I am not very fragile. It is hard to break me. I have been through countless incidents with little more than a few scratches. Things that should have killed me or broken my neck, I pulled through. I live on a large property backed on to the state forest, and I often go for long walks. On my walks, I move in a strange way and the sight of people scares me. I didn't realize until recently that I move at an abnormal speed. I draw energy from the trees.

I am good at school, even though I hate it. I never do my homework or study, but I still get A's or A-pluses. My parents don't know that I don't do half the work, and neither do my teachers. I am almost always able to get out of it or avoid detention. I often teach my teachers. Everyone tells me that I have a very deep way of thinking. I like philosophy and exploring the mysteries of life. I am not particularly religious, but I'm open to anything that might help explain me, or just to know there are others out there like me. I have instinctive knowledge about people like me. From what I know, there is a group of children born every thousand *years, children like me. These children are strange beings, not entirely human. They have paranormal gifts. Their purpose is to teach and protect.*

As we, the members of the human race, continue to pivot into newer versions of ourselves, the initial thrust of the young in breaking away from patterns several millennia old has created opposing profiles. The generations moving humankind from the plane of polarity to the plane of unity have literally become an exaggeration of the very extremes they were predicted to heal. This artifact of change demands that we face our worst nightmares and best dreams so we can determine what is real and worthy and what is not. Can opposites get along? Can enemies sit at the same table and eat the same food? Can what disgusts us find a place in our hearts? Can chaos and disaster produce the foresight and ingenuity necessary to remake our families, our communities, our culture, our world?

The answer is yes.

The question is how?

To find answers we must refocus and admit something we don't want to: *extremes can sometimes reside in the same child at the same time!*

PROFILE: THE VISIONARY

Visionary and author Soleira Green, in talking about the "supershift" people are now making in their lives, observes what she calls a global brilliance emerging from our newest generations of children.[1] She describes this brilliance as:

+ *Energetic mastery*—living as quickeners and "aliveners" of life
+ *Telepathic communication*—understanding the depth of what someone really wants to say
+ *Emotional zeitgeist*—energy fuel for personal and planetary transformation

✦ *Adventures into the miraculous*—dancing with limitless possibilities

✦ *Global contribution*—as part of daily routines

✦ *Connections to amazing, wonderful people*—all over the world

✦ *An ever-increasing sense of global community*—as people surge forward to create the NEW

✦ *The knowing of ourselves as brilliant beings*—cocreating a whole new world together

✦ *The ability to embody high vibrational frequencies*—with growing ease

✦ *The ability to help anyone transform graciously*—into their next levels

✦ *The certainty that life is never ending*—and death a simple doorway to more

✦ *A breathtaking relationship with consciousness*—as a collective, magical force within which we create, source, and evolve

✦ *A growing understanding and awe*—of our place in the cosmos

Green lives in England. She might as well be from Australia, Hong Kong, South Korea, Turkey, China, Egypt, or Dallas, Texas. This profile of visionary awareness is no longer exclusive to adults who have walked the path of a spiritual adept or reaped the harvest maturity brings. The new kids, for the most part, are simply born that way!

Vision drives them to find innovative, resourceful ways to serve, heal, and help—even if their solution has never before been tried. Fact is, they demand that their ideas be heard, and will not give up until whatever needs fixing gets fixed. Their resilience matches their tech-savvy independence and desire for meaning, a desire they value above all else.

To get a broader sense of how the visionary side of their nature operates, here are a few clips taken from newspapers, television shows, magazines, and radio programs:

Nicole Muller, a teenager who collected 47,500 pounds of food to feed

tens of thousands of people, then started Neighbors-4-Neighbors programs, which are now in all 50 states.

Alexandra LaCour, an eight-year-old who insisted that her Christmas gift be a donation to a homeless shelter.

Jackie Evancho, age ten, who amazed everyone with her strong and uplifting operatic voice on America's Got Talent.

Magnuss Knudsen, a five-year-old who asked that all his birthday money be given to Ronald McDonald House for children with cancer.

Mattie J. T. Stepanek, who lived only fourteen years, but in that time wrote poems of peace that thrilled the world, proving that disease and poverty cannot stop a messenger of love.

Matthew Berger, a nine-year-old, who wandered away from his paleontologist father's side to search for bones, and discovered partial skeletons two million years old—thus laying claim to a new species of hominids.

Kieron Williamson, eight and dubbed the "mini Monet" by British press, whose paintings are so incredible and so inspiring that thirty-three of them have sold for $235,000.

Jonathan, age three, who conducted the fourth movement of Beethoven's Fifth Symphony. Whether miming choreographed movements or creatively guiding an orchestra, what is exhibited in this YouTube video is a depth of interest unusual for one so young.

A C.E.O.'s son who created Miracle Mondays—"give a dollar each Monday for kids in hospitals."

Twelve-year-old Severn Cullis-Suzuki, who raised enough money to travel to Brazil and speak for five minutes at the United Nations Environmental Conference. She "stopped the world" with her presentation.

These teasers tell us a lot about today's children, who raise money for water wells in Africa, invent labor-saving devices, provide for the needs of senior citizens, and start businesses in their bedrooms—all before the age of nine. There are millions upon millions of these kids . . . a global phenomenon.

PROFILE: THE MISLED

The new kids are also the most coddled, cocky, reckless, impatient, arrogant, angry whiners we've ever seen. Distorted child-rearing habits, dysfunctional school programs, and wrongheaded social policies are stunting what could and should be high achievers.

Granted, there has never been a generation like this one. Because of this, they are the most protected, wanted, nurtured, educated . . . in history, and they are fast losing their way. Maybe the problem is too much too soon. Or, maybe it's the persuasive power of adults who prey on children. And, yes, the word is *prey*:

+ *Toddlers & Tiaras* is a TV show that features pageant girls egged on by obsessive mothers to strut and swagger so they will win coveted crowns. These pampered kids seldom have playtime.
+ Girls today are salon vets before the first grade. According to the market-research firm Experian, 43 percent of six- to nine-year-olds are already using lipstick or lip gloss, 38 percent use hairstyling products, and 12 percent use other cosmetics. Many frequent suntan booths.
+ According to the American Society for Aesthetic Plastic Surgery, cosmetic surgical procedures performed on those eighteen and younger have nearly doubled in the last decade.
+ Teenagers trying to look younger are also turning to Botox treatments, which paralyze the face and make normal expressions almost impossible. This desensitizes emotions as well as skin.
+ Kids overpraised by parents and educators are more prone to cheat and lie to save face, underrate the importance of time and effort, avoid challenges, falter when encountering academic difficulties, and expect rewards and prizes even when undeserved and unearned.
+ Eating disorders were rated the number-one problem in teenage girls in 2010. Most wanted to achieve the "cocaine-thin" look of their favorite supermodel or superstar.

+ Giving frequent gifts and parties that celebrate young people's specialness has produced a narcissistic generation that feels that just showing up for class should earn them a B and rate them a star on YouTube. This often leads to antisocial behavior and bullying.

+ Ad agencies target kindergarteners and up for trendy/sexy "gotta have it" clothes, jewelry, and electronic gadgets. Boys are the market for violent video games labeled as entertainment and music that promotes abusive behavior. Youngsters are encouraged to beg their parents for overprocessed foods that are high in sugar and fat, and to drink milk laced with hormones (which interfere with healthy, normal growth).

This is just a small part of the prey package that misleads our children. They believe the images they see and expect to receive what those images promise. The result is a type of deception—fueled by the pressures of growing up in families pushed to the edge—that leads to the silent scream of childhood: depression. Emotional trauma has become such a huge issue that mental capacity is at risk, leading to the inability of many children to relate to fear, express empathy, or feel pain.

Kids in general are making a game of choking themselves (for quick highs), biting each other to draw blood (a show of affection), cutting themselves (to feel relief), becoming actors and comedians (so they can pretend to be someone else), using social media to vent rage (with no respect for privacy or truth), and becoming mean girls and malicious boys (to establish self-worth). One educator told me that dissociation is a massive problem in schools throughout our nation; kids are spacing out and they don't even know they're doing it.

According to a report presented on *CBS Radio News* on October 3, 2010, suicide was found to be the third leading cause of death for kids between ten and twenty-four years of age.

The most brilliant kids ever born are killing themselves in record numbers, or being waylaid by the deceptive con of an easy way out of whatever bothers them. There is no guarantee that the Fifth Root Race will advance in numbers large enough to take our world to the next step in its development. So I'm detecting the minefields ahead of them in the next chapter. Trip wires are easier to avoid if we know what to look for.

7 Minefields

The life I touch for good or ill will touch another life,
and that in turn another, until who knows where the
trembling stops or in what far place my touch will be felt.

FREDERICK BUECHNER

Whenever there's a big shift or change in life, individually or en masse, as the old maxim says, things tend to get worse before they get better. This is typical of a *healing crisis,* a backward flip that provides needed time to readjust and reassess. Changes now, though, are evolutionary—affecting the very essence of existence. The "artifact" here is that energy is polarizing as it accelerates, and it is doing so to the extreme.

Life energy always spirals. As it does, the spiral first dips before spreading up and outward. We revisit before we climb. Progress cannot be defined until we have a better sense of territory. This creates minefields, where what seems settled and safe can become a trap in disguise. Today's minefields are off-the-wall graphic. Sex, money, and drugs, once social issues, are morphing into nightmares. Prepare yourself. This chapter will not be an easy read.

SEX

Slavery, specifically sexual slavery, generates profits estimated at $32 billion annually. It is the third-largest criminal industry in the world today according to the United Nations Office on Drugs and Crime.[1] In Thailand, this industry is number one. Teenagers traveling to other countries on retreat or spring break are often grabbed, drugged, and forced into prostitution. This trafficking could even be in your own neighborhood; maybe the girl next door or the boy down the street. Large sporting events, like the Super Bowl, draw pimps who sell "tricks" provided by their underage "property." Should the kids object, they are beaten, then drugged again. Child porn is now so widespread that the Associated Press reported in 2011 that even in the conservative state of Virginia, there has been a 218 percent increase in cases in the period between 2003 and 2009 alone.

Sexual abuse was the subject of a special *Oprah Winfrey Show* segment in November 2010. Citing the Sexual Abuse Resource Center, she reported that one out of every six boys in the United States are sexually abused by family members or trusted adults. For girls, it's one out of every three. Parental incest is on the rise. So is pedophilia. Toddlers and infants are raped and held in bondage, the crimes against them filmed for sale on the Internet as child porn. Prepubescent teens in fuzzy black-and-white photos are fairly popular, but the full-color images of torture, abuse, and sodomizing the very young are bestsellers. If you aren't screaming yet, you should be.

There's another side to this nightmare, and it addresses how children have changed because of the double standards they face daily. Take clothes: the idea is to show as much skin as possible. For girls, that means everything but nipples and pubic hair. For boys, it's the penis, although they grab it a lot to look "cool." Dating is passé. Young people get together for casual "hookups." Oral sex, the new "midnight handshake," is performed without any means of protection. Result: mouth and throat cancer are skyrocketing in the young due to the sexual transmission of human papillomavirus (HPV). Thanks to reality television, the model for teen love is now based on disrespect and bullying. Result: once inhibitions are shed, so is empathy.

Two things feed all of this: the global collapse of moral standards, and the rise of sexual activity as an economic and political asset . . . with little or no backlash. Life "on the other side of peepholes" is the new normal.

Let's broaden this subject and admit a few things. Children today are going through puberty at younger ages than in previous generations. Little ones settle, as previously noted, into sex-based play preferences at around age one, when they grasp what sex they are and identify with others like them. The new kids, though, are truly fascinated by bodies, every aspect of size and shape, and possible alterations—like surgical implants, "elf" ears, cosmetic redos, piercing, and tattoos. They tend to experiment with touch and feeling and sexual arousal. Some parents encourage this curiosity in an effort to show that the desire for sensual pleasure is healthy and sexual stigmas are not.

Creating a balance between sensuality and sex play in a loving and supportive environment—while respecting individual differences—is the kind of challenge that must be presented to the young. I say *must* because of how polarizing energy is affecting them. One of the "jobs" of the Fifth Root Race is to lead the societies of the world beyond gender-based politics and religions—a job currently in full gear.

So, as if on cue, look at what is happening globally: more hermaphrodites (people with both male and female genitalia) are being born; transgender surgery is enabling people who believe they were born into the wrong body to switch genders; homosexual and lesbian couples are becoming acceptable; genital mutilation of children, wife beating, and killing daughters who have been raped to "protect" the family's honor has become a crime; and estimates suggest that nearly half of today's young people are bisexual.

And that's not half of it. The United States averages 50,000 new cases of HIV/AIDS each year; in South Africa, it's 850 *per day*. It's the young. They're not protecting themselves, enabling HIV/AIDS to continue its rapid spread, in spite of the miracle drugs that seem to lower infection rates. Since girls are undervalued throughout Asia, female babies are still routinely murdered. The very stability of large sections of the world is at risk because *men without women become more warlike and antisocial.* Thus, rethinking the practice of abortion has become a necessity. A woman's choice during the first few months of pregnancy makes sense, but after that, the "vote" is leaning toward no. Of the new kids, not only is birth remembered by the majority, but many times so is life in the womb—*along with life before conception*—suggesting that soul physically merges with mind *at the moment of conception.* Newborns, then, are nobody's "blank slate."

Sexual freedom is a misnomer. Here's the thing: take away the moral and spiritual value of gender mixing and sexual pleasure and you condemn society to the kind of nightmares that can destroy our very future as human beings. The new kids are especially vulnerable, as their basis of information and comparison comes not from parents but a media/entertainment complex entirely geared for profit. We walk a knife's edge with this one. Loving unions and the gift of intimacy hang in the balance; so does the safety of those unable to defend or protect themselves.

MONEY

The new kids know how to make money and they know how to spend it—whether legally or illegally. Many don't care which. Yet they have little or no idea how to budget, save, or plan for the future. Their natural inventiveness and creativity bode well for launching one project after another, and one product after another. Starting their own business can begin (with a little help from parents) as early as the first grade. It is not unusual anymore to hear of youngsters who have earned enough money by the age of thirteen or fourteen to make large purchases or finance college. Still, once young adults, they barely survive on their own. A growing trend is to rent bedroom space from their parents until they are in their late twenties or thirties (with washing and cleaning "services" provided).

There's a huge disconnect between making and spending money and paying for a life . . . theirs. A lot of the disconnect wraps around self-esteem versus narcissism. Young people today have been told their entire lives that being self-confident, self-assertive, and self-aware will ensure their success and happiness. There is no arguing that self-esteem is important, but the me-first attitude that follows such advice slams them into a reality none are prepared for. The collision of self-focused entitlement with the competitive edge of the marketplace has led to a shocker: guarantees for a better life are gone.[2] Jobs aren't there. About half of today's young people are unemployed, even if they hold a college degree. Starting salaries hover around minimum wage—about what the over-fifty crowd gets these days. With an aversion to checks, they lean heavily on credit cards and computers to create the cashless society they prefer, sans needed protection.

Economists predicted in 2010 that our new kids will be the first generation in U. S. history to fall behind their parents in earning power, health, and education. Massive layoffs, weather extremes, troubles with home ownership, the burden of college debt, real hunger issues . . . the United States is beginning to look more like a third-world country than a superpower. Rich? Not like we used to be. Still, what is happening here is happening elsewhere. What government ever heard of audits or practiced accountability?

The reversal of fortune we all face is larger and deeper than predicted. At risk is an entire generation who, overall, may miss career tracks for business and research . . . unless ethics are tossed. And this may occur. Too many times it's the parents of the young who beat up or threaten anyone they disagree with, then post their gripes on Facebook. A mother about to lose her home in foreclosure went on a shopping spree with her kids, buying them new bedroom furniture because she'd had it with being frugal. What does this teach her kids? What does threatening behavior in lieu of compromise offer adults? Teens are admired and well paid for bad behavior. Why should they crunch numbers when they can party?

As a country, we appear to be going backward instead of forward. Young adults, in particular, are delaying marriage and starting a family while seriously questioning if they even have a future. Save for retirement? You've got to be kidding. They save less because they have less, except for their pile of debt.

Remember the spiral's dip? We're in a trough, a big one. Lest we forget, here's the truth: the new kids are capable of creating a parallel economy of their own. Would you believe it? Kids who graduated college in 2011 are picking entrepreneurship as a career choice! Never happened before. Not only are the new kids natural-born entrepreneurs, they are the cleverest "imagineers" we've ever seen. Give them a good mentor or coach and they'll catch on, plus institute some type of financial literacy class as a must-take at every grade level in school. This generation needs to understand what money is and how to manage it, or else they will become prisoners to debit/credit cards, quick scans, and the curse of identity theft.

Expect the new kids to "invent" their own complementary currency (sort of like bartering, only more usable on a grander scale[3]), their own banks (including student-run with microloans to high schoolers), their own investment opportunities as a counterpoint to Wall Street (so they can avoid the lure of huge payoffs . . . in favor of stock incentives and long-term planning). And watch them redefine taxation, interest/mortgage financing, governmental borrowing, and social services.

The majority are here to advance through cooperative means, not via competition. This winner-takes-all trait alone will eventually throw off global economic systems. Once today's young people recognize how the media tricks them with negative ads, how stores and restaurants falsify "fair value,"[4] they will move beyond being easy prey. People in the depths of worry, doubt, and fear are easy to control. That's why the media keeps folks that way, so they will grab at commercials and buy as advertised. It's like a mass hypnosis that spreads negativity. Kids soak it up until they crash and are forced to wake up.

DRUGS

It is commonplace for children to try drugs between twelve and fourteen years of age, the time of puberty.[5] Alcohol and marijuana are the portals most take into the vast and dangerous world of drug addiction—either to feel good or dampen stress.

Eva shares:

> I lost my job one day. My room is on the ground floor of our home and Jessica's is two flights up. I always left for work before it was time to get Jessica up for school. Jessica is my daughter and is sixteen. She's a beautiful girl too, in every way. The morning after I lost my job, I went upstairs to get Jessica up. It was 9:00 a.m. and she was supposed to be at school by 8:15. I walked up the stairs, complaining that someone had left the bathroom light on all night. Then I walked into her room and said, "Get up," and shook her. To my shock, she was cold and unresponsive. I opened the blinds so I could see. She was cold, gray, and very dead. I jumped into action, giving her CPR. Thank God she resuscitated; however, she would not breathe on her own for three days. She stayed at the ICU on a ventilator. On the third day, she awoke as if nothing had ever happened, remembering nothing. She had taken an overdose of Roxicodone and Xanax that she got from friends at her upper-class high school . . . you know, the schools where you think your kids would be safe.
>
> It came to light that my daughter is addicted to drugs. She is, as well, what people refer to as an indigo child—spiritually awake. She did not feel like she fit in; she felt different. People thought she was weird if she talked about spirituality. She could feel others' emotions, and when she asked if others felt that way, they would say no. She had been abandoned by her father. She had been violently raped and torn completely from her path of spirituality. She witnessed a tremendous amount of violence and had been used and abused. I did not know. Drugs were the self-medication for her dark night of the soul. She always smiled, she always laughed, she made honor roll, she swam on the swim team and made state championships. How would one know?

Dina has a story, too:

My older brother, Daniel, committed suicide when he was nineteen years old. He had been the brightest student in the history of the best school in this country. But he didn't study. Never did homework. What he learned in the class was enough for him. Too easy. He invented in school even ways to solve mathematical theorems in shorter paths than were taught. Teachers humbly bowed in front of his brilliance and told him to teach the class. He came home from school to play the piano, to paint, to read all the books possible, to write short stories. Nothing would stop him [from] creating. He was accepted to Yale, Columbia, and Dartmouth. He chose Columbia University in New York, where he studied one and a half years before his suicide.

One of his best friends was there and these are his words. "That night we were sitting around the kitchen table, in the ninth-floor apartment that my friend Benjamin shared with Bob, Steve, and Daniel. They had all been tripping on mescaline, and I had too, although not with them. A day or two later we were still coming down, smoking grass to ease re-entry. We sat around the table, stupefied, drifting with the remembrance of visions. Daniel slipped into the kitchen quietly, hardly making his presence felt. A Jewish boy from Bogotá, Colombia, he was wearing his wrinkled blue-pinstriped, double-breasted blazer, lightly dusted with dandruff, the too-formal jacket that had become his trademark. I also noticed he didn't have any socks on, while his shoes were very loosely tied, which seemed a little odd. He smiled absently, and everyone nodded. After a while Daniel got up, offering a last faint smile, and then he backed out of the room without saying a word. Soon after, a profound thud, a concussion, shuddered through the building. We all looked startled but did nothing. A half hour later, the doorbell rang. Bob got up to answer. A bust! Quickly, Steve flushed the grass down the toilet. Bob returned with some cops. Daniel had jumped out his bedroom window. Down the airshaft, on the concrete covered with cat shit, Daniel was spread-eagled on his side. Half his face wasn't

there anymore. Only blood and brains and one eye left half-open."
Why did he do it?

Abusing alcohol can lead not only to drug abuse but to brain damage. Binge drinking is the worst; a second binge can rack up two years of decreased attention span, thought processes, and memory. Marijuana and ecstasy are popular routes many take to giving meth a try (a frightening brain killer from the first dose).

Depression seems to be the driver. Yet antidepressants do little more than lower sex drive and make it difficult, if not impossible, to fall in love or stay in love or maintain loving relationships. More than 75 percent of the people who take antidepressants don't need them. So what type of ads dominate television and magazines? Designer drugs for this and similar ills, while the older, cheaper generic drugs that still work wonders are being phased out. "Hospitals must search for drug substitutes as shortages increase," blared an Associated Press headline from May 31, 2011. If you think this shortage is because of contaminants or the importation of raw ingredients, think again. Greed is still good. Why should drug companies offer cheaper, less harmful drugs when the more powerful concentrates—the product of lab enhancements—have become their gravy train, with every media source desperate for advertising dollars more than willing to pitch whatever is new?

Between depression and a growing list of so-called personality disorders, the overuse of psychiatric drugs, psychedelics, opiates, pain relievers, and neural toxins are causing an epidemic of drug-induced mental illness. Consider a link that has been found between school shootings in this country and young men with a history of psychiatric drug use, often antidepressants. Consider that the very drugs prescribed by physicians to stabilize mental disorders are changing brain chemistry, sometimes to the point of destabilizing mental health. Consider that OxyContin, derived from opium as a pain reliever, is so easily available that a cottage industry of "pill mills" has sprung up to supply the teenage demand, making it a "cash cow" in some areas.[6] Since it takes higher and higher doses to achieve the same result, a whole generation of kids is being lost to OxyContin (oftentimes referred to as suicide by prescription). Let's not forget the "designer" drug known as bath salts; one whiff can lead to a complete psychotic breakdown.

Drugs today are used to escape life, sometimes to end life. They have morphed into habits—a pill for everything. Drugs in older, shamanic cultures were used to enter more fully into life. Their rituals involved preparation, guidance, and elder participation to ensure protection and spiritual revelation. Mere drug highs and pill popping were never an option.

Years ago I made a statement about this subject that caused so much controversy, I had to retract it. Not this time. I said then and I say again now: *anyone who uses drugs for recreation is guilty of directly participating in the destruction of the country or place the drugs came from.* If you don't believe me, look at the opium harvest in Afghanistan that funds the Taliban, or the butchery in Mexico that fuels American tycoons and teenagers, or the crack babies and meth children who are little more than the "undead"—devoid of conscience or hope.

I warned that this chapter would be a hard read. Nothing has been exaggerated. It is an honest portrayal of the minefields confronting today's youth, and in numbers that are shocking. The biggest puzzler, though, is the "quicksand" that lies ahead in the next chapter. What will both save and demolish the world we know is so wonder-filled and exciting that the mind, everyone's mind, is staggered by the scope of what it portends.

8   QUICKSAND

*When I despair, I remember that all through history, the
ways of truth and love have always won.*

MAHATMA GANDHI

ANY SCREEN-BASED TECHNOLOGY. Computers. Television.
Movies, DVDs, 2-D/3-D films, Blu-Ray. Internet. E-mail. Websites.
Facebook. Twitter. Chat rooms. Blogs. Videos. Video games. E-readers.
iPads. iPhones. Nooks. Kindles. Droids. Apps. Cell phones. Streaming
radio and television. BlackBerries. Gaming on the run. Google. Wii.
Wi-Fi. Amazon.com. Virtual realities. Second Life. Avatars. (Can you
imagine paying $4 for your avatar, your digital representation of your-
self, to wear a cocktail dress in the virtual reality game? Or, maybe $3
for a business dress or $5 for a suit and tie? I'm talking real money
here.)

The digital world has arrived. In a short time, apps will replace
websites and iPads will replace computers. Soon after, everything will
be digital . . . no more books, no more newspapers, no more phone
directories, no more magazines and newsletters. Saving trees scores
over saving backups, scrapbooks, letters, journals, calendars, and libraries. Already our youth and young adults are completely television programmed, screen dependent. They will not miss what they are losing.
Quicksand is like that. It sucks you in before you realize what is happening or where you're headed. Gotcha.

Facebook is now a diary for people to share daily challenges, joys, thoughts, and fears. It connects people around the world like nothing else ever has.

According to Daniel Lyons, "You are not Facebook's customer. You are its inventory—the product Facebook is selling. Facebook's real customers are advertisers. You're useful only because you can be packaged and sold. The more information Facebook extracts from you, the more you are worth."[1] Newspapers have to pay journalists to get stories. Facebook gets its content for free, and can target its advertising with greater precision than newspapers.

Video games are the next big teaching tool. They will redefine education. Games teach skills employers want, such as analytical thinking, team building, multitasking, and problem solving under pressure.

This is true, depending on the game. Nonviolent puzzle and word games affect heart rates and brain waves in a way that can be used therapeutically for treating stress, anger, high blood pressure, fatigue, or depression. In April 2010, University of Virginia students and community members played *The Bay Game* (from Azure Worldwide, co-founded by Phillippe Cousteau). Every decision every player made impacted the health of the bay and showcased the concept of environmental engagement. Video games as sport or entertainment, however, quickly become addictive. They can be so addictive that children playing them develop behavioral problems. Violent video games desensitize children, especially young boys. *Grand Theft Auto,* for instance, holds players in a hypnotic trance with heavy emphasis on sex and violence. This and games like it pit free speech against the violent play of killing, maiming, dismembering, or sexually assaulting humanlike images.

Virtual realities like Second Life are now being used by the military to train soldiers. Similar reality-like scenarios train emergency first responders, show peacekeepers how to interact with civilian populations without killing them, teach us how to navigate our modern information society, and reward trial-and-error determination.

Virtual realities entice our kids to become more obedient. Through trial and error and the thinking process, the underlying game can be uncovered. But there's a catch: the game itself is the real observer. It hides its rules in such a way that it can decode the player's talents and weaknesses. Once the player accepts the system and works to succeed within it, reality scenarios begin to narrow player flexibility—molding the individual into becoming what the organization really wants.

BlackBerries, cell phones, e-mails, texting, and Twitter make access easy and quick. Says Biz Stone (one of three inventors of Twitter), "People are social animals. We need these tools to help each other become smarter and do bigger and better things."[2]

Twitter is a tyrant's worst nightmare. For the first time ever, the world's people have voices and photos to back up those voices. They can announce and record what is happening while it happens. No religion, no government, no corporation, no dictator can silence this. Not really. There is always a way to get through censorship. Yet with instant access comes constant interruption. The rapid-fire switching of attention between tasks derails brain processes that sort out incoming signals. It takes the brain a full fifteen minutes to refocus thought, even if sidetracked by something as simple as an e-mail alert. The average kid or worker spends only about eleven minutes on any given project before being interrupted or asked to do something else. The result: distraction overload and continuous partial attention. We are losing the ability to concentrate and to daydream (which is the progenitor of insight, innovation, and creative thinking).

The Internet has opened up the ears, eyes, and minds of the world, giving vast numbers of people access to unlimited knowledge, interactions, exchanges, shopping, banking, comparisons, histories, invention, lies, and secrets.

Yet opening up the world's treasury of knowledge and access has also opened up Pandora's box. WikiLeaks threatens to unveil every secret, providing terrorists and criminals with names, addresses, and codes. The Internet itself, as well as all the devices that access it, guarantee that privacy is dead. Just from a name and e-mail address it is possible to score information on a person's sexuality, employability, health, body type, and intelligence, as well as locate his or her social security number, address, and telephone number.[3] Fraud is rampant. Copyrights are tossed. The new kids see nothing wrong with using the Internet to cheat on school exams or phony up research papers.

Social media has taken the best and the worst aspects of the Internet and used them to create a unique culture that exists without borders or boundaries.

Whatever is posted on the Internet remains there . . . indefinitely. Curse someone, say things you wished you hadn't, expose yourself, ridicule in anger, share your uttermost dreams and fears, launch an attack campaign—no matter; there's no going back. This is confusing kids big time. They don't understand the full weight of their actions (neither do a lot of adults). Example: a thirteen-year-old boy was accused of threatening to inflict injury "by means of electronic communication." Now called cyberbullying, his threats are subject to police action, not just being kicked out of school.[4] Teens have been driven to suicide by such slander. Even thoughtful kids are guilty of wallpapering their Web pages with gutter filth and arrogance. Then there's sexting. Sending a digital photo of anyone nude or in a sexual pose, or even inviting sex through a text message to someone who does not welcome the advances is *against the law* in several states. The new kids are getting caught sending or receiving nude photos, then being jailed for child pornography. On the *Today* show (February 2010), an expert in teen behavior said that 25 percent of the kids are guilty of sexting and 47 percent thought it was a perfectly okay thing to do. We live in a voyeuristic society where reality television and YouTube make "personal" a thing of the past. Pirating another's name, reputation, story, website features, and blog is becoming all too common. PhotoShopping and airbrushing seals the deal . . . we can be phony; we can lie. Few even notice.

The industry behind movies, television, DVDs, and streaming videos is flooding our screens with nonstop entertainment of every type imaginable that seems as real as the real thing—thanks to HDTV, 3-D, Blu-ray, and goofy glasses.

But what seems good has several catches. The way the brain reacts to radiant light (from television and computer monitors) is one of them. After a few minutes of exposure, the brain nods off. The industry counters this by the use of startle effects (unexpected sounds and actions) to trick the brain into paying attention. Eventually, the brain zones past false alarms into a hypnotic state. This means bigger and bigger startles are necessary. Today, even children's cartoons and family fare average around sixteen startles per half hour of viewing time. The most common startle used is violence, which throws the heart and emotions into overdrive and releases the stress hormone cortisol into the body. Most kids have watched between five and six thousand hours of TV by the age of five or six. This massive, no-letup, overstimulus is causing maladaptation of the brain. Example: from a twenty-year study by the German Psychological Institute, four thousand kids per year, average hours of TV watched by age six (between five and six thousand hours)—two-thirds lost the ability to detect shadings of color, 20 percent had a reduction in awareness of the natural environment and showed a tendency toward anxiety/boredom/violence when deprived of high-density stimuli such as television.[5] As if this isn't enough, *family movies* feature one female character to every three male characters, and those females are often scantily clad or wear sexy, tight, alluring attire. The upshot: a 2003 Kaiser Family Foundation survey found that the more television a girl watches, the fewer options she believes she has in life; the more a boy watches, the more his views become sexist. And while TV teaches girls to become onlookers, it teaches boys to go out and do interesting things. Disney announced in May 2010 that it will no longer make traditional films, but will focus instead on animation, franchises, and superheroes. Maximum startles.

What about 3-D films and television? According to movie expert Roger Ebert, 3-D is a waste of dimension, adds nothing to the viewing experience, can be a distraction, can create nausea and headaches, dims lights and colors—and also increases sales of digital projectors, enables theaters to slap on surcharges, allows Hollywood to avoid serious dramas, and is a gimmick Hollywood uses to excite people.[6] Translation: it hurts your eyes, is hard on your brain, and costs more. What do the best-selling books, movies, music, and television shows from 2009 indicate about the type of entertainment people prefer? Seventy percent favor violence. If you don't believe me, note that *Piranha 3D,* a bloody summer 2010 thriller, raked in megabucks . . . and not because it was clever and funny.

The quicksand of technology—the reality of how it really works and how we respond to it—is rewiring our brains and our hearts. Too much too soon too often results in shorter attention spans, less exercise, superficial relationships, loss of self-control and sustained thought, hearing loss (from volume and duration of sounds delivered via earbuds and headphones), fried brain cells from cell phones held too close to head, isolation, sleep disorders, shallowness, plagiarism, disrupted hormones, obesity, and a fear of silence. High-density stimulation emboldens hurtful speech and abusive behavior while decreasing empathy and the ability to recognize emotional facial expressions and voice tones.

Surprise! The toggling the brain has to do while multitasking actually dumbs down intelligence levels. Texting skyrockets phone bills while enforcing a "hive" mentality. This can lead to a type of "digital Maoism" where the few entice the many to swarm in flash mobs or gangs for specific purposes. There is no arguing that the new technologies promote the power of group effort. Because this is so, individualism is fast disappearing, along with musical and literary classics that inspired generations of people for countless centuries.

How tricky is this quicksand? The convenience of e-commerce and e-books is designed by teen tech companies to permanently eliminate jobs on a massive scale. In a 2010 *Newsweek* article, commentator George F. Will predicted that in four years half the U.S. bookstores (about 50 million feet of commercial real estate) and two-thirds of the music stores would evaporate.[7] As of the time of this writing, it looks like he may be right. Casting a shadow on any idea of better ethics, top management at Facebook hired a public relations firm in May 2011 to pitch disinformation about Google to journalists. They claimed this was not meant to be a smear campaign, but clearly it was.

The real truth is that the will to connect is the primary driving force in the digital age, not the will to compete. There are solutions to challenges. With kids, model down. They don't need the fancy gadgets until they are older. Don't expose infants and toddlers to technology, and from ages three to six, limit exposure times to less than two hours per day. Increase slowly after that until puberty. Balance usage with plenty of exercise, fresh air, nature walks, friendships, conversation, household chores, pet care, gardening, and learning how to cook. There are other great ideas in the book *Generation Text,* so get a copy.[8] Most of the scary stuff with quicksand can be avoided if you do your homework and prepare.

9

THE IMAGINAL WORLDS

The Universe is full of magical things, patiently waiting for our wits to grow sharper.

EDEN PHILLPOTTS

The antidote to overstimulation and the addictive qualities of the electronic world is its opposite . . . the imaginal realms of spirit. Our new kids may be in lockstep with digital nanoseconds, but they flow just as easily through the hidden nooks and crannies of worlds within worlds. Silence may be threatening to them, yet the very thing they fear is the doorway all must enter in order to be healthy, at peace, and have a sense of personal value and purpose.

THE FRONT DOOR TO SPIRIT

Open it—your front door. Breathe deeply. Eyeball what's there, especially in early morning or at eventide. The natural world does not betray or pretend. It is what it is . . . noisy splashes of life so vast both mind and body are assaulted with the rawness of its sensuality: squishy mud, floods of flower scent, luscious pop-ups from garden patches, sticker-bush and weed tangles, slaps of clay, spooky full moons, rough bark and soft petals, splinters and scraped knees, scary storms, bug "bands," leaf piles, stacks of wood, streams for toes, pomegranate seeds, claws that draw blood like the color of those seeds, the smell of death, the cry of new life.

Nothing can compare with the pleasure and pain the natural world offers. Without the wide range of sensations we can experience from nature, we would grow up insensitive, unfeeling. Without the challenge nature's minions foist upon us, our ability to care and be compassionate would suffer. Did you know that bats rock their babies and sing to them? Did you know that elephants can recognize themselves in a mirror, have incredible abilities to reason and remember, honor their relatives, and grieve a death? Science has now established that animals have an inner life, somewhat similar to that of humans.[1] Animals are among our first teachers as children; so are spirits of woodland, desert, mountain, sea, river, canyon, tundra, island, volcano, grassland, ice pack.

You heard me right: spirits. They are everywhere—the souls of all things and the energy beings with lives of their own, busy with tasks, as much a part of Creation's story as we are. And kids see them regularly. Do they look like us? Not unless we want them to. Name them elves, gnomes, fairies, sprites, goblins, devas, tricksters, wind walkers, tempters, jinni. Doesn't matter. In nature's world, all exists, all has meaning and purpose, and all serve in a Hidden Order.

A HIDDEN ORDER

In the evolution of the human family on earth, legend tells us that another line of similar manifestation also occurred. J. R. R. Tolkien's *The Lord of the Rings* chronicles what he believed happened when the race of elves and the race of men divided, each going their own way, with the coming of the Fourth World (a perfect counterpoint to what is now happening as we all make way for evolution's Fifth World). Most important to me of Tolkien's visionary work is his book *The Silmarillion*. Published after the rings saga, this work contained the original revelations given to him about why Creation ever occurred and how the worlds of heaven and earth would eventually cycle through the timetables of a Greater Plan.[2]

Folklore from every culture we have knowledge of and every religion known to exist has stories about such a Greater Plan or Order and the Third Order of Creation: not angels, not demons, not humans, but a hidden peoples who appear and disappear at will, pass through physical matter, and violate the laws of physics. Not aliens in any sense; rather an elder race who are engaged in a symbiotic relationship with us, their "first cousins." Speculation is that we share a common ancestry.

Gregory L. Little, Ed.D., an expert in brain processes and author of *People of the Web,* reminds us that humans see only 5 percent of what exists in the electromagnetic spectrum.[3] The rods and cones in the human eye respond only to that 5-percent range. Beings normally not visible to us, worlds and realms beyond regular perception, seem to exist, in his opinion, on the ultraviolet and infrared ends of the spectrum. "Just because we can't see something, doesn't mean it's not real."[4] (Refer also to the books *Subtle Worlds* by David Spangler and *Beyond Shadow World* by Brad Steiger.[5])

That a hidden order exists, I have no doubt. The currently popular bloodlust of vampires and werewolves requires that we take a deeper look at folklore for whatever truth lies at the core of these stories. The difference between imaginal worlds and imagination goes a long way to explain a host of misconceptions.

IMAGINAL WORLDS/IMAGINATION

Imagination has two aspects: 1) intentional fabrication, where we make it up from our own minds and feeling sense; and 2) what is presented to us, intact, from a world that is as real as what we see, touch, hear, feel, and know intellectually.

French scholar and mystic Henry Corbin, coined the phrase *imaginal worlds* to describe realms that exist above and beyond the three-dimensional world, where things are *real* in the sense that they are not being imagined. Imaginal imagery has integrity and exists apart from what we create or control.

Let me reframe this difference. *Something imaginary is **created by and comes from us**. Something imaginal **comes to us from another realm** beyond our own. When an imaginal image presents itself to us, we may be awed, afraid, surprised, puzzled, confused, or emotionally moved. It stirs something deep within us. It awakens us to a feeling or emotion. The imaginal realm carries within it "thoughts of the heart" that can awaken universal archetypes and deeper processes of creativity. Archetypes, as defined by renowned psychologist Carl Gustav Jung, are "symbols with meaning" that can take on a life of their own and exist outside of individual consciousness, thus bridging the gap between objective reality and what is imaginal.*

Our intellects can grasp this, whether or not we fully understand. Kids get it instantly. They know if they've conjured up something via their own effort, or if what came to them did so of its own will and volition.

PSYCHIC KIDS

Litany Burns, the author of *The Sixth Sense of Children*, feels that creativity, psychic abilities, an expanded perspective, a sense of higher purpose in life, wisdom, unconditional love, compassion, and what we can imagine and innovate are all "gifts of the spirit," proof positive of the immense value of the ability to participate in imaginal/imagery worlds within worlds.[6]

Children regularly talk to their toys and hear voices and see beings that both delight and frighten them, and play with either imaginal or imagined playmates. They occasionally chase winged ones and bright orbs (plasma/spirit effects), or cry when the "red man" comes (the harbinger of high fever and sickness). These kids—most kids—are not learning disabled and in need of drugs. The new children are highly telepathic, psychic/intuitive, and precognitive. And many can, with practice, move objects without touching them—including cursors on computers. Faculties typical to humankind are expanded at birth (or via conception) with these kids.

We need to admit something here. . . . *Psychic abilities are really survival abilities.* Our ancestors survived and thrived because they were smart enough to listen to their instincts. What do you think instincts are? They are exactly what our ministers, parents, schoolteachers, counselors, doctors, and psychologists tell us is bad or the work of the devil or nonsense. Everyone possesses psychic sensitivities to some degree. It's what we use them for that establishes value or hindrance. Case in point: out-of-body experiences. For most children, these are a natural extension of play or curiosity. If a child is ill, the ability to leave his or her body becomes a quick aid to relieving discomfort, or a reassurance once parents are "located." While being molested or hurt, withdrawing from body confines can be a way to save one's sanity and endure the pain until escape is possible. Many children's near-death experiences result from situations of this sort.

Face it: *if you are breathing, you're psychic.* (There are excellent books now on how to teach children to use their inborn abilities in positive, helpful ways, as well as summer camps where this type of learning experience is the camp's goal.[7])

GHOSTS AND SCARY STUFF

Children see and interact with ghosts—sometimes the newly dead or those who passed on years ago. This is almost a given if the child had a near-death episode. Deceased pets, even spirits of animals in general, can cozy up to kids. This can be advantageous if the spirit form is protective. Sometimes the souls of animals or birds become wise guides or mentors while the child is young, and pass into memory once he or she matures.

Ghost are no joke. Sightings are commonly investigated, from the noisy ghosts of the undead to those who scare or interfere or are simply lost and in need of advice or counseling. What was once a fun idea of "Ghost Busters" has given way to investigators of paranormal science. People armed with electronic devices have verified that ghosts emit distinctive electromagnetic fields that can be sensed or felt by individuals, charted on field detectors, and recognized on film.

For everyone's peace of mind, get the book *Kids Who See Ghosts: How to Guide Them Through Fear* by Caron B. Goode, Ed.D., NCC.[8] Dr. Goode is a certified psychotherapist willing to step out and explore how and why a child might see a ghost. She is a godsend for parents confused by this, and a friend to every child who sees and interacts within the invisible worlds of spirit. A real plus: she is experienced in dealing with what can go wrong . . . and a lot can.

Scary stuff includes kids who take levitating objects too far and become a threat to themselves and others. My youngest and a friend of hers did this until I made it clear to them that anything they could do, I could do, and better. They immediately quit. Don't forget: you're the parent. Act like it. Take charge. If you don't know how to handle situations like this, learn. Classes are universally available.

But the really scary stuff is far more sinister. As the psychic/intuitive abilities of our new children continue to expand (we've hardly glimpsed what they will be able to do with their minds), they can and will become increasingly susceptible to what is oftentimes called the dark forces. These forces are spirits who can attach themselves to an individual and take over his or her personality in an act of possession. They can even be souls of the dead who want back into a warm body. Tricksters (spirits who enjoy confusing people) exist as well, as does spirit residue (leftover emotions and thoughts that hang around a house once the resident has moved away; this stuff can "infect" or influence new tenants. Cleanse the home with prayer and herb sprays such as sage, cedarwood, tea tree, geranium, rosemary, rose, eucalyptus, or camphor). There are black magicians—those who as part of their religion or rituals or out of curiosity or unchecked desire seek to harm or enslave another. This preference for things negative can arise from a steady diet of violent video games/movies/television, drugs and alcohol, bullying, parental mistreatment, and/or the deceptive rhetoric spewed by extremists over the Internet. Some blame fallen angels, giving the presence of dark forces a biblical twist.

No matter how you define the darkness that can trap the innocent, what I believe underscores this whole quagmire is what results when children are raised with little or no love, encouragement, or support. Happy, well-adjusted kids with a good sense of spiritual/religious values are seldom victims of anything dark.

A HANDY GUIDE

Here is a way to discriminate between those beings who are basically helpful and supportive (like guides or guardian angels) and those who seek to confuse or possess (like mixed-up or angry disincarnates). Hesitation is healthy, especially if channeling is involved (where voices or thoughts other than your own seek attention or try to express themselves through you). "Gifts of the spirit" are not always what they seem; neither are they necessarily positive.

SUBJECTIVE VOICES, SUBJECTIVE VISITORS: DISCERNING THEIR TRUE SOURCE

Lesser Mind	Greater Mind
The Voice of Ego	The Voice of Spirit
Personality Level	*Soul Level*
Flatters	Informs
Commands	Suggests
Demands	Guides
Tests	Nudges
Chooses for you	Leaves choice to you
Imprisons	Empowers
Promotes dependency	Promotes independence
Intrudes	Respects

Pushes	Supports
Excludes	Includes
Status oriented	Free and open
Insists on obedience	Encourages growth and development
Often claims ultimate authority	Recognizes a greater power (God/Allah/The Divine)
Offers shortcuts	Offers integration
Seeks personal gratification	Affirms Divine Order along with the good of the whole

The word *magic,* by the way, comes from the Babylonian and Persian word for *receptive* which is *magno* (*magnet, magnetic,* and *magi* derive from the same term). These ancient peoples knew that when someone was receptive or displayed receptivity (a willingness to receive), the person could then draw to him or her all manner of unique or desirable happenings with little or no effort, almost as if charmed (possessed of magic). Today, the word *magic* is used most often to indicate influential powers recognizable by the "color" of how they are used. Examples:

Magic Type	Basis	Purpose
White magic	Spirit based	Healing self and others; emphasizes growth and guardianship; enhances, charms, protects
Black magic	Ego based	Enhancing self-importance; emphasizes possessions and status; indulges, exploits, enslaves

Gray magic	Belief based	Acquiring attention or imposing a point of view; emphasizes wishful thinking and cultural fixations; entices, coerces, programs
Real magic (transparent)	Feeling based	Developing an open and receptive mood; emphasizes receptivity and sensitivity; enables, readies, resonates
Soul magic (luminous)	Source based	Learning through experience so the soul can evolve; emphasizes self-empowerment and personal responsibility; uplifts, frees, brings together in wholeness

As these examples show, what establishes the power behind spirit manifestations (what seems magical), is actually the degree of vulnerability we feel when interacting with spirit. Intuition and psychic ability, the wonderful worlds of spirit, are only valuable to us if we remember to ask questions and reserve the right to challenge answers. Surrendering to a higher power (God/Allah/The Divine) does not require blind obedience.

MORE SCARIES

Although the new children seem "right there," touched by a power beyond that of generations before them, don't let this fool you. Discernment skills take years to develop, even for them. Behind closed doors, depression and loneliness can become an issue. Kids who stand out as different are still branded crazy and ostracized. But the opposite also applies . . . the child can be the perpetrator.

Severe psychosis is striking at younger and younger ages—sometimes as young as age three. Parents who notice excessively angry, aggressive behavior in their child or an unusual desire for isolation should check with a qualified professional for advice. If the child is older and suddenly acting strangely, for no apparent reason (more noticeable with tweens, teens, and those in their early twenties), the specter of possession could be present. Psychiatrists and other mental healthcare professionals who use hypnosis rather than drugs have a better success rate "releasing" individuals of interlopers. The book *Freeing the Captives: The Emerging Therapy of Treating Spirit Attachment* by Louise Ireland-Frey, M.D., is based on her considerable experience using hypnosis for this and constitutes a wake-up call for professionals.[9] Disturbing memories from past lives respond effectively to hypnotherapy, as well.

REINCARNATION

Past lives . . . children remember these without pretense, almost as if reincarnation is the way souls move throughout time and space. Listen to them jabber, especially when they are playing. You'll be surprised, maybe shocked, at what they say. Children under the age of five are more inclined to have recalls. Anything they express is usually done in a matter-of-fact tone, with stories consistent over time that have behaviors and traits corresponding to a particular historic period. The knowledge they convey is outside their frame of reference. So far, complaints that these stories are mere fantasy have fallen short to considerable research showing, among other things, that past lives have a greater influence on a person's character than either heredity or astrology.

The most credible pioneer in this field of study is Ian Stevenson, M.D., yet there are others who have made important findings.[10] The topic of reincarnation will become increasingly important as science turns to the reality of the soul as a basic truth underscoring the human condition and all things of spirit.

Spiritual traditions tell us that each lifetime is but one segment in the soul's continuing evolution. The claim is that the past does not define where we're going; rather it is an expression of the soul's eternalness.

10 A DIFFERENT BRAIN

Born this way.

LADY GAGA

"Thirty thousand years ago, we were wandering around in small groups and not thinking much about the future," notes Robert Gifford, an environmental psychologist at the University of Victoria in Canada. "Everything that was important was within a few kilometers or so. And that is the brain we still have."[1]

Correction: *once had.* Giant leaps in brain development have already occurred in the twenty-first century and more are coming. Demands and pressures are accelerating at rates that are so rapid, brain structure and function are literally forced to alter. The brain, as an "ongoing construction" site, is being reshaped by the digital world *and* by a barrage of chemicals few need. The result? Quirky kids and pooped parents. The entertainer Lady Gaga is hot not just because she's bold and brash but because of what the reporter Ramin Setoodeh noted in an article he wrote about her: "She's become an evangelist of self-acceptance, preaching to an audience of outcasts."[2]

The new kids think differently. Their language is different. They respond to different cues. It has been said that they are the dumbest generation ever—can't reason their way out of a teapot—and have been stupefied by tweeting and texting to the point that they no longer maintain a memory of things past. Really?

Okay, so multitasking is harder on the IQ than pot smoking, and without rest and simple time-outs like staring into space or watching clouds drift by (flow states), the brain is unable to organize itself and process what it has learned. But a biggie we're overlooking is kids who play dumb because they're bored, don't fit in, or are just plain uncomfortable in their own skin. And then there's the issue of thirds, a surprisingly important slant to the challenge of altered intellects.

THIRDS

By the time children turn five their brain is 90 percent formed. "Early experiences are so powerful," cautions pediatric neurobiologist Harry Chugani of Wayne State University, "that they can completely change the way a person turns out."[3] At age six, then, you are you. That's why the very young should never be involved in wars or gangs or drugs or sexual trafficking or overexposure to digital screens or media sales tricks or lousy diets and processed foods. Potential can be betrayed or destroyed if they are.

As the human race evolves so does the brain. Even in our less-than-perfect world, where children are regularly squandered, take a look at what else is occurring:

+ Two key gene mutations to "build a better brain" (around for thousands years) are suddenly "on the move." Our scientific community estimates that 70 percent of the world's population now evidences one of them; one-third have both. Other genes, more than a thousand of them, help with brain building, but what is happening with these two mutations lies beyond prediction.[4]
+ In 2002 British newspaper *The Guardian* scooped headlines by announcing that in countries using standard IQ tests, there had been a sudden unexpected rise of around 27 points on test scores. One-third of the kids scored between 150 to 160—genius level. Improvements in education, permissive parenting (where

the child leads), better nutrition, and a sudden rise in gene pool capacity were all eliminated as causes. American psychologists Bill Dickens and James Flynn offered another answer. Known today as the Flynn effect, the theory posits that kids exciting other kids in a stimulating environment raises IQ. This falls short, though, of explaining why even isolated children without any extra stimulation scored the same as the advantaged.

✦ Another IQ puzzle cropped up in 2007, concerning the two tests that are used to score intelligence: Wechsler measures "crystallized intelligence"—what a person has learned; Raven measures—"fluid intelligence," what a person can learn. Not a single autistic child taking the Wechsler test has ever scored in the high range. Yet with the Raven test, one-third scored between 150 and 160—genius. Why haven't parents noticed this? One reason may be that a low score guarantees special services and public assistance. Another reason may be that with autistic kids, finding hidden sparks can be difficult. Still, Raven scores prove that such efforts can be more than worthwhile.

So why, consistently, are gains in thirds? There is a "Rule of Thirds," natural markers that ensure balance, ascetics, and endurance, that may explain this. For instance, healthy individuals spend one-third of their life asleep. And a study done by Matt Ridley of the period between 1955 and 2005 found that the average person made three times more money (corrected for inflation), ate one-third more calories of food, and lived one-third longer.[5] Progressions tended to occur in thirds.

The Rule of Thirds in art applies to composition and how to make things visually more interesting and attractive. With video and film, thirds make reference points easier to find. Divisions of thirds and triangles strengthen materials used for long-term stability in construction, repair, and design. In Christianity, the Holy Trinity illustrates the triune aspect of God—while providing a measure for what has value. The third law in spiritual/mystical traditions refers to karma (cause and effect) and the Golden Rule (do to others what you would have them do to you). The Rule of Thirds traces back to the rhythmic proportions of the Golden Mean (Golden Ratio/Golden Section), which is nature's preference for harmony and beauty and the baseline of all things sacred and balanced universal order.[6]

That human intelligence would advance in step with natural harmonics tells me that the evolutionary leap we are now witnessing is unique in history.

SMARTS

The smartest kid in the world was identified in the 1977 *Guinness Book of World Records* as Kim Ung-yong, a Korean boy with an IQ score of 210. Before his fifth birthday he spoke three languages besides his own and was solving complex calculus problems. That score of 210 was matched in my research by child near-death experiencers who had their episode between birth and fifteen months and were immersed in a rich, warm, dark or black light (as opposed to the more familiar white or bright light). Linda Silverman, an expert on giftedness, discovered IQ scores of 238 and above in certain children who had been born premature or undergone birth trauma. Her discovery, based on her unique way of testing children, underscored mine, as many near-death cases arise from the same type of birthing crises.[7]

What becomes of these profoundly gifted children? Their parents keep their existence hush-hush and have them homeschooled or educated over the Internet. They fear the government or the military finding out about them and robbing them of a healthy childhood and families who love them. Overriding this parental caution, however, are regular YouTube videos that spotlight the feats of child prodigies.

Einstein was thought to have used between 10 and 12 percent of his brain capacity; most folks, maybe 3 to 5 percent. Considering the current global rise in intelligence, we could see some people able to utilize 30 percent or more of their brains by 2133. I base this not only on the Rule of Thirds, but also on the fact that 97 percent of our DNA, considered "junk" because no scientist can map it, is plugged directly into the mind. They can't map the stuff because the mind itself cannot be mapped.

Know this about DNA: thanks to its coiled design, vibrational spin, and built-in "electronics" (electronic devices today mimic the way DNA functions), it acts mainly as an antenna for communication exchanges and interplays between body, environment, universe, and the memory fields of mass consciousness. DNA is a biological Internet.

Mind and brain are not the same. Mind is nonlocal; brain is the physical organ in our heads. Mind exists as intelligence, a consciousness that pervades Creation. The DNA Internet knows all the codes for any form of contact with any level of consciousness. As we plug into our own potential—who we really are and what else we might be capable of—we begin to activate more of those codes. We expand. We grow. We become smarter. The best way to tap potential is through the right-brain environments of imagination, creativity, intuition, innovation, and inspiration. This can lead us to the higher action of things spiritual and mystical and otherworldly. We bypass brain when we do this and flow into mind. Junk DNA is the "equipment" we have to navigate the realms of mind.

When we're talking IQ, it would behoove us to embrace the whole package. Thanks to visionary Soleira Green, we have an idea of what that package is.[8] Based on her hands-on experience investigating the range of human consciousness and how intelligence quotients are evolving, Soleira has identified five forms of intelligence.

INTELLIGENCE EQUALS EXPANDED CONSCIOUS AWARENESS

Intelligence (IQ)	Measures mental processes of thought and rational analysis
Emotional (EQ)	Measures intuitive, emotional understandings of the heart
Spiritual (SQ)	Measures wisdom found in connecting with the higher self

Wholistic (WQ)	Measures profound connections to potential/knowing/others
Quantum (QQ)	Measures superspeed creativity, connection to Allness

MUSIC, MATH, LANGUAGE, EXERCISE

The aftereffects experienced by children who undergo near-death states include marked changes in brain structure/function; the younger the child, the greater the shift. I found that enhancements in music (85 percent) were almost as high as those in math (93 percent). This is important because the centers for math and music are next to each other in the brain. When one accelerates, the other tends to as well, as if they were a single unit. (Good mathematicians are usually music lovers, and often musicians.)

Music, math, brain, mind, language . . . *inseparable.* Some examples: neuroscientist Andrew Newberg found that if you *sing* your sacred words, not just pray them, they become like a poem that enhances memory and opens up new structural connections in the brain . . . which expands language skills.[9] Back in 1988, Dr. Susumu Ohno of the Beckman Research Institute in California converted the chemical formulas of healthy living cells from various parts of the body into musical notes. He found that DNA molecules of different bodily areas had their own musical melody; some had an uncanny resemblance to the works of the great composers. A decade later French anthropologist Jeremy Narby discovered that DNA emits and receives both phonons and photons (electromagnetic waves of sound and light)—verifying a shamanic teaching that it is impossible to enter the world of spirits and remain silent, for everywhere there is *visual music* and *endless sound.*[10]

What's with that 97 percent junk? DNA, besides being a biological Internet, forms a text, a keyboard, a musical score that *exactly follows the rules of grammar and language* (that's why affirmations and chants are so powerful). It was Pythagoras who claimed that "all things are numbers," that "every structural form is frozen music." And Goethe who declared that architecture is "crystallized music."

Connect all of this with language. If bilingualism (the immersion in and regular use of more than one language) begins before a child is four, not only will this instill a global consciousness early-on, but the practice also enables the child to focus better, make more efficient comparisons, and easily release what is no longer useful. These three bonuses form our "executive functions." And those little ones, babes even, are surprisingly sophisticated mini musicians, prewired in the womb for music and math and language.

The kicker is exercise. The brain/mind assembly will not operate right if the child doesn't jump around, dance, climb, leap, move hand over fist while hanging from contraptions like monkey bars, run, walk, reach, fall down, and get up again. Developmental advancements coordinate together and become advantageous only if *put to work through the human body*. Math classes miss the boat if there aren't gym, sports, music, art, band, and marching, too. With art classes, be sure to include finger painting and pottery making, if at all possible, because there's nothing quite like slapping around wet paints and globs of clay to reduce stress.

THE GREATEST ADVANCEMENTS

The greatest talent of the new children is the ability to abstract and function from the conceptual level. These children are not concrete thinkers. They are adept at the art of conceptualizing, dealing with broad ideas and notions. Forget thinking outside the box; for them, the box was never there to begin with. They can tie facts and figures and ideas together and rapidly produce solutions that fit, without having to go through conventional routines. Their minds leap instead of think. That's why they buckle under tried-and-true methods that demand rote discipline. Kids who abstract get from here to there as if by magic, not because they are wise but because they do not recognize limits. Their play is the search for better, easier ways of doing things. Their play is their genius.

A two-year-old child I know was in a conversation one day with her mother. She stopped midway and impatiently stomped her feet; then, with pointer finger aimed at her mother's nose, she yelled, "I don't know the word for that yet." Stop for a moment. How does a child of two know she doesn't know the word she wants to use at the precise moment she wants to use it? We mistakenly think the new children are wise old souls. This isn't wisdom at work here; it is the amazing, almost unbelievable ability to abstract knowledge, to know things without knowing. These children are conceptualizers, made to order for the Conceptual Age.

And the greatest advancement of all advancements in our brains is the prefrontal lobes (both left and right).

The prefrontals are behind our foreheads and sort of flow into the brain proper. They're dubbed wings of the brain, not because of their shape, but because they represent the highest and best in the human family. They operate as the seat of judgment, morals, empathy, compassion, and well-being; and they moderate social behaviors, decision making, and personality expression. The prefrontals developed late in the evolution of humankind, becoming a signature feature for distinguishing higher brain development. They are physically apparent in some kids—their foreheads either protrude or are quite rounded, curving back in over the nose. Yet the majority exhibit the character traits without differences in forehead shape. There are many scientists and educators studying the prefrontals. The best is Joseph Chilton Pearce, author of many books including *The Biology of Transcendence*.[11]

What people like Pearce tell us is that the mother's state while carrying her child determines the brain the child will have. Everything hinges on her perception of safety. If she feels threatened or if her environment is stressful or fear- or anger-inducing, her child will be more apt to develop the lower or reptilian brain (conditioned for fight, survival). If she feels comfortable, safe, it's as if the fetus gets an all-clear signal to go ahead and develop the prefrontals, the higher brain. The first three years are the most important for the "flowering" of the prefrontals. The second most important time is puberty. The brain does not fully mature until we are around the age of twenty-five.

Here are some striking comparisons: after the Iranian Revolution in 1979 that overthrew the shah, a mandate went out offering financial and government support for Iranian women to have more babies. These children were wanted, loved, well-fed, educated, and, for the most part, had supportive home environments. The mandate ended in 1990. During this period, prefrontal lobe development soared, producing the young adults who started the peaceful Green Movement, to object to the corrupt elections of 2009 and 2010. During this same time frame, Soviet forces invaded Afghanistan, tension built between Iran and Iraq, and the two Gulf Wars occurred. The constant fighting, intrigue, suicide bombers, carnage, and butchery on a massive scale—all in the name of Allah—destroyed families and family life. Prefrontal development plummeted, producing young adults who today are more radicalized than their elders. Their lost potential has become a global nightmare.

Decreased prefrontal lobe development can be turned around. Since the heart and prefrontals are in constant dialogue, the key to a healing environment is loving kindness. Meditation and mindfulness training (the practice of sitting quietly and observing thoughts and perceptions without judging them; learning to be in the moment) can repair damage to the prefrontals quicker than most other therapies.

Research on the prefrontal cortex has revealed that the lobes cannot process more than seven items at once (plus or minus two). That's why anything to be remembered (like codes and strings of numbers) seldom exceed this natural cutoff, and why all the religions of the world and all the spiritual traditions known to have existed have always regarded 7 as a sacred number and the key to unlocking divine truth (seven heavens, seven chakras, etc.). Attention given to prefrontal development in children will become a priority in the decades to come.

THE GREATEST CHALLENGES

Brain disorders and learning disorders seem to be the curse of being a new kid. The stats are worth repeating: in the United States, two out of every five children have a learning disorder, one out of every ten are mentally ill, cases of ADHD are up 600 percent since the early 1990s, and autism spectrum disorders are now so pervasive that they're considered an epidemic. The majority of brain mess-ups are in boys. A question to ask: Is this somehow related to the increasing feminization of nature, where animals (such as frogs), plants, and fish are beginning to revert to the female gender? Scientists are even finding that some sharks can now give birth without the necessity of male fertilization. Puzzles like this are mushrooming; answers are not.

Symptoms of the newest disorder include irritability or frequent displays of anger, excessive talking, racing thoughts, increased activity, decreased need for sleep, elation and silliness, grandiosity or excessive self-esteem, very intuitive and very creative displays. The diagnosis is . . . bipolar disorder (similar to ADHD, attention-deficit/hyperactivity disorder but with swings between highs and lows). Treatment: powerful antipsychotic drugs.[12]

Did you know that kids today are medicated at the same rate as adults? No long-term study has ever been done on the drugs we give our children. According to Joseph Chilton Pearce, in a talk he gave, some schools are said to get a bonus for every child they put on drugs. Whether this is true or not, no incentive seems to exist to encourage educators to recommend drug-free treatments. Insurance companies are well-known for giving incentives for drugs and disincentives for therapy. Who is the winner here? Pharmaceutical companies who are championing the latest diagnosis from what has become the "psychiatric industry,"[13] with declarations like "shyness is a sickness"[14]—one of many "abuse excuses" that threaten the legal system and society's moral equilibrium.[15]

For the first time, someone who was put on medication at a very young age—in this case because of ADHD—has written a book about what it was like to grow up on drugs. Kaitlin Bell Barnett never knew what it was like to feel love, to enjoy sex, to make the kind of personal choices most of us take for granted. Life to her was staring at a lineup of pill bottles and doing what she was told. She talks about a "lost youth" and gives the kids' side to this issue. Every parent and doctor should read *Dosed: The Medication Generation Grows Up*.[16]

What follows are some glaring observations one can make about the "disorders" that are being medicated:

+ Kids who have not mastered the ability to focus are said to have ADD or ADHD, but kids who have figured out how to focus are called geniuses.

+ Kids who are comfortable with limitlessness but haven't figured out how to experience this successfully in a physical body are called autistic, but kids who have figured out how to experience limitlessness in physicality and how to focus and utilize that awareness are called messiahs or Christed Ones.

+ Autism concerns extremes of the left hemisphere of the brain. Tiny details predominate, and extreme specialization in narrow ranges. Relationships and communication are difficult; autistic kids must hone in on a topic and comb it for details. Autism is diagnosed more often in males.

+ Dyslexia concerns extremes of the right hemisphere. These kids are usually smart, spatial, nonlinear, more intuitive, often left-handed, and late blooming. They show a tendency toward alcoholism, stuttering, and reversal of words. Although dyslexia is diagnosed more often in males than females, we know that girls compensate more readily than boys, leading to the suspicion that female cases are underreported.[17]

Add to these observations one more: 70 percent of the children who have autism are male, and 30 percent (one-third) female. The Rule of Thirds applies. I suspect it is the same proportion, only in reverse for dyslexia, although this is unproven as of this writing. Known causal factors for brain/learning disorders (percentages vary):

+ Metal toxicity, organic toxins, lead paint—especially in toys
+ Pesticide exposures, including prebirth exposure[18]
+ Artificial food coloring, chemical food additives, fruit sprays, hormones and antibiotics used in animal production[19]
+ Smart meters, cell phone towers, Wi-Fi, and electronic grids[20]

Action can be taken regarding these factors. Check on which chemicals are used in your food, and switch to organic milk. Pesticide usage can be traced, as well as exposure to incoherent energy sources (digital devices, smart meters, cell phone towers, electrical transmission lines, Wi-Fi, etc.). Have paint and metals tested. You can either lower exposure risks to all of these health hazards or eliminate them altogether. Investigation pays off.

The brain is malleable. *It is capable of healing and recovery—sometimes partially, sometimes all the way.* Research shows that it is possible for at least 10 to 20 percent of children with autism to completely recover as they mature.[21] Occasionally kids simply outgrow either ADD or ADHD as well. Changing sleep habits and getting more rest helps. (If you haven't tried Brain Gym techniques, please do, as they are quite remarkable—notably with dyslexia.[22]) Among the drug-free treatments, the more universally preferred is neurofeedback. The book *Healing Young Brains: The Neurofeedback Solution* by Robert W. Hill, Ph.D., and Eduardo Castro, M.D., is well worth reading.[23]

The most exciting news in this field, though, is the therapies developed by Anat Baniel and detailed in her book *Kids Beyond Limits: Breakthrough Results for Children with Autism, Asperger's, Brain Damage, ADHD, and Undiagnosed Developmental Delays.*[24] Baniel emphasizes in her work that *movement is the language of the brain.* Through slow, gentle hands-on and verbal techniques, she is able to awaken the brains of children, even tiny babies. The results of her therapies are undeniable, bordering on the miraculous.

Another surprise: nonverbal autistic people are responding to keyboarding on a computer in ways that are shocking scientists. It's as if they wake up (as per the teachings of Baniel) once they discover this "way out." Sue Rubin, a film writer with autism, is one who made that leap once she began listening to the news and reading the newspaper, thanks to her newfound keyboarding skills. Today she's a junior history major at Whittier College and lives semi-independently with an aide in her home a few blocks from campus. "Tell everyone," she types, "that nonverbal autistic people are intelligent!"[25]

Another real surprise: "brain-disordered" people have saved the world in the past and they still do. If you don't believe me, turn the page.

11

A Different Perspective

No child is a mistake; no child is broken.

SALLY PATTON

Patton's statement above backs up this reminder to "recognize the spiritual truth of your children and do not focus on brokenness and deficits."[1] Her message is more than powerful because ample proof exists in history that "mad men" (and women) made better leaders than normal folk.

Abraham Lincoln suffered deep depressions, heard voices, and had startling visions. Winston Churchill suffered from bipolar disorder. What these men struggled with made them sharper and better able to recognize and act on problems. Franklin Delano Roosevelt and John F. Kennedy Jr. dealt with the specter of mania, which enabled them to become resilient, to learn from failure and start over. Gandhi, Martin Luther King, General William T. Sherman, and Ted Turner benefitted as well from "unconventional" brain function. The research of Nassir Ghaemi and his team in the Mood Disorders Program at Tufts Medical Center is a testament to what can become of people with "brain glitches."[2] Consider also Albert Einstein and Issac Newton. Both exhibited the classic signs of autism spectrum (more specifically Asperger's syndrome), as did Nikola Tesla.

Nothing amazes more than the flip side of ADHD. Its positives are striking: creativity, energy, intuition, nonlinear minds that abstract, risk taking, entrepreneurial spirit, adventurousness, courageousness, curiosity, daring, cunning, and ability to thrive on the new and different.[3] ADHD is actually a gene mutation that first appeared in the human family about forty thousand years ago when the human race was faced with extinction (weather, earth changes, famine). Genetic scientists dubbed it the Hunter's Gene for the way people who had it struck out on their own and became hunter/gatherers. The gene then became quiescent in the human family, showing up in large numbers only when populations were threatened (war, famine, disease). Thus whenever the human family faced a "crash," the gene would pop up, then fall back in when need lessened. Today, the ADHD mutation has suddenly leapt sky-high, up 600 percent in the U.S. population since 1990, with a significant rise in other countries as well. Thomas Edison had it; so did many other inventors and far thinkers. For this reason, it is also called the Edison Gene.[4]

Is Mother Nature trying to tell us something about the future with the recent explosion in ADHD cases? Are we drugging into submission the very people gifted with the specific energy and daring needed to once again save the human race?

Any society labels a free thinker a "deviant." Yet such folk tend to flourish when others struggle. Find a deviant thinker who is positive and you have someone who can not only fire up a community, but draw from the wisdom of the group to organize potential, reduce violence, and put those to work who will. These individuals find unique ways to handle seemingly insoluble difficulties. They spread and sustain needed change. And they are everywhere. In September 2010, *Ode Magazine* ran an article about outliers who succeed against all odds; it referenced the book *The Power of Positive Deviance: How Unlikely Innovators Solve the World's Toughest Problems.*[5] Consider this book a must-read if you want to understand the new kids. They literally use their own bodies and lives as the "tool box" they experiment with to see what works and what doesn't and what can be done to change outcomes. Their perspective (*how* they think) wraps around a unique fulcrum point that deviates from society's norms . . . that of the outlier.

Take Mozart. He was said to have once mused, "We would not be creative at all if it were not for all these boundaries and limitations." And he pushed them, every boundary he could find, driven to capture the soul of how music *felt to him*. A Fifth Root Race type, he lived at a time when Europe was abuzz with souls just like we have now—then for the Renaissance; now for the coming change in human consciousness.

Thomas Armstrong explains it this way: "People with conditions like ADHD, dyslexia, and mood disorders are routinely labeled 'disabled.' But differences among brains are as enriching—and essential—as differences among plants and animals. Welcome to the new field of neurodiversity."[6] He shows how your brain is a "rain forest" with a tremendous ability to transform and alter with changing times. To medicalize and pathologize differences misses the point, and puts society itself at risk of losing the very diversity needed for enriched and healthy continuance. For example, dyslexics often have minds that visualize clearly in three dimensions, those with ADHD have a more diffuse attention style, and the autistic relate to objects better than to people. We need them, all of them, for the human brain is not a machine. An authority on neurodiversity, Armstrong adds this about the brain: "It is a biological organism—not hardware or software, but wetware. And it is messy."

Seven basic brain disorders exist: ADHD, autism, dyslexia, mood disorders, anxiety disorders, intellectual disabilities, and schizophrenia. All of them create distinctive ecosystems that make the "tolerance mantra" of the new children an authentic, in-your-face truism. "We're differently able," they assert. "Reordered, not disordered." They insist that "your weakness is uniqueness." Children with varied abilities star in concerts all over the city of Chicago. Why not elsewhere? Television ads, if you really study them, actually program people to become disordered, overstimulated, and at risk. Turn off that television set. Once you do, you'll recognize something quite remarkable. Our children are multi-sensory multichannelers, who live in a multiverse. They instinctively bond into . . . *Generation WE*.[7]

Catch this: the majority of today's children are not just groupies. They tend to think as if in unison, as if a "we," and make choices as though in step with a level of consciousness they hardly notice. Social networking is part of that; still, it's almost as if the young possess a "hive mind" that thinks, moves, and acts on cue, *irrespective of iPhones and Twitter*.

Do you remember the 2005 news coverage of the young women lacrosse champions from Northwestern University that met with the president in the White House? Almost all of them wore flip-flops. This was not prearranged. They just showed up that way, causing a dress-code controversy that continues to this day.

Social etiquette in movie theaters and concerts flip-flopped around the same time, when the young refused to obey common house rules. Today many rant, rave, text, or "YouTube" even the slightest affront or retort—as if giving full attention is a thing of the past, sitting in a chair a waste of time, and silence somehow obscene. Everything to them— movies, sporting events, concerts, church services, lectures, speeches, tours—is interactive. Distraction comes with the show.

Youthquakes are worldwide. Elite orchestras are now being led by vibrant, passionate, totally unconventional, even manic, directors who are just as likely to drag their musicians into markets and grocery stores for shopper serenades as they are to explode concert halls with the sounds of "punk" programming.

The young so believe in file sharing, a practice tied to the idea of "we" (we have, we think, we do, we share), that they almost dismantled the music industry by giving away their music files, ignoring copyrights, contracts, and the right of artists to be paid for their work. This is now happening with books, thanks to technologies and services that enable anyone to pirate the work of others. This type of piracy is global, turning file sharing into outright theft. What is instinctual to them, what seems fair and right and good . . . has another side.

Keep in mind how our young people are polarizing: coming together as if one, yet expressing that unity in opposite ways. What happened in August 2011 with the London riots and the massacre in Oslo, Norway, illustrates that contrast.

London riots: Some blame the protest on a backlash to the government's austerity program. After days of unparalleled violence, looting, firebombing cars/businesses/homes, killing some, injuring many, the upshot hung on the discovery that the unrest was largely the work of children. Although started in impoverished sections, a flash-mob mentality quickly took over and the riots spread. Police were overwhelmed. Locals had to protect their own. Initially a protest against taxes and the rich, the real cause of the anarchy became blatantly obvious: the kids were bored.

Norwegian massacre: A young Norwegian dressed as a police officer set off an explosion in Oslo to divert police so he could hop a boat to the island of Utøya. Once at the popular camp/retreat, he opened fire. Death toll: 91 teenagers. He was protesting Norwegian immigration laws that allow what he felt was too many Muslims into the country. His actions so shocked people that Norway, already known as a land of peace, transformed itself. Liv Evensen was there.

We left roses all around town—stuck in construction-site fences, on street columns, around statues, floating in Oslo's fountains . . . so beautiful. I walked with people to the National Theatre. Three ambulances were parked there and they were covered with roses in appreciation by people. Farther up the main street people had stuck roses down in cracks in the street and at Parliament Hill, a sea of flowers and lit candles. People are hugging each other and speaking to each other and rooting for even more tolerance, even more freedom of speech, even more love and caring. The Crown Prince said it: "Today our streets are covered by love. We will not be silenced. We will not hide our sadness nor grief. Some will need longer

time than others, but our streets are covered by love." Our politicians are
kinder now to each other. I hugged two of them today.

In London, when a young girl was asked why she was rioting, she replied: "We want our taxes back. The rich must pay." In Oslo, Liv asked of a young man on the street, "Did you lose someone close?" He replied through tears, "We all lost all those youngsters." Another person asked if he was with anyone. He replied, "We're all together."

In London, social networks were used to generate flash mobs, which spread senseless destruction. In Oslo, social networks called forth people to hug each other and spread love.

Yes, the new kids feel entitled. They claim the right to express themselves in any manner they so choose. But because of short attention spans, lives stuffed into the "blanket" of incoherent digital energy now covering our planet, our children are easily frustrated . . . and a frustrated child is easy to anger and be manipulated. Hence they harass, stalk, plague, and threaten each other with a recklessness on the scale of a nightmare. According to Joseph Chilton Pearce, "Between 1990 and 2000, 55,000 children killed each other. Nothing like this has ever happened before in history." The mantra of "I can't think"[8] has become a scream against information overload, a state affecting everyone. With kids, though, this directly impinges on brain development. The prefrontals have a limited capacity of working memory: seven items, plus or minus two. We all hit this wall. When it happens to children, they lose the ability to read faces and body language and the tone of one's voice. They lose empathy.

The Rule of Thirds applies to what I keep finding. This natural measuring stick works as well with negatives as with positives for deeper insight. What follows is a whole string of them, and a lot of surprises.

One-third of our children harass and threaten others according to survey estimates—usually through social networks, but just as often in and through school and home environments. This is the act of bullying.

One-third of our children are considered "lost," too violent to rehabilitate by the mental healthcare community. It is said that predictive behavior for this can begin with babies as young as fifteen months— those who cannot stand to be touched and are inordinately upset by normal sounds and gestures.

These estimates illustrate something very unusual: the difficulties the new children face, whether acquired or inborn, are in proportion to the startling rise in their intelligence. Downturns are moving in rhythm with uplifts.

But here's the eerie part.

For most of my adult life I've been asking questions of young people, simple questions like "What do you want to be when you grow up? Do you want to marry? Do you see yourself ever becoming a parent?" The usual "I want to be a fireman [or a nurse] and have four kids" abruptly changed in the eighties. From then on, the answers I received came from a decided knowingness about things future:

> One-third had no sense of living a full life (nothing morbid, just factual). None seemed worried about this, nor were they interested in assigning a reason.
>
> Two-thirds had no intention of ever marrying, going to college, or becoming parents. They were more attracted to a simple life with few possessions or debt. (Remember, these kids can and do go in opposite directions at the same time. Even though they can be consumed by consumerism, they can just as easily walk away from the tenets of "success.")

I started doing this long before the economic downturn, intensifying my focus once my research also included near-death states. In the past few years, however, studies about the Millennial Generation (born from 1982 to 2001) now echo what I previously noticed. Generational researchers blame the two-thirds majority on the high divorce rate of parents and on the Great Recession, which most tag at beginning in 2006. In other words, they see the young as too spooked to plan long-term. As a basic assessment, their explanation works; still, it does not address the comparison I can make between children of the '60s and '70s, and what I noticed with basically the same type of kids (plus near-death kids) during the '80s, '90s, and early 2000s. The difference was a uniquely odd and eerie perspective.

And it was off-angled, as if they possessed a second set of eyes and another bank of memories tied closely to broad sweeps of time and space. Without meaning to, they behaved as if prognosticators of a future they already knew and had previously agreed on. Wave after wave of children are coming in like this now. Many are quite open about it. They may not consciously know what will happen in their lifetime, yet somehow, in ways no one can fully understand, they do know the future and their place in it. This alarms parents, not kids.

This odd perspective is attuned to what in esoteric traditions is called the natural order. Within this aegis they want to change the mainstream, or at least build parallels to it based on alternatives and sustainability measures that bypass the mainstream. They sometimes turn to telepathy to communicate with each other because it's faster and easier, and consider intuitive/psychic promptings of importance. They listen to a guidance not their own.

Their version of the natural order is plain enough:

+ You know what is right. It's stamped in your heart.
+ Return to an awareness of consequences. Are you aware? Do you care?
+ Expect to live your life with others who are different from you. It's okay.
+ We all make mistakes. . . . Admit, apologize, correct, move on.
+ Guilt serves no purpose. Blaming and obsessing are a waste of time.
+ Your intention is who you are. No need to defend this.
+ Life is about focus, who you are inside, your intention.
+ There are no free passes. We're all in this together.

There is not a leader alive who is prepared to handle this crop of citizenry—not politicians, heads of state, religious figures, or corporate executives.

An immense plus many bring with them that skirts the way leadership roles have been conducted in the past is their ability to form holons. A holon is a situation where opposing sides come together to accomplish a given task or project that is of mutual benefit for the greater good. Young people understand that opposing forces are not going to change. Trying to get along usually backfires. Their idea of diplomacy differs in that they have no need for sameness. They want solutions that make things better. Their approach: get all sides together, figure out what needs to be done and how to pay for it, empower the people in the group to make work assignments and figure out details, do the work, finish the job. By working together to accomplish a task at hand, progress becomes an organic mix of discovery—that opposing forces are really the same at their core. The greater good wins. No one changed, yet everyone changed. A holon was created. . . . *The strength of a whole comes from the diversity of its many parts working together.*

Underlying all these thirds is a secret: *the new children hold pain deep inside.* It's as if they carry into this world all the suffering of past worlds, past lives, past identities, past histories of one sort or another. They seek permission to let this out, heal it. Listen to what kids have to say. Listen deeply. As they heal, worlds of hurt heal. Give them permission to be who they are and they will help us heal the problems of a globe in transition.

All things move and have their being—their life—through what is termed the spiritual, that sense of a higher reality and a greater order. Our children are connected to this in a way previous generations were not. The older kids define spirituality as alchemy without props. Only a small fraction relate to church and the religious experience, and follow a preset dictum of behavior and belief. Many of the others simply feel God, breathe God, know God, talk to God as an ever-present reality. They heal and help in the name of the God of Love they intimately know, as if this was part of their job specs in being alive. Even the differently ordered hold to this same sense of truth, as William Stillman says when speaking for those with autism in his small but powerful book *The Soul of Autism*.[9]

In *The Bond*, Lynne McTaggart explains scientifically what the new kids are born knowing: "The idea of the individual is a fallacy."[10]

12 GENERATIONAL FACTORS

The visible world is part of a more spiritual universe from which it draws its chief significance.

WILLIAM JAMES

Mystics tell us that souls tend to incarnate in groups. John Van Auken, when interpreting the readings of Edgar Cayce, noted, "Nearly all souls on the planet today were together in past ages of human history. As a result, the relationships among the people of the world today are a reflection of the past. It's not just personal, it's *cosmic*, and *regional* within the Cosmos. For example, the souls who came in to this specific *solar system* comprise a subset of all the souls ever created. This solar soul group can then be divided into the subgroups we call 'the generations'. . . . In a manner of speaking, such groups form a distinct *collective consciousness* and *spirit,* much like the souls who gave us 'the spirit of '76.'"[1]

It fascinates me that generational researchers like Neil Howe and William Strauss, in their seminal achievement *Generations: The History of America's Future, 1584 to 2069,* arrived at a basic theme or shared mentality for each generation in our history—based on the forces and challenges faced by that generation during their growing years—*that almost exactly dovetails with the astrological cycles of Pluto (now* downgraded to "dwarf" status), *plus the spiritual understandings of soul group incarnations* (similar to what Van Auken described).[2]

It is not a stretch, then, to say, that what we call generations are groups of souls who come and go in waves of intent and purpose, each marked by an imprint or energy pattern that distinguishes that wave's members from those who came before and those who will follow. Tradition marks a generation at thirty-three years, yet most seesaw between fourteen and twenty-six years, depending on the impact of historical events.

The best way to explore this is through the lens of astrology, which affords a clear view of time cycles through the aegis of symbolic metaphor, human behavior, and historical occurrences.

THE MARCH OF GENERATIONS

Believe it or not, the erratic dwarf called Pluto casts a dynamic influence on generational trends and changes and the mass movements that shape society itself. I first wrote of this in *Beyond the Indigo Children*.[3] This time, however, I will weave in some of the comments and ideas of astrologer Theresa H. McDevitt (author of *Why History Repeats: Mass Movements and the Generations, Past-Present-Future*[4]) with my own. Her work tracing the historical influences of Pluto's passages from before the first century CE to the twenty-third helps evolutionary patterning make more sense.

Theresa explains that "the cycle of the planet Pluto shows our group karma, or the purpose of our particular generation and the part we must play as individuals. It specifically shows how one generation impacts the next and what to expect when each one begins to stamp its mark on the world. . . . Hence, people feel motivated or compelled to express the issues related to the particular sign being activated by Pluto at the time. Likewise, the generation born absorbs the pertinent qualities of the sign that will identify them as part of a specific group for the rest of their lives."

Using the model developed by Strauss and Howe, here is a keyword description of the part Pluto plays in the march of generations. Notice that each generation encompasses dual passages of Pluto through zodiacal signs, except for three with the Millennials and only one with the Aquarians.

1901–1924: G.I. Joes (Builders)

Dubbed the greatest generation, this group, toughened by the Great Depression, fought two world wars with the "right stuff." *Pluto in Gemini until 1913* (experimentation, invention, ideas, communication, restless, changeable); continued breakout from restrictive past, including the Roaring '20s, explosion of scientific genius, New Thought movement, Industrial Revolution, Women's Suffrage. *Pluto moves into Cancer* (family, protection, hard work, loyalty, patriotism, emotion, dedication, possessiveness); immigration increases, women's rights expand, women take part in the war effort, building boom, labor unions, patriotism and creativity on a grand scale, progress as conditional, alcoholism.

1925–1942: Silents (Care Givers)

A time of broken dreams; faithful workers either ignored, skipped, or forgotten. Took care of others. *Pluto in Cancer until 1939* (extreme patriots, care givers, the military, sacrifice for country, changing family roles); birthed the largest group of future women prime ministers in history, women's rights, Wall Street crash, the Great Depression, psychiatry, psychoanalysis. *Pluto in Leo begins* (pride, drive to perform, self-identity, independence, media savvy, energy, powerful creativity and innovation)—the rise and fall of egocentric leaders and dictators, the holocaust, Pearl Harbor, War bonds, Walt Disney, Hollywood glamour and showmanship.

1943–1960: Boomers (Rebels)

A me-first, narcissistic trend that resulted in a youthful upheaval. In huge numbers and with a spiritual euphoria unknown before, they burst the seams of every social institution and fabric. *Pluto in Leo until 1958* (self-expression, entertainment, visionary sense of purpose, dictatorial, lavish spending); a television set in most homes, self-help, free love, drugs, Woodstock, space program, Civil Rights movement, Peace Corps. *Pluto entered Virgo* (service, healthcare, dedicated workers, analytical, efficient, pragmatic); Leo extremes hit hard with AIDS, drug addictions, alcohol abuse, bankruptcies, draft dodging, issues with children.

1961–1981: Generation X (Survivors)

Our nation's thirteenth generation, dubbed the lost generation. A star-crossed bunch challenged by poverty, drugs, and parental neglect. *Pluto in Virgo until 1972* (technical, studious, clever organizing, perfectionism, activism, political leanings); the "latchkey kids" with no real sense of family, Vietnam War, skyrocketing divorce rates, corporate takeovers, failing schools, hypocrisy, instant gratification, abortions, identity theft, computer viruses, androgyny, strong survival instinct. *Pluto enters Libra* (partnership, relationships, balance, law, diplomacy); marriage changes, team players, social "tribes," tattoos/body piercing, cult leaders, court challenges, rising military complex alongside peace movements, the "smiley face," clever perversions.

1982–2001: Millennials (Fixers)

New traditionalists consider themselves "generation fix," here to repair the excesses and cynicism of the past. Innovative thinkers, they abstract easily, have high IQ scores and wisdom beyond their years. *Pluto in Libra until 1984* (vanity, the arts, sharing, sociability, ethical, legal); nicknamed the "mini me's," consumerist, wealth oriented, engage in business startups, develop new technologies, view the world through screens, expect instant communication, are exposed to constant sound. *Pluto in Scorpio until 1995* (transformation, sexuality, political manipulation, taxation, life extremes, mysteries); shrinking middle class, authority figures crash, small groups/smart mobs/coalitions, "evil empires,"

political wars, Iran-Contra, money laundering, drug lords, riots, geno-
cides, New Age rise and fall, famine, child porn. *Pluto enters Sagittarius*
(religion, beliefs, judgment, adventure, luck, privilege, idealism); foreign
interests, quick tempers, sharp words, science/sports dominate, humani-
tarianism, volunteerism, gambling, UFO cults, religious fanatics/mar-
tyrs/human bombs, ethnic controversies.

2002–2024: 9/11 Generation (Adapters)

A clash of cultures underscores much global unrest. Excitement of can-
do optimism and extraordinary advancements in technology gives way
to a deep distrust of government, banking, corporations, and religious
institutions. A growing need to understand what is feared and to heal.
Pluto in Sagittarius until 2008 (the world as one family, global perspective, expansion, faith, morality, publicity, the "party animal," nature, the
environment, careers); massive concerts to raise aid money, entertain-
ers as global ambassadors, starvation and education global issues, ethnic
violence, terrorism, gay rights, a desire to embrace "other," safety issues.
Pluto enters Capricorn (slowdowns, ambition, conservativism, discipline,
limitations, greed seen as deserved); senior-citizen rights versus young-
adult resentment, recession/depression a national disgrace, return to
basics, unique types of housing, sustainability, educational turnaround,
global economic restructuring, constitutional threat, inspired/common-
sense solutions to problems.

2025–2043: Aquarians (Connectors)

Initial beginning of Aquarian Age. Ongoing religious reformations,
global campaign for human rights. Although Aquarian energy does
not permeate our planet until between 2132 and 2150, awareness of
the coming Age of Enlightenment spreads across all sectors. Aquarian
characteristics (diversity, revolution, reform, progress, the individual,
science, technology, invention, change agent, unconventional, erratic
genius, visionary thinking); cloning, body part replacements, universal rallies the norm, lunatic fringe, less government controls/more

individual responsibility/individual accomplishments, alien connection, robotics, plagues/blood diseases, departures in genetics.

The world as we know it is rapidly disappearing. As illustrated in the march of generations, each wave of souls entering the earth plane moves into place, taking on traits necessary for both individual maturity and collective evolution. We tend to be a little myopic when we focus most on what straddles our vision line, rather than taking the time to study history and gain that longer view of what is valuable and what is not.

I want to take a moment here to review some of the popular labels applied to certain of our new children. There's an astrological interpretation worth considering before we tackle the energetics of generational *signatures*.

THREE WAVES

Reverend Alice Miller, another astrologer, mentioned three waves of special children entering the earth plane in an article. "Humanity is growing up," said Miller, "beginning to take responsibility for its own choices. Gradually, true Spirituality is replacing organized religion. It has served its purpose, and served it well, but the time has come for us all to take responsibility for our own moral choices." She continues, "To this end, new generations of more-evolved children began to be born, first a sprinkling, then a small stream."[5]

The first wave began in the late seventies, according to Miller, and continued throughout the eighties with the emergence of indigos. She calls them *system-busters,* pioneers here to plant seeds of change and jolt elders out of past ruts. They have been condemned, praised, and branded learning disabled. "Think of them as college graduates sent back to kindergarten," she advises. "They cannot slow their minds sufficiently for working so far beneath their capabilities."

The second wave she pegs more for the nineties and into the 2000s. She sees these as the "crystal" children—inclined to use passive resistance and ignore what ruffled the indigos. Many are autistic, she cautions, or at least so supersensitive that they build defenses around them as protection from the mental and emotional chaos of their environment. She claims that the third wave is imminent, the "rainbow" kids. It is her belief that these children will balance the active and passive traits of their predecessors, bringing in a type of wholeness more indicative of "Aquarian Age humanity."

Miller will be the first to admit that no line can be drawn between soul waves as to who enters when or how. I think she would also agree that no label, no matter how popular, is really that useful. Thanks to Pluto, though, we can recognize the energetics of mass movement and the larger patterning that gives us.

There is a point to be made: foundational energy changed three times during the birthing years of the Millennial Generation. That's stress. It's no wonder that people born during that time are so changeable, restless, and sometimes lose their way, or that parents, schools, and employers are to this day still confused about them. Millennial brilliance and disappointment are almost equally mixed. The 9/11s entered under the shadow of historical retribution. Mass mind altered sharply on September 11, 2001, as if creating a portal where the unfinished business of the past several thousand years could be noticed, admitted, and healed.[6] Because of this generation's efforts to put things right, the groundwork will be laid for the single-minded, decidedly different Aquarians—the true mavericks.

GENERATIONAL SIGNATURES

Signatures are concentrations of particular traits or characteristics of an energy patterning that undergird the cycle itself. They define core essence as well as the thrust of the cycle in positive/negative terms, revealing potential—the range of how that energy patterning could manifest. The chart below shows each of the generations mentioned thus far and the signatures they carry.

Generation	Positive Signature	Negative Signature
(1901–1924) G.I. Joes	Perseverance	Stubbornness
(1925–1942) Silents	Compassion	Disillusionment
(1943–1960) Boomers	Enthusiasm	Selfishness
(1961–1981) Generation X	Resourcefulness	Suicide/depression (self-condemnation)
(1982–2001) Millennials	Tolerance	Anger (a peculiar impatience)
(2002–2024) 9/11 Generation	Adaptability	Fear (insecurity)
(2025–2043) Aquarians	Humanitarian	Instability (crisis)

A note about Millennial anger: *listen to them*. They are good observers with a lot to say. Their hot buttons are lies, deceit, manipulation. Unlike children of the past, these kids are quick to object to what they see as unfair—no matter where.

About 9/11 fear: *be a mentor to them*. Few are allowed to have the freedom to be a child. What used to enthrall past generations scares them. They need a lot of assurances to know that it's okay to explore and take a chance. About Aquarian instability: *help them to feel*. There is a fine line between genius and mental illness. Volunteering is a must, as it enables them to experience personally what others face on a daily basis. Physical labor and the arts are their release valves.

MILLENNIAL VOICES

Newspaper Article on Aaron McGruder, Author of "Boondocks" Comic Strip

[A young man by the name of] Aaron McGruder has been called a "genius" and "the angriest black man in America" as he skewered everything from the Bush White House to Black Entertainment Television. His comic strip premiered on the Cartoon Network's Adult Swim in 2005, and he has gone on to even more acclaim for his work. "For me," says McGruder, "it really first has to be a good story and be funny. If you're doing sincere comedy, the edgy stuff kind of happens on its own."

He continued, "For you, some 10-year-old kids talking about hoes may not [be] that big of a deal. But someone out there is gonna flip. There's no way to know. So I just try to deliver an amusing and decent story and leave the shock and awe to whatever people have in their own heads."[7]

Brooke Mahanes

For a good part of my life, I have been flooded with horrible images, dreams, PTSD-type experiences of war and torture, unspeakable cruelty against humans and animals. During my time of the month I get to see all kinds of suffering of women.

Finally, last month as that was happening, I saw the images begin swirling around me and they lifted up through my central core and went out my crown, as Legions of Michael and Grace, Purity, and Rapture Elohim took those energies along with the Violet Flame of Transmutation into another realm for healing. I wasn't sure if it was good to have all those energies go through my body, but I figured if all these wonderful Angels and Elohim are involved, then it's probably okay. I figured it was what I was supposed to do with those things all along. I read about how some people are here to help clear the human genetic consciousness and I guess that is how I am experiencing the clearing. I hope to help teach people to do this because it's really easy and a gift from our Creator, [a necessity] for our times. It is great that all the "junk" was helped to be released by 9/11, and now we gotta clean it up!

Grandfather Edwin Silverheels (the Millennial pattern can apply to any age)

My spiritual mother Emily General gave me a tape that she made before she died. In it, she explained how our people from the six nations were known as Light Walkers. She gave a brief example using me, and asked if I ever wondered why she and the chiefs and clan mothers would spend so much time with me. She also mentioned that they could only "hold a mirror to my face," as it was up to me if I could someday look beyond what I didn't want to see. Her tape did help me understand why I could seemingly do a lot of things, as if I were trained. If there are more people out there who feel compelled to have a duty in life, then I am so very glad of that. I could sometimes feel people's pain and fear or happiness when I held their hands. I had to stop that. It would drain me.

Monica Majewski

I myself have a lot of psychic tendencies, and experienced warnings of something horrible to happen the weekend prior to April 16. The morning of the sixteenth I did everything as I normally did, but before I left for class I noticed I had a tiny blood spot on the knee of my jeans. I tried to rub out the stain; the odd thing was that from that small spot, the bathroom filled with the odor of blood. I drove to the campus of Virginia Tech and parked right by the Duck Pond. Every morning I would meet my good friend there. We got to class about fifteen minutes before 9:00, and even as I sat there I could still smell the blood from my jeans. Halfway through class, I noticed a guy sitting in the first row, who never took off his jacket or hat, get up and quietly leave. I watched him walk up the steps right outside our room. As class ended a girl announced that she got an e-mail from the school stating that there had been a shooting on campus. It wasn't until we all walked outside that there was chaos. Even before the casualties were reported I called my parents to tell them I was all right. I mentioned about the male in my class that suspiciously left early, wearing clothes that I later learned matched the gunman's. Just recently the police have begun to investigate the Duck Pond; a witness said they saw Cho there throwing something into the water. It upset me that I could have crossed paths with Cho that morning. I ignored all the warning signs that God was trying to give me, from the anxiety of feeling death around me the weekend before to the mysterious spot [on my jeans] that reeked of blood.

13   Puzzled Parents

Kids go where there is excitement. They stay where there is love.

Zig Ziglar

How do you raise a child smarter than you? Well, you don't. In truth, they raise you. And that is exactly what is happening in the majority of households. Adora Svitak, a twelve-year-old, has written several books about this and produced a video called *What Adults Can Learn from Kids*.[1] She's one of many with a clear mind, who sees past the gullibility of adults who react rather than respond.

Consider their parents. Most come from Generation X, with a few late boomers in the mix. This generation was almost forgotten, wedged as they were between boomer splash and new-kid upstarts. They have been edgy and tired for years, waiting for the widespread recognition due to them but that wound up going only to a few. The feeling of having the rug pulled out from under them pervades their sense of security and self-worth even today. So let's begin with them.

FIRST AID FOR PARENTS

We know now that men's testosterone levels decrease once they become fathers (easing out aggressive tendencies, making it more comfortable to "stick" and "stay"), even more if they participate in child rearing—proof that men are designed to take part in raising their children. I want to say that right off, so when I refer to parents you'll know I mean both men and women. Meg Blackburn Losey, Ph.D., wrote a book about the struggle of child rearing called *Parenting the Children of Now: Practicing Health, Spirit, and Awareness to Transcend Generations.*[2] She admonishes parents to "get real and accept yourself," as she zeros in on every flaw and fumble of raising yourself . . . alongside your kids. Another important read: *Joyful Evolution: A Guide for Loving Co-creation with Your Conscious, Subconscious, and Superconscious Selves* by Gordon Davidson.[3] The author has dedicated his life to supporting individuals as they seek to fulfill the highest vision for their life while exploring and accepting the truth of who they really are.

Both of these books center around the same point: know thyself. Babies are not pets, reality shows on television are performance based, and the party scene is a seldom seen, if you're smart. Don't be so busy looking *at* your children that you miss the view you could have had if you looked *with* them.

Simple is best. Don Miguel Ruiz in *The Four Agreements* and *The Fifth Agreement* made core truth the ultimate in simplicity:[4]

+ Be impeccable with your word
+ Don't take things personally
+ Don't make assumptions
+ Always do your best
+ Be skeptical; learn to listen

Admit it . . . you work out the problems you had in your childhood through your relationships as an adult, especially mom-and-dad issues. *Know thyself* is no small order, yet it is the most important journey anyone can undertake. Parents get double duty: discovering who they really are while helping their kids explore the life they now have. The best "first aid" for this is having the presence of mind to ask questions, as no one source has all the answers you will need.

RECOGNIZING THE TERRITORY

Kids lie and siblings fight with each other. Insufficient sleep messes you up. White parents rarely talk about race; blacks and Hispanics/Latinos do—a lot. Tests for giftedness are not as accurate as observation. Children learn more from what they see than from what you say. Love doesn't solve all your problems.

Basic truths like these about stressors in family interactions are still the same old basic truths. They haven't changed just because the human race is evolving. These positive, workable solutions are true—today and always:

+ Stay calm; turning up the volume scares or angers people.
+ Stop arguing; adult logic doesn't translate to kid speak.
+ Give everyone a chance to be heard; encourage listening.
+ Have some fun; laugh more; hug often; lend a hand.
+ Efforts count more than results.

The key to a successful life, whether or not you are a parent, is balance. The new kids haven't discovered this yet. Let's help them.

A HOST OF SUGGESTIONS

Hold on to your chair. I intend to stuff this section with everything I can cram into it, beginning now.

+ True for all ages: for the six weeks before your birthday, your energy is at its lowest ebb of the year. For the six weeks after your birthday the reverse is true—your energy can peak. Opposite your birthday (on the calendar) is a time when you may need to struggle and put in more effort, yet possibilities are greater. Aim expectations to match the basic energetic rhythms of human capability.

+ How a person moves (also his or her posture) says volumes about self-esteem and health. This is crucial with the new kids, as they tend to slouch for hours using their cyber toys, which puts their spine and lungs at risk, not to mention the image of them that's perceived by others. Double the trouble if high heels are worn.

+ The job of a child is to play. Kids need time, books, nature, and love. Don't waste your money on gimmicks or in producing the next great genius. Some children's book publishers are now doing away with pictures as a way to cut costs. Complain.

+ Encourage your children to read a book a week during summer. Set the stage for them to present written or oral book reports on a regular basis to the family.

+ Today's kids size up their parents by the age of two or two and a half. They know who you are and what they have to do to raise you so they can get what they want. You can bribe them, make deals, negotiate, explain—for they can think things through. Don't hide anything from them. Be honest. Be authentic. Let them know what you expect from them. Follow through on what you say.

+ No junk food under the age of three. Natural sugars only. Children's bodies today do not process foods like their parents' or grandparents' did. Processed foods today are also more unhealthy than those of the past. Young people's intestinal tracts are often unable to absorb needed nutrients. Food allergies are now so pervasive, some psychologists believe it to be a major cause in learning disorders. If in doubt, have your child tested for allergies. Cut down on fruit juices and soft drinks. Cut out fructose and aspartame completely, and most food colorings. Eat very little processed foods. Read every label. Educate yourself.

+ Sugar addiction is a leading cause of the obesity epidemic, but so is keeping kids inside. Kids must be allowed to be kids and participate in roughhousing, outdoor games, making forts, rock climbing, nature walks, taking care of pets, explorations, building things, cloud gazing, local jobs, family chores, and hikes. You can actually improve cognitive function and concentration skills just by immersion in nature. An added benefit: peace of mind and a sense of the sacred. The parent's challenge is to show a generation of kids how to be active and how to appreciate the novelty of real-life adventures.[5]

✦ Consumerism has taught children to expect to get what they want when they want it. Many kids now regard being taught how to work a form of child abuse. This should be a wake-up call for every parent to make a few changes:

❖ No computers in bedrooms for any family member. Keep them centrally located.

❖ No television sets in bedrooms. They too must be centrally located.

❖ Radio is still the most reliable communicator. (Plus, you're dealing with less incoherent energy fields.) These can be in any room.

❖ Teach/learn basic homemaking skills—cooking, nutrition, budgeting.

❖ Teach/learn mending and first aid, as well as how to care for those who are ill.

❖ Cleanliness and good housekeeping skills are a must.

❖ Household chores begin when the child is big enough to put away toys.

❖ No news shows or watching fast-paced television before bedtime; this includes cartoons like *SpongeBob SquarePants*. Lights out means lights out: texting or playing video games or with apps on any electronic device not only robs kids of sleep (and adults too), but also puts the nervous system and brain function at risk. Lack of sleep is a major problem. You may have to get tough with this one.

+ The more bells and whistles smart phones have, the more likely the young are to become attached to them. Not only does this cause sleep loss, but "separation anxiety" when the child is away from his or her phone. There are other factors too, like overexposure. The new kids photograph and document everything. Have a heart-to-heart about the following:

  ❖ Federal law states that a child must be thirteen to have a page on a social media site or website. Kids defy this. Parents let them, effectively teaching their children that lying is okay.

  ❖ File sharing is another form of theft. Check before you press Send.

  ❖ Cyberstalking is bullying carried to extremes. Don't do it.

  ❖ Personal computers for toddlers improve dexterity while dumbing down overall intelligence and creative genius. Forget about getting one.

  ❖ Prospective employers are now checking social media outlets before hiring to see what kind of person you are and how you handle yourself . . . going all the way back to first use when a kid. There's no get-out-of-jail-free card with this.

  ❖ Excessive text messaging causes more problems than it's worth. It's an endless source of distraction.

  ❖ Data on Internet social media sites is regularly sold to "persons of interest."

  ❖ Whatever is posted remains; many deletions are not true deletions.

+ Bring back character building.[6] Encourage volunteerism, participating in social responsibilities, and viewing only those movies and television shows that teach integrity, self-worth, and respect. Instruct in how to say no and risk the consequences; and how to argue so expressed viewpoints can be negotiated. A wonderful way to do all of this within the family unit is to hold weekly (or monthly) "town hall" meetings. The family gathers around the dinner table. Each in turn reports on any problem, argument, or accomplishment. Others ask questions. Discussion, debate, and negotiation follow, and votes are taken when a decision needs to be made that involves the entire family. The importance of each member is honored.

✦ Teach your kids about money and thrift. This is absolutely essential. Some tips:

❖ The child portions out all monies received. Ten percent off the top goes back to God/Allah/The Divine in a church setting or is donated to a charity or to someone who needs help. Ten percent goes into long-term savings, 40 percent is saved for future education, and 40 percent goes to the child to spend now or later on. Illustrate the power of budgeting.

❖ A savings-account passbook is the child's and should be kept in the child's room. Parents can monitor this, but hands-on activity with it is always the child's.

❖ Household chores never involve money. Income derives from gifts, extra jobs, allowance, and work outside the home. Discuss this, especially ways to increase income. Many kids develop businesses they conduct over the Internet. Let your kids feel the pinch if budget measures fail to cover actual expenses.

❖ When shopping, give the money to the child. The child then pays the clerk, checks the change, and returns it to the parent. If children never touch or count money spent on them, if they don't have a feel for actual bills and coins, they tend to grow up with a detached/distorted sense of values and meaning—and little regard for planning ahead or impulse control.

❖ No credit card for a child under 18—ever. Payments on credit cards should never be made by parents, except in the case of a valid emergency.

✦ Maintain control and discipline through cleverness, not punishment. Bargain, negotiate, compromise. Establish turf rules: parents and kids have quiet rooms. Privacy is earned. Praise children for their efforts, not for talent.[7] This is especially true of anger issues; praise the child for learning to control his or her anger and act appropriately.

- ❖ Show children how to use respectful language, even when arguing.
- ❖ Instigate time-out and discussion periods. If they mess up, they clean up.
- ❖ Teach anger management and mediation skills by the first grade, if not before.
- ❖ Enact honesty codes. Listen carefully to kids' sides, their assessments, and any correction they agree is needed. Help them to see what happened from all sides. Show how anger can be a prelude to courageous action.
- ❖ Depression is anger turned inward. Move it out with art, pets, journaling.

+ Eat together as often as possible. Have something lovely for a table or countertop centerpiece, like flowers or candles or seasonal decorations. Say grace—acknowledge a higher power and gratitude for food and family.

+ Electromagnetic radiation is a real issue. Do not allow SmartMeters in your home. Their pulsed radiation is harmful (counter to electrical company claims). Check your home's exposure to Wi-Fi routers and cell phone towers. Also, the new money-saving lightbulbs (CFLs) can create larger disruptive fields than the incandescent bulbs they replace. Buildups of this incoherent energy affect the nervous system and the brain. Use an EMF meter/radiation detector to measure the fields in your home if you have concerns. Electrical sensitivity is especially an issue for those who have had near-death experiences, but it is also becoming a concern for the public at large.

+ Middle school is when substance abuse problems spread (access the website www.drugfreeamerica). Alcohol is the most lethal of available drugs. Even a single teen binge can result in permanent brain damage, yet such binges are tolerated as coming-of-age antics. Injecting young girls to protect against the human papilloma virus (HPV) as a way to prevent cervical cancer, and now the head and neck cancers that can result from oral sex, misses the point—like ignoring teen binges.[8] Unprotected sex of any kind can kill; so can drinking yourself silly. Get the facts/discuss them.

✦ Monitor vaccinations and drug prescriptions for the young very carefully. Physicians often prescribe high doses in a single vaccination. Double check. This holds true with learning-disorder pharmaceuticals. Aden, an eight-year-old I know, had been chemically treated for ADHD and bipolar disorder since he was a tyke. Recently he also developed Tourette's syndrome—*because he was prescribed too many strong drugs when too young*, a sorry admission from his family doctor. When the drugs were withdrawn, all his "disorders" disappeared. This never made the newspaper because the overdosing of the child was never considered a medical mistake.

✦ The new children will fail in their tasks without mentors. Kids blame themselves if something in their environment goes wrong. Parents, educators, and adults are needed to set things straight and guide kids. Show them; don't just tell them. Be there for questions, listen, encourage solution finding. It no longer takes a village to raise a child; it now takes the world.

✦ No one can appreciate light without acknowledging shadows. The guises the shadow side of our nature hide behind show up in the "monsters" we create to scare us. That's why monsters are so popular. What scares us is the possibility of facing whatever is within us that we don't want to face. Childhood is filled with what is rational beset by the irrational, especially in war-torn countries, military families, ghettos, gangs, and housing projects.

Help kids to face their monsters (fears), so they can conquer whatever depresses or limits them.

+ Take classes in developing your own psychic/intuitive abilities, so you can keep up with your kids. Do not be shocked or upset by their ability to occasionally know the future. Be detached, objective, calm. This trait is normal and natural for them and it can be for you too. Because many can see almost holographically (with multiple angles/dimensions), widescreen television, 3-D effects, and fluorescent lighting can hurt their eyes. Forget all this nonsense about ESP. *Extended sense perception* is the real ESP—the extension of faculties normal to us. Get over the idea of special, gifted, cursed, overly imaginative, or phony. Our new kids demonstrate this simple fact: as energies change, perception changes; as perception changes, what appears impossible becomes commonplace.

+ We are losing family histories. How sad for mothers or fathers to die without passing on their story; the same with other relatives. We never know what excited them, their loves, passions, disappointments, horrors, how they hurt or why. We never know the spiritual side of their lives or what advice they could have passed on. Please record your story and/or what life has taught you—on some pages or digital recorder, a video, a book, memoir, diaries, scrapbooks. Ken Jablonski did this in *A Letter of Love: A Gift for Your Loved Ones.*[9] He explains: "The idea first came to me on 9/11/2001, after I survived that tragedy. I thought, if I had died on that day, what would my daughters remember about me? How can I offer advice on this life and the next if I am not here?" Because of the high divorce rate, changing partners, sperm bank donors, and adoptions, it is more important than ever before that we have some sense of lineage, of family histories.

+ Up to ages five or six, when the temporal lobes are in full developmental "flower," reports abound of kids who have invisible friends; who see demons, angels, fairies, and aliens; have near-death episodes and undergo an experience of enlightenment so profound that it becomes a major influence in their lives. If we knew more about our families' stories we could trace this and learn a great deal about ourselves and the effects of spiritual phenomena over time.

+ Speaking of the spiritual, the best book for parents about this is *The Secret Spiritual World of Children: The Breakthrough Discovery That Profoundly Alters Our Conventional View of Children's Mystical Experiences* by Tobin Hart, Ph.D.[10] He was forced to face the truth of childhood illuminations when his own daughter told him about the angels she regularly conversed with. The result: aids for parents in understanding the phenomenon, and steps parents can take to make spirituality a regular part of their own lives.

+ Some gems:

  * Teach your children to use a M.A.P. for spiritual guidance: **M**editation, **A**ffirmation, **P**rayer.

  * Teenagers who join together in spiritual worship or activity within a community have substantially lower suicide rates and incidents of drug use or crime.

  * Cincinnati Children's Hospital Medical Center is part of a growing list of medical/therapeutic facilities using meditation as a healing modality.[11]

  * The Center on Spirituality and Psychology in West Roxbury, Massachusetts, teaches mindfulness and is dedicated to bringing about a spiritual revival in the field of psychology.[12]

  * One House of Peace has clever ideas for children and families to invoke peace and spirituality. Check out www.onehouseofpeace .org.

  * Parents especially should try soul writing (not to be confused with automatic writing, where another entity takes over one's mind). Soul writing is a meditative/prayerful practice of connecting to the sacred wisdom within—that part of us that has our answers for guidance or assistance.[13]

❖ There is a new type of music available, using the Solfeggio frequencies found in the ancient Gregorian Chants and other sacred works. There are nine such frequencies, aligned in repetitive patterns of thirds (following the Rule of Thirds) for healing and uplift. What is created are not songs, but, rather, continuous wave forms of sound, dubbed DNA music. They are excellent as background sound for home, office, or car.[14]

A change in consciousness restructures the brain and reawakens the heart. *Know thyself* is where this begins for parents.

14 EDUCATION ROCKS

*Our education system has been fundamental to our success
as a nation, but it has barely changed in 100 years.*

BILL GATES

Schools are caught in a time warp. They are still rooted to the simplistic basics necessary to turn out good factory workers. Billionaires bulldozing the system, convinced that the tools of the boardroom (boosting incentives, instituting new technologies, bringing in innovators) would transform education forever, have, for the most part, fumbled or failed. A study by Stanford University's Center for Research on Educational Outcomes[1] found that 37 percent of charter schools produced results worse than public schools; only 17 percent performed significantly better. Michelle Rhee, who tried to revamp how schools were run and subjects were taught in Washington, D.C., but was later fired, had this to say: "The truth is that despite a handful of successful reforms, the state of American education is pitiful, and getting worse. Spending on schools has more than doubled in the last three decades, but the increased resources haven't produced better results."[2]

Let's dwell on the dismal a little longer.

+ A five-year-study in Denver, Colorado, beginning in 1999 found a 65 percent flunk-out rate, thirty thousand illegal aliens speaking forty different languages, crowded classrooms, over-the-top violence, and 30 percent of teachers who quit vowed never to return.[3]

+ One-third of all our nation's high school graduates lack the skills they need to either handle a job or live a healthy, productive life.[4]

+ Two-thirds of Wisconsin eighth-graders cannot read at their grade's proficiency standard (notice *thirds:* in this section they consistently point to failures); *yet Wisconsin receives more money to educate their students than any other state in the Midwest.*[5]

+ Children as young as six are being arrested at school for excessive infractions and have a police record by the time they leave elementary school.

+ In a news radio report on August 15, 2010, the United States was named the world leader in school dropouts (one in three quit). U.S. schools also rank 23 and 25 out of 30 in reading and math on the list of the world's most developed nations.

+ One-fourth of all U.S. school kids *do not see anything wrong with cheating*. They regularly photograph tests with their cell phones and text message answers. To them, this is sharing and helping, not cheating. They have a different sense of honesty—*the group first*—even if the action taken is wrong.

+ For the first time in American history, the newer generations (Millennials and 9/11s) may be less educated than their parents (boomers were the best educated of all the generations), and are projected to earn less and die earlier than their parents. They are labeled the dumbest because they lack problem-solving skills and depend too much on digital "toys."[6]

Beyond dismal is the legacy of No Child Left Behind—the worst thing to have happened to U.S. schools in recent history. Teaching to tests totally ignores the fact that today's students are not the people our educational system was designed to teach. Evolution's "curveball" added yet another setback: where 80 percent of school curriculums are geared toward the verbal learner, 80 percent of the new kids are visual/spatial learners.[7] Kids drop out in droves because they're bored.

The tragedy of Hurricane Katrina created an opportunity to scrap the former educational system in New Orleans. Administrators did, replacing it with a specific type of charter school system that uses Promethean ActivBoards (interactive whiteboards that engage students with vivid images, video, and audio). Test scores that were once among the lowest in the nation soared to the highest percentiles because of this, proving that poverty, homelessness, hunger, and even lack of parental help and parental illiteracy *cannot and will not stop a child who is provided an environment where curiosity is encouraged; effort is praised; and the abilities to self-organize, question, and problem solve are taught.*

FRAMES OF MIND AND THE CHILD'S MIND

Howard Gardner, in his seminal book *Frames of Mind,* established that there are seven forms of intelligence: linguistic, logical-mathematical, spatial/visual, body-kinesthetic, musical, interpersonal, and intrapersonal.[8] We know from previous research on several fronts, including intuitive observers such as Soleira Green, that there are five basic levels of intelligence: mental (IQ), emotional (EQ), spiritual (SQ), wholistic (WQ), and quantum (QQ).[9] This breakthrough research extends and enlarges our knowledge of intelligence measures and the increased capabilities implied by them. Important to know.

Tobin Hart, Ph.D., in a talk given November 9, 2007, at a conference on childhood learning I attended in Tennessee, put the whole question of a child's mind into perspective. "Children are on the front edge of evolution," he stated. He then went on to show how children regularly use arrangements of mental functioning in such a manner that it is almost as if "mind" exists in multiples.

He identified the multiples of a child's mind this way:

+ *Rational mind*: helpful for daily tasks, numbers, rules, and school, but insufficient for meaning or fulfillment or the reality of the future.

+ *Imaginative mind:* differently real, builds bridge between the known and unknown, adjusts to larger fields of consciousness and the world "soul."
+ *Beautiful mind:* possessing a certain presence, openness, awareness to what is lovely to behold and what will help and nurture others.
+ *Natural mind:* able to discern good versus not good, moments of wonder, triggers of spiritual experiences; reacts to overscheduling, and wants unstructured time and to be closer to the earth.
+ *Embodied mind:* makes no distinction between mind and body; unity consciousness.
+ *Empathic mind:* has a sense of what's going on and difficulty with discernment/shutting off/ letting go, highly sensitive and loving, seeks to understand others and go from "I" to "we"; humanitarian.
+ *Contemplative mind:* functions as a "valve" that reduces stress and tension, contemplates, opens up the mind in new ways through the power of silence; gateway to the blessings of spirit.

Once you get what reality is to a child of the rational mind, used in tandem with other realms of mind and a total acceptance of the many types of intelligence, you begin to understand why the whole-child approach is the only form of teaching that produces a truly educated and integrated youngster.

WHOLE-CHILD APPROACH

Kids have been pushed too hard, too fast, too long. The body-mind-spirit connection has been ignored. Because of the way the limbic system in the brain works (it caps off the brainstem), full use of faculties and body movements *as part of the learning process* is essential if a child is to comprehend and remember. Most youngsters today burn out by the third grade. With recess, music, art, social studies, geography, and sports being replaced with writing drills and spelling quizzes and tests about every ten days (in accordance with budget cuts), kids are getting their first taste of personal failure practically before they learn to tie their shoes.

The whole-child approach builds on the child's natural curiosity and expands that into a world alive with rhythms, mysteries, sounds, histories, and puzzles. Schools worldwide are switching to this system and, in doing so, are banning standardized testing of kids between ages five and seven. They are also putting more emphasis on social and emotional development during those formative early years. High-stakes pressure comes later, once good skills are developed and the child is motivated to speak up and question.

Facts: If you want good mathematicians and scientists, you must have music classes. If you want good designers and architects, you must have art classes. If you want good leaders, you must have sports, debate clubs, and marching bands. If you want good engineers and tradesmen/women, you must have old-fashioned shop classes, box-car races, field trips, and experiments with building techniques. If you want good bankers and investment brokers, you must encourage student-run banks and stock market studies using pretend money. (Students at Tullar Elementary School in Neenah, Wisconsin, won a statewide stock-market investment challenge in April 2010 by turning $100,000 in pretend money into $160,218 in ten weeks. The kids beat out seasoned investors and brokerages.) If you want voters who are interested and active, you must teach history and civics. If you want healthy brain development, you must include running, dancing, jumping, hanging from monkey bars, gym (no Wi-Fi substitutes), and bilingualism. Bilingualism? Ah, this one may surprise you.

FULL IMMERSION/DUAL LANGUAGES

Learning another language at any point in life confers an advantage. But here's the surprising part: there's another way to do this. Facts are now in about full immersion/dual-language learning, and they are astounding. Nix your previous class experience with languages; full immersion is different and it begins in kindergarten (or nursery school). For half a day school is conducted in, let's say, Spanish, and the other half of the day school is conducted in English. So during each half of the day, only one language is spoken or written—all discussions, all explanations, all responses, anything said or written down or read corresponds to the language in effect at that time of day. No exceptions, not even for the frustrated.

Children don't take long to catch on. Yet during that time, *they develop two mother tongues—which means two languages of origin, two unique ways of seeing the world and understanding cultures other than their own.* Full immersion increases and expands the capacity of the brain. The brain's ability to do this has always been present; we just didn't know. Now we do. A natural benefit of this is kids developing skills similar to that of an executive. They become more resilient, compassionate, versatile, flexible, self-reliant, observant, able to let go and move on. If there's a downside, perhaps it is the cost of full-immersion teachers versus school budgets. Get the DVD of the documentary on this subject, *Speaking in Tongues.*[10] Full immersion is a major step toward *enlarging brain capacity.*

To be sure, parents are doing everything they can to give their children a competitive edge in the global job market, and that entails becoming bilingual. Some are moving to other countries and enrolling their youngsters in the schools there. The most popular choice: China. By 2025, when the Aquarian generation emerges, dual language could be a necessity . . . in kindergarten.

CHILD-LED LEARNING

To know is one of the very first verbs a person learns to conjugate when studying a foreign language. "I know," we all say often. "I want to know" might as well be the mission statement of the new kids. Although they come in "knowing," wanting to know more consumes them. Education's purpose is to awaken this inner teacher. "Unschooling" (which is entirely child-led) and homeschooling (which is primarily child-led) emphasize more natural approaches to self-motivated learning. Kids turned off by rigid rules turn on when the pace alters; this is also true of classroom study.

Since so many of our new kids are being educated online or at home, go to www.guidetoonlineschools.com for tips, then explore The Natural Learning Research Institute and their "guided experience" approach at www.naturallearninginstitute.org. Both sources are helpful for youngsters and their parents in making better choices.

Even allowing children to have more say in standard classrooms and giving them ways to express novel and original ideas reaps huge dividends. Here are some examples.

+ John Hunter, a fourth-grade teacher in Charlottesville, VA, devised the World Peace Game, a huge, stand-alone, four-tiered Plexiglas tower game filled with countries, dramas, weather developments, mercenaries, temples, and so on.[11] It completely dominates the middle of a classroom, lighting up children's eyes with absolute wonder—until they play it. Kids divide up into teams and are given a global problem they must solve, taking into consideration all aspects of each action they might take. They must learn to collaborate within their team, think critically, examine possible solutions, complete for answers, and do the research for outside-the-box problem solving. It takes eight to ten weeks to play.

+ Marietta McCarty, outspoken in her insistence that philosophy needs to be taught in grade school, pegs the subject as the art of clear thinking. She believes it gives kids a toolbox full of ideas on how to critically examine what is essential to healthy living. She wrote the book *Little Big Minds* to show that children by their very nature are ready to question life issues and discuss what occurs to them.[12] Serious and deep thinking actually begins in kindergarten through the third grade. For older kids, she recommends philosophy clubs after school or during lunch.

+ The 2007 movie *Freedom Writers,* directed by Richard

LaGravenese and starring Hilary Swank, showed how a teacher unable to engage her students asked them, as an experiment, to write the story of their lives, then read in class what they wrote. The results were palpable. Not only were the kids able to break through to what was really in their hearts, but they also discovered the reason why fellow classmates acted the way they did. With no previous interest in learning and no relationship to paper and pen, each teenager opened a door to self-expression, compassion, truth, and forgiveness that ignited a desire to learn. Writing stories or expressing the self through poetry is a way for the young to say, "Hear me. See me. I have something to tell you." Art and music classes offer similar opportunities—creative self-expression tethered to the discipline of form and method.[13]

✦ Class courts are a necessity from the third grade on. Children need to decide for themselves what their honesty codes will be. If there is an infraction, court is called to order. Although the teacher remains as supervisor, the kids themselves take charge, investigate all sides, listen, discern, vote, and carry out decisions in a fair manner. Children are much better at this than teachers are. Another student-led initiative is "Bully Nots," a unique program that makes it cool for classmates to wipe out bullying. Students conduct annual antibullying programs for schools and parents. Agendas feature humor, rap, catchy songs, acrobatic flips, pithy speeches, and skits demonstrating how to squash bullying. "Upstanders" are those who volunteer to tell bullies to stop, befriend the victims, and seek out an adult if intervention is needed. Another of their goals: convince guys that beating up their girlfriends is not an act of love. (Note: conflict resolution and problem-solving skills are especially important in sports, as competition can bring out the worst in a person, as well as the best. Give youngsters an opportunity to figure things out and express what they are feeling. Anger and fear are big issues for Millennials and 9/11s.)

✦ The Adawee Teachings learning program (*Adawee* is Cherokee for "guardians of wisdom") was developed by Linda Redford and her daughter Anne Vorburger.[14] It is a classroom program that enables children to address their personal concerns while disciplining their minds and restoring a sense of honor and value to their world. The course consists of a self-discovery book and a T-shirt that says *I am important to the world. The world is important to me.* The Honor Code is also included, addressing such topics as humility, responsibility, respect, honesty, generosity, forgiveness, and wisdom. Most effective in elementary grades, this course does wonders at the third-grade level, when so many youngsters experience burnout from typical curriculums.

MYTH, MINDFULNESS, CREATIVITY

I think you recognize by now that creativity in some form is not an "extra" schools can toss aside because money is scarce. What can bridge the gap between needs and funds are "citizen teachers"—people with particular talents, skills, and interests who are willing to help out at school, some without charge. It works this way: after school is over kids stay for extended classes taught by people who come in and share what they know. These programs are highly successful at every school where they have been tried.

Townspeople are rich sources of talent. They can bring mindfulness training into the classroom (which improves focus and concentration skills), as well as expertise in subjects such as music appreciation, dance, singing, theater, photography, painting, wood carving, writing, making tied flies for use in fishing, mountain climbing, gardening, cooking, building, repairs of any kind, astronomy, ham radio, design, storytelling, clowning, yoga, and fun exercises. Miracles happen when people help each other.

Using mythology to illuminate human behavior is a stroke of genius, for myth highlights the intuitive and makes real what moves our passions. Without the guidance possible from this source of wisdom, we are like a ship without a rudder. "Teachers" from the invisible worlds, our muses, inspire or frighten for the purpose of demonstrating value. Examples: *the mythology of the world tree* helps us to understand the importance of the religious/spiritual urge, our interconnections; *the hero's journey* enables us to recognize and learn about the passages we all undertake in our lives; and *calling for a vision* expresses the primal urge to know our mission in life. When you pry open the mind's door to mythology, you link with universal archetypes, imaginal worlds, and the very soul of existence itself. Children pick this up immediately. Forget Dungeons & Dragons. Feast instead on *The Power of Myth* by Joseph Campbell;[15] the "social artistry" of Jean Houston;[16] Malidoma Patrice Somé's *Ritual: Power, Healing and Commmunity;*[17] and the insightful programs developed by David Oldfield and others at the Midway Center for Creative Imagination.[18]

Fertile ground for the wild and wonderful world of creativity is the free CAD (computer-aided design) program Minecraft. Its Sketchup feature enables virtually unlimited imaginings, scripts, plugins, graphics, and shortcuts. Even the sun's position can be adjusted based on various locations to show shadows. A popular tool in homeschooling or for play time is the book *Google SketchUp 8 For Dummies* by Aidan Chopra, which explains the how-to's in addition to showing how Minecraft encourages the intuitive urge.[19]

A child's desire to learn is ignited by creativity, fed by hands-on experience, disciplined by exercises like mindfulness and poetry, expanded by the intuitive urge to connect with larger vistas of possibility, and tested, continuously, through the rigor of questions and solution finding. Bypass any of this, and learning distorts.

CHANGING EDUCATION

If you haven't seen the 2010 movie *Waiting for Superman,* access the website www.waitingforsuperman.com. It's a powerful film about the need to change the school system. Good education for children cannot be deleted from tight budgets or thwarted by religious zealots without a country's prosperity and very existence suffering. Because this is true, I'm going to tease you with some unique ideas that are already in use and achieving incredible results.

+ From kindergarten to senior high, the Kids Teaching Kids (KTK) program promotes the sharing potential of children when coupled with resources they can use. See www.intuition.org/ktk.pdf, or call Hollie Webster at (925) 254-8054; holliewebster@comcast.net.

+ Extending the school day through the Knowledge Is Power Program (KIPP), a network of free, open-enrollment, college-preparatory public schools dedicated to helping kids in underserved communities: www.kipp.org.

+ "Teaching Naked," an idea that originated at Southern Methodist University and is spreading, means no computers, no PowerPoints, no technology, and no lectures. Instead it utilizes innovative interactions, discussions, projects, debates, and creativity: http://chronicle.com/article/Tech-Naked-Effort-Strips/47398/.

+ Innovative school and classroom designs at Ordrup School, Charlottenlund, Denmark, including upholstered reading tubes, sunken "hot pot" circular seating areas for concentrated group work, colorful concentration booths, and other inventive spaces designed to accommodate diverse learning styles. For more information, look up the school at www.imagineschooldesign.org.

+ As reported by futurist and life coach Annimac Consultants, elementary schools in Perth, Australia, made simple yet unique changes where children can talk quietly (this discourages mind-to-mind communication), rooms have movable walls so environments can be altered, classrooms are called neighborhoods and teachers are "guides." Just doing this raised test scores and decreased dropout rate.[20]

+ By nurturing the inner life of children through myth, storytelling, and creativity, Rachael Kessler discovered that kids can embrace shadows and the depression they bring in healthy ways. Her book *The Soul of Education* offers in-depth ways to listen, speak, and interact in the classroom.[21]

+ Issac Newton, one of the greatest scientists of all time, was an alchemist and intuitive mystic. Shutting out intuitive ideas and responses or demeaning them turns creativity into mere exercise sans passion or feeling or truth. There are constructive ways to handle this.[22]

+ As learning potential steadily decreases in colleges and universities, three-year degrees are offered as an alternative. Exciting schools like Bainbridge Graduate Institute award an MBA in sustainable business.[23] Community colleges are partnering with high schools to enable ambitious students to graduate from both *at the same time.*[24] Schools for social change are now worldwide. For example, the Community and Individual Development Association (CIDA) in Johannesburg, South Africa, is a business school for the underprivileged that teaches entrepreneurship and considers every student an agent of change. Access their website at www.cida.co.za.

+ Bill Strickland, a genius who sees the genius in everyone, discovered how to build successful schools in broken-down, dangerous communities and to inspire others to learn and excel. With the theme of "environment drives behavior," his schools are filled with art, lunches are served as if in a fine restaurant, doors are never locked, and students are regularly praised and treated with respect. His schools defy all statistics of educational failure and prove the impossible on a daily basis. His book is *Make the Impossible Possible: One Man's Crusade to Inspire Others to Dream Bigger and Achieve the Extraordinary.*[25]

+ Sustainability Workshop of Philadelphia was the brainchild of Simon Hauger. His goal: teach students to change the world. He is doing this by giving high school students real problems with real tools to tackle them. Privately funded, the school is designed around three simple principles: *put the work first* (this drives curriculum knowledge, and skills), *trust students to make decisions* (make, explain, and justify decisions), and *make the most out of failure* (failure is not an option, it is a necessity). The Sustainability Workshop is solving real life problems while changing kids' lives.[26]

TRANSFORMING EDUCATION

What works, what could transform education itself, is to lay aside the act of teaching, per se, and offer instead a game of rotating responsibilities and tasks—a project called BeLonging. Based on the principles of Mereon, an integrated model of existence that provides a link between living and lifelike systems, BeLonging is more than a vision. It is an operational project that begins with *educators as lifelong learners*. This three-day course is for teachers and anyone else who works in schools. During this course, real issues are tackled straight on. This is followed by introducing teachers and parents to the classroom project "Learners Learning to Lead." None of this impinges on the formal school curriculum.

Learning to cooperate and share responsibility for the social dimension of their learning environment is the student's ongoing lesson in leading. As the learners have new experiences and see themselves, their peers, and their teachers from a new perspective, change happens quickly. Tested successfully in Mirano, Venice, Italy, pilot programs have since been initiated in North America and Switzerland. To find out more about BeLonging programs and the Mereon principles of existence, visit www.mereon.org and www.essenceillumined.com. A book about this new system of learning is in progress.

Today, people of color do the worst in school because of poor language and math skills. By 2040, half the U.S. population will be brown or black. We can no longer afford to wait. All kids deserve better. Education for *all learners* must be transformed . . . now!

15 FOOD/HEALTH AND THE ENVIRONMENT

Never doubt that a small group of thoughtful, committed citizens can change the world; indeed, it's the only thing that ever has.

MARGARET MEAD

Give an A to schools that replace vending machines with water coolers, hamburgers and french fries with fresh veggies, fruits, whole-grain bread, and a salad bar. For this school, though, make it a A+++: *ten years ago, Dr. Yvonne Sanders-Butler, the principal of Browns Mill Elementary School in Lithonia, Georgia, banned sugar. Results from this schoolwide ban on sugar were that reading improved by 15 percent and behavior issues dropped by 23 percent.*[1] This change is so dramatic, the whole world is paying attention.

The average school-age youngster consumes four cups of sugar per week. High-fructose corn syrup, trans fats, vegetable oils, refined grains, energy drinks, flavored milk—these flood all of our diets. Even most hamburger patties have 1/2 teaspoon of sugar in them. It's no wonder folks are getting fat and irritable. Sugar substitutes? Don't believe the assurances you read in various studies (always check to see who funded that study). Aspartame, the most commonly used sugar substitute in the food industry, is a neural toxin with a multitude of adverse side effects (like short-term memory loss, forgetfulness, fuzzy-headed feelings, seizures, numbness, muscle spasms, or headaches).[2]

The latest statistics peg one in every thirteen U.S. kids with a food allergy. The most common: gluten, peanut butter, and milk. Other common sources of allergies include the yeast/fungal presence in kitchens (we don't clean surfaces nearly enough), food dyes, mercury and aluminum poisoning (from cookware, dental fillings, some fish, toxic vaccinations, antiperspirants), ear piercings (it's the nickel), pesticides, and plasticizers—anything hormonelike.

Get this: asthma is the most common ailment reported today . . . by schoolchildren *and* school maintenance workers. Hello? Is anybody looking at the chemicals schools are using for pest management? Numerous learning disorders can be traced to pesticides, as can the deaths of bee colonies. Monosodium glutamate (MSG, a known nervous-system toxin) is now used as a spray on fruit, vegetable, nut, and grain crops, especially those headed for baby food.

We are assured that all is well, that nothing exceeds tolerance levels, and then we learn about bisphenol A (BPA), a plastic hardener found in baby bottles, water bottles, and as a resin lining most food cans. This compound mimics hormones and is linked to autoimmune disorders, neurologic diseases, and cancer.

Hormones are regularly fed to the poultry and livestock we ingest, then pass through us and the toilet with each flush. The feminization of nature can be understood if you consider these factors. Devra Lee Davis, director of the Center for Environmental Oncology at the University of Pittsburgh, admits: "We've changed the nature of nature."

THE VITAMIN CONTROVERSY

New realities are emerging from food, health, and environmental changes. Girls as young as seven start puberty. Windstorms spread nuclear particles. Fragrances and perfumes in products make people sick. Chem trails expelled from airplanes dust large areas with contaminants.

Lead is still the number-one environmental threat to children—whether people live in public housing, in suburbs, or on farms.

The bottom line, irrespective of governmental regulations or violations, is always the individual choices we make. So why is it that state and national legislatures and the United Nations, are bending over backward to force people to rely mostly on pharmaceuticals for their healthcare needs? Certainly the supplement industry needs an overhaul and better standards, *but this does not and should not deny individuals the freedom of choice.*

The Codex Alimentarius, developed by the World Health Organization of the United Nations, has, through its recommendations, redefined vitamins, minerals, and herbs in ways that either lower dosages to nearly useless levels or ban items. Any country accepting the codex has effectively denied their citizens the right to make choices about their own healthcare, criminalizing nature's best. The codex is supported by international banks and multinational pharmaceutical corporations. So far, local citizens like you and me have managed to keep the codex out of the United States. Keep monitoring state legislature; preserve the right to choose.

Are we free to choose? That can be tricky. We know that levels of vitamin D correlate with sun exposure. The farther north you live or the more time you spend inside, the more vitamin D you need as a supplement. Standards cannot be trusted, though, *because the only way you can tell how much you need is to have a blood test.* For black people, the situation is serious, because the melanin in dark skin, which protects them from harmful rays, *blocks their defense against diabetes and cancer.* Deficiency rates of vitamin D are shocking for black women (80 percent) and their babies at birth (92.5 percent); for black men, the deficiency is a major cause of aggressive forms of prostate cancer.[3] In 2011 the recommended doses of vitamin D were downscaled nationwide, but no mention was made of the stark divide between whites and blacks. Full disclosure of healthcare information is a right we all have that is not freely given or often claimed. Insist on that right.

CORN VERSUS COWS

"By some estimates," says Rob Dunn, the author of *The Wild Life of Our Bodies,* "75 percent of all the food consumed in the world comes from just six plants and one animal."[4] You know that animal is a cow. And you know that a diet that is primarily animal based can mess up your health. Cut down on the amount of meat, poultry, and fish eaten, and health improves. Yet the real culprit is industrialized farming, along with the way foods are processed. These methods lower nutritional value, add too many chemicals, can mistreat animals, and hurt the environment.

Eating only vegetables isn't necessarily the best dietary choice, either. There are antinutritional factors, chemicals and toxins in grains, nuts, seeds, beans, the nightshade family (potatoes, tomatoes, eggplants), and various other fruits and vegetables. The way around these "inhibitors" is to cook, ferment, or process the foods. Improper preparation is one of the main causes of leaky-gut, an immune system reaction common in many of today's kids.[5] The job of "plants that bite back" is to save a species from being overconsumed. So if you're going to be a vegetarian, be informed. A balanced, natural/organic approach to what we eat makes more sense than whether one is vegetarian or a meat eater.

At issue with what we consume is a two-fold threat: lobbyists trying to convince Congress to outlaw organic farms and gardens, and the need to create alternative/biofuel sources. Using corn and other foodstuffs to make ethanol is leading to global food shortages—and this doesn't need to happen. Scientists at the Royal Institute of Technology (KTH) in Stockholm, Sweden, have shown that fossils (animal and plant remains) are not necessary for the production of oil, nor is biofuel a better alternative. There are many global sources of untapped oil. KTH professor Vladimir Kutcherov emphasizes, "The oil supply is not about to end."[6]

The steady depletion of topsoil, the conversion of cropland to nonfarm uses (in the United States, Egypt, China, and India particularly), large-scale farms killing the land as well as small towns, and Wall Street experts buying up acreage in a wide swath—all of this spells out a single message: profit trumps starvation.

LEARNING FROM NATURE

We have seven billion people on our planet, with India and China about to overtax their supply of natural resources. But there are solutions. Count the new kids and their parents as "shovel ready" for launching new projects (and expanding already-existing programs) that make a difference, like the upswing in farmers' markets, community-supported agriculture programs (wherein residents buy shares in local farms), a switch to majority perennial crops that pull animals out of meat factories and put them back on farms where they belong. Think these are minor measures? Take a gander at the small and large of the "green revolution":

+ A whole new interest in cooking is inspiring the younger set to make it from scratch and raise it from seed. See *The Edible Front Yard* by Ivette Soler for some ideas.[7] Look at the vertical gardens (plants on walls) at www.plantsonwalls.com and the "window farms" at www.windowfarms.org. Get seeds from Southern Exposure at www.southernexposure.com. Help farmers when crops are ripe with Crop Mobs to the Rescue, www.cropmob.org. Partner up with nature via *The Joy of Hobby Farming* by Michael and Audrey Levatino,[8] then accompany Lisa Taylor in touring *Your Farm in the City*.[9]

+ Entire cities are getting on board too, converting vacant lots and abandoned properties into gardens to raise vegetables for city residents and restaurants. The most ambitious so far is in Cleveland, Ohio, where more than 60 acres are currently under cultivation. Cities in Australia, Chile, and Spain are vigorously converting not only to green roofs but to rooftop gardens and vertical gardens as well.

+ Some of the best sources for information about what really works in building up soil, raising food, and working with nature and the spirits of nature, beyond organic to the healing of the land, food, economy, and culture, are Joe Salatin at Polyface, Inc. (www.poly-facefarms.com); Perelandra Gardens (www.perelandra-ltd.com); Findhorn Gardens in northern Scotland (www.findhorn.org); One Straw Revolution by Fukuoka through his student Larry Korn (www.onestrawrevolution.net); the permaculture experts at www.permaculture.org; the sustainable agriculture experts at www.attra.ncat.org, www.wwoof.org, www.ifoam.org; the acoustic gardening experts at www.care2.com ; the kids who participate in hands-on learning at the Green School in Bali (www.greenschool.org); agrarian philosophy, a set of values deeply rooted in place and soil; *The Essential Agrarian Reader* by Norman Wirzba;[10] and *The Green Intention* by Sandy Moore and Deanna Moore.[11]

✦ And don't forget one of the best gardening books available, *The Resilient Gardener: Food Production and Self-Reliance in Uncertain Times* by Carol Deppe,[12] and the shocking story of how many environmental policies are counterproductive and wind up costing us *more*—not less—energy to comply with, outlined in the book *Green Gone Wrong: How Our Economy Is Undermining the Environmental Revolution* by Heather Rogers.[13]

The more we learn from nature, the more we realize there is to learn. This has given rise to new fields of study that in future years will accelerate the kind of innovative changes that directly affect life on earth. Some of these:

Biomimicry: studies nature for solutions to human design and engineering

Bioengineering: discovers solutions to engineering problems and applies them

Plant neurobiology: studies plant biochemicals that mirror animal/human brains

Geobiology: research on the influence of Earth on the life forms that inhabit it

Agroecology: application of ecology to the design of sustainable agro-ecosystems; seeks to restore small farms and organic gardening

Ecomysticism: the profound experience of nature as a spiritual guide[14]

BIOFUELS AND OIL ALTERNATIVES

The world can produce plenty of food for its people. The problem is not food shortages, but *incompetent leadership* (e.g., President Robert Mugabe's mismanaged and disastrous land reforms in Zimbabwe), *speculation in the commodities market* (where people gamble for profit without regard for outcomes or distribution of foodstuffs), and *the rush to biofuel production* (already proven insufficient as a dependable source to build a postpetroleum future).

Professor Kutcherov is right. There are indeed many places on Earth with huge oil and gas reserves. Some countries use this advantage to "whitewash" their own dictatorships. For instance, the rogue regime of Myanmar, which has huge natural gas reserves, brokers fuel deals that require silence about their human-rights violations. In our own country, a practice known as fracking is used to reach deep pockets of oil and gas. Fracking shoots high-pressure toxic chemicals and water beneath ground levels to release these deposits; contaminated groundwater and low-level earthquake clusters often result from the practice. So many regions and cities now ban fracking that irate gas-drilling corporations are countersuing. Their new claim is: "We've learned how to do it differently. No more shallow pockets—we're now aiming several miles down." Doing just that, drillers have hit a gigantic oil deposit in Williston, North Dakota—unequaled in modern times—creating an equally unequaled jobs rush.

What is happening in Williston, North Dakota, is the beginning of a new "gold rush"—a global one that will last for decades. Supposedly the greater depth of drilling protects aquifers and groundwater, but what of fault lines? A time when the Earth became more prone to earthquakes began in November 2004. Events have been steadily on the increase ever since. Underground pressures will not abate to any appreciable degree for the foreseeable future. Geobiology, the interrelationship between earth and its inhabitants, will prove to be an invaluable measure during this stress cycle.

The rush to biofuel production will give way to more electric and solar-battery power. Even with continued discoveries of new oil and gas deposits, the demand for other alternatives will increase—and I do not consider coal to be one of them. The U.S. Patent Office ignores "overunity" devices (machines that run from "unacceptable" energy sources like cold fusion[15]); this "glass ceiling" will be broken within the next thirty years, opening the door to vast and exotic sources of energy.

THE PROMISE OF BETTER HEALTH

Twenty-five of America's top business giants have already converted to green energy, from solar panels, renewable energy sources, free electric-vehicle charging, and so forth. Savings in time, money, and healthier environments have been impressive. What is now done on a volunteer basis will soon be a necessity. Buildings themselves can be and should be self-sustaining ecospheres, off-the-grid in every possible way (while still universally interconnected to electrical circuitry as backup).

Overall health is improving. We're taller now, more apt to exercise and eat right, and we're living longer. Life spans of 120 to 150 years could be typical by midcentury. The fly in the ointment is the current way medicine has been co-opted by pharmaceutical companies and management groups. According to chemist Shane Ellison, "Rather than being funded solely by taxpayers, our drug administration is being paid by the very industry it's supposed to regulate. This is legal courtesy of the 'Prescription Drug User Fee Act.' Today, the Center for Drug

Evaluation and Research at the Federal Drug Administration is dependent on drug companies for nearly half of its funding."[16]

Fact: we've squandered the effectiveness of our antibiotics through overuse (in animal feed and in trying to cure what can't be treated with these drugs, like the flu). Because of that, we now have bacteria resistant to our best and most powerful medicines. Cheaper but still effective and necessary drugs are being ignored by pharmaceutical companies because the profit margin to make them is too low. Doctors are now prescribing drugs to treat the side effects of other drugs; no studies have been done on this, or on the overall effect of unrelated drugs/supplements taken together over time.

Fact: a biochemist by the name of Stanislaw Burzynski discovered a nontoxic gene-targeted cancer medicine in the 1970s that was shown to be an effective aid to curing some of the most incurable forms of terminal cancer. His discovery was promptly banned by the Food and Drug Administration. In 2011 Dr. Burzynski finally won his battle against his accusers, too late to have saved the millions of lives that could have been saved. Yet in winning the lawsuit, he lost ownership of his work. This injustice was featured on the popular television show *The Dr. Oz Show,* and is the subject of a documentary.[17]

Fact: On April 30, 2004, BBC television news in England told of a British trucker by the name of Brian Bennett who, by tinkering around in his Warwickshire garage, came up with a cream that would help his wife's skin condition. She had MRSA (*Staphylococcus aureus,* a skin-eating bacteria). His success proved that the incurable can be cured, even by a truck driver with no scientific education.[18]

We are plagued today with "diseases of affluence" unknown in ancient times. The way we address this quandary fails to honor the intelligence of the human body or of the human mind (look at what Burzynski and Bennett did). Natural, more effective, and less expensive measures are proving in most cases not only to be the better choice but also the way of the future. Educate yourself about practices such as Reiki, homeopathy, acupuncture, aromatherapy, craniosacral therapy, biofeedback, deep-tissue bodywork, qigong, osteopathy, naturopathy, yoga, therapeutic touch, and Pilates. This is the world of alternative/complementary healthcare. Three books will acquaint you with this growing field: *Radical Medicine, Prescription of Natural Cures*, and *Homeopathy for Today's World.*[19]

Back in the 1800s medicine was based on a bioenergetic/electromagnetic model, recognizing that electricity is part of the life process. Robert O. Becker, M.D., an orthopedic surgeon, discovered this missing chapter in biology and medicine and began to experiment. He found new pathways in our understanding of evolution, acupuncture, psychic phenomena, the mysteries of cancer, and how a severed limb can be regrown. His *The Body Electric: Electromagnetism and the Foundation of Life* is the work of genius, his experiments unequaled.[20] For this he was cursed and reviled and later shunned as a charlatan. Today we are finding that he was right on all counts.

Energy medicine, the practical application of Becker's work and the work of those like him, is growing in viability and acceptance. Medical intuitives, trained to recognize bioenergetic field strength, body currents, and blockages, are taking their place as partners to physicians in patient healthcare and during surgery. Energy medicine and energy psychology, along with other alternatives to allopathic (standard) healthcare, are coupling with the continuing advances made in the medical field to create what is called integrated medicine.[21] In less than a decade, integrated medicine will be mainstream, with bionics, cloning, and robotics not far behind. And music will be piped into surgical and critical-care units, as findings continue to show that music accelerates healing and pain control.[22]

When you explore the field of energy psychology, you will realize the power of words and how what is said to a patient has more to do with recovery than medical treatment. The "talking cure" encourages one to write things out in a personal journal or discuss problems with a practitioner, nurse, or physician who takes the time to listen. Just signing up to receive enlightening monthly e-zines like Reality Shifters can be a source of encouragement (www.RealityShifters.com).

Since placebos outscore drugs and antidepressants in clinical settings, we can now say that pharmaceuticals are not necessarily the best choice . . . nor are hospitals.[23] In the November 2011 *Prevention* magazine article "Fourteen Worst Hospital Mistakes to Avoid," Joanne Chen reveals that one out of every seven hospital patients nationwide undergoes unintended harm during their stay—everything from surgical mistakes to serious life-threatening infections. One solution is the mobile health clinic, similar to a family van but that takes physicians to patients. (In Iran, nurse practitioners make such house calls, door to door if necessary. The results of this practice are dramatic.)

THE BROKEN PROMISE OF BETTER ENVIRONMENT

You knew this was coming, so I won't keep you waiting any longer. Global warming is real. What is happening is part of a natural cycle, exacerbated and accelerated by conditions such as greenhouse gas emissions, modern lifestyles, concrete "footprints," deforestation practices, factory farming, and mountaintop removal (puts entire watersheds at risk while spewing toxins into the air). Climate change is a given. Reducing carbon footprints will not stop the extremes of storm, drought, and Earth changes that are now occurring—they may slow things down on occasion, but that's it. Weather on the order of biblical prophecy continues. This puts global food security and water supplies at risk.

The only environmental safety anyone now has is . . . adaptation. The sooner we revamp building codes, grid lines, transportation, banking, business, and lifestyles, the better. The world we know will not only survive but thrive, *if we let go of the need to control outcomes—if we bend, if we compromise, if we negotiate, if we adapt.*

An example of this: people in an area with excess water made a deal with those suffering from drought. Thus, Blue Lakes water in Sitka, Alaska, is being siphoned into tankers and shipped to a bulk bottling facility near Mumbai, India. There it is dispersed to thirsty Middle Eastern cities. Three billion gallons of water a year are transferred in this manner, giving rise to a $90 million industry.[24]

This example of the entrepreneurial spirit is a win-win, with entrepreneurs thriving in conditions of challenge. Monopolies are the opposite. Even if their stated goal is to capitalize on improvements they make to enrich and enhance the common good (a great goal), the end result far too often twists the bottom line away from good products, good benefits, and good profits to a few making out like bandits. The business of food, health, and environment is awash in this "logic."

For example, Monsanto, DuPont, and Syngenta AG have tried to corner the market on insect-resistant, herbicide-tolerant plants and seed technologies. According to Timothy A. Wise, policy research director at the Global Development and Environment Institute of Tufts University: "U.S. anti-trust law has always recognized buyer power as an anti-competitive practice, but authorities have rarely taken the issue seriously when reviewing the agribusiness mergers that in the last two decades have placed the majority of the world's food in the hands of a small number of corporations" (from MinutemanMedia). Monsanto, especially, "has used heavy-handed investigations and ruthless prosecutions that have fundamentally changed the way many American farmers farm. The result has been nothing less than an assault on the foundations of farming practices and traditions that have endured for centuries in this country and millennia around the world, including one of the oldest—the right to save and replant crop seed."[25]

The real crux of this situation is the ability to patent living organisms (which dates back to 1873) and seeds (permitted since 1930). Scientists at Monsanto genetically modified a plant cell in 1982; by 1996 they introduced the first biotech seeds to market—soy beans and cotton. The U.S. Supreme Court affirmed in 2001 that plants can indeed be patented. This decision created what we face today: incredible gains in modeling foodstuffs to changing conditions while at the same time putting the health of people, livestock, plants, and entire ecosystems at risk.

Here's what I'm talking about. Superweeds now threaten the super-plants. Infertility in livestock fed these plants is rising at the same time as immune- and insulin-regulation problems, accelerated aging, and changes to major organs and the gastrointestinal system. Food-safety expert Dr. Árpád Pusztai stated during an interview, "Even Monsanto's own research showed significant immune system changes in rats fed Bt corn."[26]

Today there are genetically engineered tree plantations, the result of massive deforestation projects to produce biofuel, and genetically engineered pastures that expose cows to pesticide-laden plants. France and Germany have outlawed GM foods and plants. Yet in America an estimated 75 to 80 percent of the processed foods eaten contain GM ingredients. According to journalists Ronnie Cummins and Ben Lilliston, you eat the food and you expose yourself to the toxic herbicide Roundup engineered into the plant seeds.[27] The World Bank vigorously promotes this. U.S. diplomats with ties to corporate interests peddle these seeds worldwide.[28] On January 18, 2010, *Forbes* magazine came out with an investigative piece exonerating Monsanto of all charges, calling them a victim of mass hysteria and naming them "Company of the Year." I question the research used for this article. It does not match the reports I see.

What is the greater challenge with the environment: climate change or companies that modify nature to accommodate climate change? Not just our children, but the genetic makeup of the entire human race and all living things hang in the balance with this conundrum.[29] Be careful how you answer the question, though, as there is more to the story than what I presented here. I'll sprinkle the rest of the story as I go along, culminating in the last chapter.

16 Community

Where there is no vision, the people perish.

PROVERBS 29:18

A news headline from 2011 blared, *Shanghai Student Test Scores the Highest in the World.* Why? We are told kids there love to learn, are highly disciplined, know how to beat tests, have classes nine hours per day, and have few breaks except to exercise. There is also greater emphasis on teacher training and pay. Are these the reasons why? No. Their *entire* community—not just parents—support education. Japan has similar community involvement and its schools graduate outstanding students with incredible scores, too.

But there's a catch. Several, actually. Japan has one of the highest suicide rates in the world, and, historically, Chinese whiz kids often lack creative vision. There's no artistry to this type of uncanny brilliance, no emotion, no culture bending on the level of Steve Jobs. While China is bringing back calligraphy to nurture feelings (patriotic, they say), we on the home front are tossing cursive writing, claiming we don't need it anymore, forgetting as we say this that handwriting is an extension of who we are, our personality. It flows as it does because we do. We limit the human responsiveness and sensitivity of our skin by becoming wholly digital.

Libraries now "inhabit" a single disc. Efficient. Yet as we lose language and touch in the digital age, we find ourselves caught in a loneliness loop, longing for contact and community and that which bonds. We are social animals and we need each other.[1] We are not as individual as we may seem. Rather than an instinct to dominate and compete, the impulse of life is the will to connect. Vision is an outgrowth of that connection: the emergence of emotional artistry in tandem with the opportunities community provides.

THE NEW COMMUNITIES

They are called work clubs, swarm power, recycle groups, flash mobs, crop mobs, Occupy Wall Street, democracy now, freedom groups, date groups, zippies, smart mobs, party-time, and tribal clans—whether they're made up of nerds, geeks, goths, freaks, punks, preps, born frees, or tweens. Collectively, these groups comprise the largest social movement ever to have happened on earth, a movement that has no name, no leader, no consistent location.[2] Together, they are dedicated to uplifting and helping each other, restoring environmental integrity, social justice, democratic governance, and a form of capitalism that is fair. (A few are freaky anarchists, but, fortunately, they are in the minority.) With the ping of a cell or iPhone, maybe via e-mail or social network, anyone so moved can invite one or a hundred or a thousand or more, to gather at a certain time in a certain place for whatever reason.

Yes, social reform is front and center to many of the calls for a meetup or a demonstration, but hellos and how-are-yas and how-about-a-dates are just as common. The new kids are "groupies," and to them the group is their community—the new kind, like Facebook and Twitter folk—who bond in a moment's call for unity. They understand each other, even if different languages are spoken, and they share a common instinctual need to connect.

The new kids' need to connect, to gather in a community, is turning bookstores into community-gathering centers and co-ops and neighborhood gardens/festivals into class acts. And—surprise, surprise—they are reclaiming public spaces such as street corners, parks, squares, coffee shops, plazas, fountains, bridges, sidewalks, and lawns—public spaces throughout history were where gatherings solidified into commerce, community, and democracy. The new kids are going back to these early beginnings of social movements and reestablishing the importance of individual voices within the power and solidarity of community.

I offer a caution here: whenever everyone in a group or gathering or community, starts moving their arms and legs in unison with a repetitive chant, especially if done in rhythmic rhyme, get outta there. Run, do not walk, to the nearest exit. If you don't, you will find yourself doing things you never intended or may not like. Group power is greater than that of the individual. You can be swept away by the overwhelming and later regret having been involved. The power of groups and gatherings, of community, is now and will continue to transform our world. Remember this, though: *solidarity is one thing—blind obedience is another.*

INTENTIONAL COMMUNITIES

Intentional communities (people of similar minds who come together with common missions, needs, callings, or goals) have been around forever, it seems, but since the sixties they have flowered in great abundance, mostly as communes where all monies and decision making passed to a central authority. Few of these survived. Yet the idea of intentional community—choosing to be near, aid, assist, and enjoy others in a community of free souls—in essence a village created by and for its inhabitants, is making a comeback. Big time.

"If you take a few steps back and ask what a village is," says Jay Walljasper, author of *All That We Share: A Field Guide to the Commons,* "you'll realize it's a place where you have face-to-face encounters."[3] There is a Village to Village Network (VtV) that offers information on how to get a village started; see the website www.vtvnetwork.org. For a list of a thousand such communities worldwide, access www.ic.org. Solar-powered communities are also springing up; to reach one in Sage Valley,

Nevada, try www.earthloving.com. Here are two spiritual communities that operate more as self-sustaining ecovillages: the Transcendental Meditation Center in Maharishi Vedic City, Iowa (www.sthapatyaveda.com), and the far-out, endlessly fascinating Damanhur near the Italian Alps (www.damanhur.org).

THE OLD COMMUNITIES

Families, relations, the legacy of bloodlines—who knows when that began? (Maybe on another planet?) What we do know is this: if you go back just twenty-nine generations, *we are all related* (the math is based on squares—we each have four grandparents and they each had four, and so forth). Populations are exploding. And with this explosion comes unbelievable poverty. Suburban communities in our own cities are now the fastest-growing clusters of poverty. The Millennials are the first generation ever that has to choose whether or not to have children, and if so, how many (in China, the choice is made for you). History has shown that wherever women are educated, the birthrate always falls; still, with sinking economies, even the family unit as it currently exists has to change. . . . And it is.

Generations of families are starting to live together as they once did. From birth to death, they are sharing the same house or remodeling or redesigning the place so they can. This divides up expenses and chores, enables the elderly to stay home as long as possible, guarantees child care, and spreads out chores in an equitable manner that enables more leisure time and makes vacations possible. In families where meals are shared, children tend to grow up happier and better adjusted. Conversations at the dinner table bond the family (and can teach self-worth).

For those who can't stand the thought of staying with their parents one more night, there's cohousing. This is where several people, maybe a group of folks, sign their name on a dotted line to either rent space or co-purchase space, with each person having his/her room (or section) and arrangements made for the sharing of common areas, chores, and household bills. The agreements must be kept legal and always have an "out clause," as just shaking someone's hand doesn't cut it. Cohousing is growing in popularity between siblings, a child and a parent, relatives, or between friends. Divorced women with young children are finding that cohousing solves an infinite number of problems while maintaining a sense of home and security. An added benefit: kids are more apt to learn "whole thinking" when encouraged in familylike environments to converse in whole sentences.

The days when parents could afford to overindulge their children are fast fading. What is more common now is the reverse: children having to raise or take care of their parents. The majority of boomers and Gen Xers either lost their money during the recession or never had much put aside to begin with. Changing roles around while being careful to keep everything open and reasonable relieves much of the burden.

Marriage for Millennials is a coin toss. Most are looking for a union of equal and devoted partners, not the humble-pie kitten and dominant pack leader of the past who agree with an "I do" at the altar. Go back to the Bible and be honest about the stories there. No place can you find a single example of a healthy marriage or healthy sex. The same is true with the Qur'an and other religious texts. No blame here, as ancient teachings fit the needs of ancient times, while still applying to the present in respect to one's overall relationship with God/Allah/The Divine. But truth is truth. Children of today want a partner who has an established identity outside the marriage (or union) and who comes from a place of strength, not weakness. Watch this new preference completely transform the institution of marriage and having families in future years. Even the idea of committed partners and extended families (those who come together by choice) will shift, and continuously, as need and preference do.

Immigrants will keep populations lively. Community embraces the gamut of skin colors and body types—not as a swing toward multiculturalism, *at least not if we're smart,* but rather in recognition that strength comes from diversity. The different skills we have and the unique stories we tell are much too valuable to dilute or absorb or forget or blend or legislate.

HOMES AND SACRED DESIGN

I love the way today's young think. Faced with the choice of either downsizing and being debt free or drowning in debt as a buy-buy consumer, there is an across-the-board awakening to the value of "less is more." Even with the madness of consumerism-gone-wild, some are waking up and connecting the price of what they buy with the cost of how they live. Take Tammy Strobel, for instance. She put it this way: "Rethink normal." With that in mind she and her husband downsized and restructured their lives, reconsidered their priorities, and in doing so discovered endless potential and the freedom to be creative. Their house is tiny, I mean teeny tiny; go to http://rowdykittens.com and see for yourself. The concept of simple living graces their lives. They have bicycles instead of cars (they rent a car when needed), unplugged the television set (she found that each person who watches TV shows on a regular basis is exposed to hundreds of ads every day—especially ads that portray women as soft, skinny, and worth little more than easy sex). She and her husband said no to wasteful habits and accumulating possessions, and yes to spending more time with friends and doing what they really wanted. They have ordinary jobs but live extraordinary lives and are very happy. We can learn from them.

Carolyn North grabbed the proverbial gold ring herself and decided that what the world needs is a serious dose of fun. In *Serious Fun,* she shares ingenious improvisations on money, food, waste, water, and home.[4] Carolyn and Tammy are teaching others what worked for them. They are preparing the way as our culture moves from borrow and consume to repair, fix, and invent. A thought: take foreclosed homes and repair them for disabled vets and the homeless. Some banks are actually doing this.

The home of the future for the majority of people will be a rental, maybe a flat, or an efficiency (room pared down to basics). Some apartment complexes, though, are going all out to attract the "green" crowd with every type of holistic, sustainable feature imaginable (such as lighting systems designed to sync with your circadian rhythms and electromagnetic-free zones). *Newsweek* magazine devoted a page to this in their May 21, 2012, issue with the article "Apartment Therapy" by Rebecca Dana.

Owning your own home is not necessarily any kind of dream come true. (Have you ever stopped to consider the maintenance costs and labor attached to home ownership?) Use feng shui to turn any hovel or arrangement of rooms into that dream you wanted. The practice of feng shui goes back a thousand years or more and is based on the idea that when energy flows smoothly through a space, it feels serene and balanced. Its principles for rearranging stuff or adding color are excellent, and the ideas can be adapted to your own tastes.

If home ownership doesn't scare you, go the way of the future: "Earth ships" (www.earthship.com), or homes off the electrical grid. Architecture is headed in this direction, in the way of sleek, innovative, quiet, and self-sustaining ecospheres or haciendas (where rooms circle around private gardens). Baubiologie makes this possible. Although a German idea, Baubiologie, like feng shui, is ancient. The tradition recognizes that in order to have healthy, nontoxic structures you have to use healthy, nontoxic materials.[5] Also consider "pocket neighborhoods" (http://pocketneighborhoods.net) where smaller, community-oriented homes are built, maybe eight houses on four lots, that surround green spaces.

Whatever you do in the way of design and construction, use sacred geometry for proportions. Special numbers and ratios have been applied throughout history and have influenced everything from art and architecture to the development of religion and secret spiritual societies. Ancient temples and megalithic sites were also constructed utilizing what we today call acoustic technology, which shifts prefrontal-lobe activity in the brain to right-brain/emotional processing (at 110 hertz).

Check out www.landscape-perception.com/archaeoacoustics/ for details. The entire universe and all that is rhythmic and orderly, all that is beautiful and inspiring to look upon, all that enhances and strengthens natural forces and natural sounds, all that honors movement and flow and the Source from which all things and all life springs—reveals its proportion and vitality through sacred geometry. As the new kids take their place in the community of nations, sacred geometry will become the preferred measure in the construction of buildings and homes. Experts in the field are John Michell, Scott Olsen, Stephen Skinner, and Richard Heath.[6]

RELIGIOUS COMMUNITY

All religions are an attempt to help humankind evolve to perfection. They each consist of a doctrine of philosophy, mysticism, and the paranormal that includes a spiritual hierarchy. Without some type of spiritual/religious foundation in a society, confusion reigns in social discourse and relationships, ethics, and morals. The question of the twenty-first century is, *Can diverse faiths live together?*[7] For all that can be said about communities of believers, tolerance is still a struggle.

Individual believers are questioning their own faith today as never before. Hindus, for instance, are no longer as strict about how their deities are depicted. Lord Krishna is just as apt to appear on a computer mouse pad as a coffee mug. Christians have discovered that 666, the "mark of the beast," actually spells out a man's name—that of Nero Caesar—in the alphabet used at that time in history (each letter had a numerical value). They've also discovered that *Lucifer* refers to the first star of the morning, metaphorically *the king of Babylon. Hell,* by the way means "trash heap" in Peshitta/Aramaic. Egyptian Muslims formed human shields to protect Coptic Christians who were being attacked in 2011. When a Somali-born teen tried to bomb Pioneer Square in Portland, Oregon, in November 2010, local Muslims ascended on the place, passing out cards that read: *This man isn't like us.*

Can diverse faiths live together in community? The answer to that hangs on a central belief that is still held in trust: sacred violence.

For Muslims, the movie *Of Gods and Men,* directed by Xavier Beauvois, says it all. In a true story from the 1990s, monks serving the poor in Northern Africa were murdered by a Muslim insurgency. This powerful film shows that the right to murder, kill, maim in the name of one's deity is a false teaching that shames the very deity it supposedly honors. For Christians, Rocco Errico, Th.D., Ph.D., had this to say in his article "Did Jesus Die for Your Sins?": "Jesus' death on the cross was to end sacred violence. His teachings are dangerous because they are subversive and undermine our violent cultural and religious notions that so many live by. God's mercy and compassion do not work through revenge or violent wrath. God is love and love does not act through violent, death-dealing cleansing of any kind. Love is healing, forgiving, and harmonious. Love unites and God is that very love."[8]

SPIRITUAL COMMUNITY

The idea of church as a place of common worship is radically altering to fit the views and needs of the new generations. "Spirit-led" assemblies shake and yell; "house churches" operate from individual homes or bars; "techno mass" is turning sanctuaries into raves with techno sounds and ultraviolet light; meditation groups, pilgrimage travelers, metaphysical study groups, orb and crop-circle investigators, intuition camps, Earth energy seekers, participants in sacred service via computer, global prayers and chants and joyful voices singing in praise, even atheist student groups and atheist churches—all of these and more are the new houses of worship. Any religion that does not embrace and welcome this change will either die off or slowly wither from a lack of relevance. While the Islamic faithful finally admit their need for reform and allow their communities to modernize, many Christian sects are doing the opposite—devolving into the Army of God and the New Apostolic Reformation Movement (stricter types of fundamentalism).

Here's a new maxim: *spirituality*—questions that may never be answered; *religion*—answers that may never be questioned.

This maxim defines the divide. Power is swelling. The stages of belief, of conscious awareness, are moving toward the enlightenment that becomes possible when freedom of choice is honored. Countries with the lowest rates of social dysfunction are those who squeeze the least. Far from causing collapse, freedom of choice leads to self-responsibility, creativity, invention, compassion, and a greater and deeper love of one's god. "Coerced belief is no belief at all; it is tyranny."[9]

The growth of power is the sum of millions of the young, and others as well, who are bringing back the Goddess—woman power—and asserting themselves mightily in their choice to leave organized religion and opt instead for a closeness, an everyday, everywhere, personal walk with their god as the core reality in their lives. The gurus of the past—those charismatic leaders and teachers who seduced us by saying how wonderful we are and that we'll live forever—are falling by the wayside. They are being replaced by smiling folk who already know they are okay, who know we can do this, we can be better, we can help each other.

An amazing number of children are born knowing. It's as if they remember a truth from another world of being. The mythic and the legendary speak more directly to them than catechisms and biblical verse. Yet in their incredible knowing and psychic awareness, their confident self-assertion of belief, the new kids are strangely hesitant and uninformed. The visionary boomers who have a lock on the transcendental often mistake the bravado of the young for something other than what it is. Yes, the new kids, many of them, are wise beyond their years, yet they are almost desperate in their need for mentors. Not teachers, but mentors who can help them remember even more of what they already know and apply it to daily life. A more valuable type of worship for them is the play-shop (as opposed to the workshop) model, where they can experiment, debate, act out, organize, produce, create, dream, dance, sing, and serve.

Yes, serve, for their main avenue of worship is in service to others. Theirs is the living church. Examples:

+ Volunteering at the antihunger Heifer Ranch
  (www.heiferfoundation.org)
+ Offering solutions to World Changing
  (www.worldchanging.com/seattle/)
+ Watching the film *One Peace at a Time*, then acting
  (http://nobelity.org)
+ Working with AmeriCorps (www.americorps.gov), City Year,
  (http://cityyear.org), Habitat for Humanity (www.habitat.org),
  Peace Corps (www.peacecorps.gov), or Teach for America
  (www.teachforamerica.org)
+ Passing it on through gestures of generosity
  (www.servicespace.org)

A national service of volunteers *is* their call to worship. The location of their church is wherever they can help make a difference. Put them in an environment where their voice matters and their bodies can move, and they will be at ease and happy.

GETTING ALONG

Spiritual communities are where we go to be inspired, encouraged, and nurtured. They foster accountability and the sustenance needed for an awakening consciousness. It is where you become the "yeast" in the "rising bread" of enlightenment (for little ones, *The Joy of Affirmative Prayer* is a wonder[10]).

Prohibition, back in the 1920s, taught us that you cannot force people to be good. The unintended consequences of enforced morality turned law-abiding citizens into criminals. Organized crime began during that period; so did higher rates of alcoholism in women. What does this have to do with community and getting along? Everything.

It brings to the fore the question of shadows, the darker side of our nature, and the basics of civility—how we treat each other.

Carl Gustav Jung, the famed psychoanalyst, identified shadow as the dark side of each human being that contains repressed weaknesses and shortcomings. Don't think for a moment that our new kids are squeaky-clean. They can have personal vendettas and axes to grind. If you don't believe me, visit some of these Occupy Wall Street encampments. Starhawk, a well-known group-dynamics leader, says, "It happens over and over again—a group of people come together, fired up with passion to create change. They begin with huge inspiration and enthusiasm—and a year later, it's all floundered in the mire of conflict. We could have changed the world ten times over—if we didn't have to do it together with other people, those irritating, self-righteous, controlling, fluff-brained, clueless idiots who are our friends and allies."[11]

So how do we handle the shadow side of our natures and get along?

+ For the Maori people of New Zealand, "a 'community circle' session opens with perpetrator talking about what happened and then all the participants—victims, parents, bystanders—are invited to discuss how the crime affected them. It's a little like a drug intervention, except that it ends with everyone coming to a written agreement, which invariably includes an apology and some form of restitution."[12]

+ Ho'oponopono of the Hawaiian Islands is very similar. It too is a way for participants to solve problems, not by apportioning blame but by making right any relations that have gone astray. The parties involved meet face-to-face with a facilitator to talk things through. Everyone has a voice and everyone has a vote as to outcome and the results of that outcome.

+ Real yoga is far more than a relaxation technique. The emphasis is on self-realization and knowing who you really are, then moving past identifying with the ego to a consciousness more integrated with that of humankind and the natural world. The higher levels of yoga move in and through deeper levels of the meditative journey—a surrender to the silence and wisdom of soul.

Getting along with others means realizing that contrast, conflict, differences—the shadow side—have a purpose. According to Debbie Ford: "We wouldn't discern courage if we hadn't known fear. We wouldn't seek kindness if we didn't know meanness. We wouldn't appreciate selflessness if we hadn't experienced selfishness. This is how humans learn. Having this awareness helps us appreciate both sides, both perspectives, both polarities."[13]

We integrate polarites by moving from "I" to "we." We are the light of God on a journey—so say our children. Experience is what defines our deity for us. We get from here to there through *choice*—the power, opportunity, and right we each have to choose what we think, what we say, what we believe, what we do.

Choice operates best through the Rule of Thirds:

1. Seek your best response, thought, or action by first being honest with yourself. What is it you want?
2. Consider any alternatives, then make your decision.
3. Before you act, give yourself three minutes, hours, days, or weeks. Live with your decision a while. Swallow, clear your throat, recheck, then act.

Only by taking the third step will you know if your choice is worthwhile.

17

The New Business of Business Politics

People are taught to look for jobs, not opportunities.

JESSE GABY-HUGHSON

I met Jesse in northern New York State. He is a young man who decided he wanted to be his own boss, so he created a company where he could do just that. He loves his work and has been very successful, to the point where he can hire a few others to help him. He's one of our new entrepreneurs.

Jobs are out there. Opportunities literally crowd the scene—but not in the manner they did in the past. The U.S. Bureau of Labor Statistics' Occupational Outlook Handbook 2010–2011 lists those jobs expected to shrink in demand during coming years. They are: judge, fashion designer, insurance underwriter, travel agent, newspaper reporter, broadcast announcer, plant manager, chemist, economist, and chief executive officer. These are high-paying jobs our government has pegged for "no future." Also on the agenda: a paperless society. (The trees are clapping.)

Civilizations don't decline; they collapse. What has enabled most of us in the Western nations to skate along at a pretty good clip compared with other countries are these powerful advantages: competition, scientific breakthroughs, rule of law, modern medicine, consumer society, and a work ethic that enables wealth accumulation—hence the creation of a large middle class. Yet we could lose it all; sooner than you may think. And not just because Republicans and Democrats hate each other. There are extreme forces at work, both here and across the world—new ones we haven't faced before—like the tragedy of around 40 percent of our young being unemployed (included in that figure are newly minted college graduates who carry debt loads of around thirty thousand dollars in student loans), and the angry shouts of the Occupy movement (the same young saying "Enough is enough. Banks are monsters and capitalism is evil").

What lies ahead of us? A world that is already surprising even the psychics.

FOUR BASIC ECONOMIC CYCLES

Expansion	Begins at a low point; steady growth as change takes place
Peak	Reaches a time of overall prosperity, employment, spending
Contraction	Slowdowns, declines, cutbacks, recession
Recovery	Hits rock bottom; may be stagnant or depressed for a while before the next expansion begins

You guessed it: we're currently in a contraction cycle. Can we skip the bottoming out trough of recovery and scoot straight to expansion? No, but we may be able to ease up on the rough stuff ahead of us. Robert J. Samuelson, a political columnist, gives some perspective on this: "The problem isn't that the economy occasionally goes bust. It's that it doesn't go bust often enough." The deal is, when governments deliver as much prosperity to as many people as possible for as long as possible, instability results—an unhappy truth. Ups and downs enable systems and citizens to self-correct and realign.

OUR COUNTRY AND OUR CONSTITUTION

Sorry to topple a few myths, but we live in a constitutional republic, not a democracy. Most of the founding fathers of our republic were Deists, not Christians. (A Deist is one who believes in God based on religious truths discovered through reasoning or from nature.) Many were Masons and mystics. It is said that Benjamin Franklin himself suggested that the constitution of the Iroquois Confederacy be used as a model for what later became the Constitution of the United States.[1] Although hard facts are missing to back up the many claims about America's secret past, architectural designs, currency, rituals, symbols—the very legitimacy of our government—are all contained within and formed around mythical principle and sacred design.

Chief among the factions devoted to correcting what they feel were mistakes made by the founding fathers are the Army of God and the New Apostolic Reformation Movement. Some goals of these organizations are to replace the Constitution with a biblical one, and to do away with the "pagan goddesses" of Lady Liberty/Lady Columbia/Lady Freedom. They teach believers to defeat evil by taking control over all sectors of society and government, ensuring mass conversions to their brand of Christianity.[2] This is laughable—except that two candidates running for president in 2012 associated with these groups; so did the unstable evangelical who tried to assassinate Obama on 11-11-11.

Yet the big question is, Has the Constitution become a joke? John Whitehead, founder and president of the Rutherford Institute (a civil-liberties organization), has this to say: "For all intents and purposes, the Constitution is on life support and has been for some time now. Those responsible for its demise are none other than the schools, which have failed to educate students about its principles; the courts, which have failed to uphold the rights enshrined within it; the politicians, who long ago sold out to corporations and special interests; and 'we the people' who, in our ignorance and greed, have valued materialism over freedom."[3]

Whitehead hits the nail on the head when talking about the Constitution and how our Congress is busily reducing and weakening the rights enshrined within it. Please remember that the Constitution not only sets up federal government; it also fetters it with enumerated powers, three branches of government, two rival legislative wings, supermajorities, judicial review, and presidential veto power.

So who do we vote for to represent us? In 2000, 373 of the 535 congressional members had records as criminals, drunks, or cheats. We looked the other way when congressional members gave themselves the right to trade stocks and land deals while considering major bills—essentially insider trading, a crime outside Congress. Just to run for office, candidates must now spend 90 percent of their time raising money instead of working on the nation's business. Television has skewed elections by making big things small and small things big. The result? We no longer elect the best person for the job; rather, we choose whomever puts on the best show and has the most shocking ads. Even when our sovereignty is at risk, the mandates that pass both houses wind up based on politics, not what is in our best interests. Legislators routinely spend more time on vacation than on the job.

"Throw the bums out," you say? Hey, government is us. Our Constitution gives us the power to change things. How? VOTE! Organize. Study who is running. Run for office yourself. Have mock electioneering as a project in school. Encourage every child to follow a bill from Committee to House or Senate floor and testify about its merits or demerits. Restore patriotism and love of country.

And, admit the truth. The Equal Rights Amendment to the Constitution lost because the final three states necessary for ratification never came forward. Should any of the federal legislation protecting women and minorities ever be challenged, this amendment would have guaranteed protection. Don't believe anyone who says we don't need this. We do. It is folly that in America, of all places, equal rights are still blocked from Constitutional coverage. Women are now poised globally to become the most important economic engine ever known.

Until women are accepted as true partners in the human race, females will never be secure.

BUSINESS POLITICS

January 21, 2010, the United States Supreme Court overturned a twenty-year ruling limiting political soft money and television advertising during elections. Certainly, for most of our history, election campaigns have been unrestricted. But in this case the Supreme Court ruled that corporations had the same rights as an individual to make political donations, and could do so without revealing identity. Unlimited political donations work *only* if every dollar given is declared publicly for all to see. This way, funny money and mysterious contributors become public knowledge and perhaps campaign issues. Doing this would ensure transparency. As long as corporations can donate money without restriction, *they own our country*. Already we are a global embarrassment for funds we allow to be spent on political lobbying—when that same money could be spent on infrastructure projects and restoring some semblance of a middle class.

This one act merged business with politics to create business-politics, the new capitalism—the beginnings of a corporate state. During the '60s, '70s, and into the '80s there existed an unwritten social contract between labor, business, and government that created and maintained a balance of power and responsibility. At that time the salary span between top executives and the lowest paid was 40 percent. Today it's 256 percent.[4] Popular reform bills that would create a public-consumer advocate, close small loopholes in taxation of the wealthy, and make it harder for employers to circumvent labor laws have consistently been defeated. There's no incentive to try again now that corporations rule. But do they?

The headline reads: *Municipalities Take on Corporations*. Allen D. Kanner observes, "Since 1998, more than 125 municipalities have passed ordinances that explicitly put their citizens' rights ahead of corporate interests, despite the existence of state and federal laws to the contrary." At issue are corporate practices such as toxic-sludge dumping and fracking. The Community Environmental Legal Defense Fund, a nonprofit public-interest law firm, jumped into the fray to defend the rights of municipalities to govern themselves, above that of corporate interests.[5] Firms like this will mushroom as people wake up and stand up.

Because of long-standing and unchecked business-political influence, along with a 35 percent rise of unionized workers in the public sector (whose pensions, by the way, are lavish beyond any sense of fiscal discipline), the United States has become a two-tiered society: the very wealthy, and the middle/lower class. Families are now segregated according to income. This debacle, to my way of thinking, began in the '60s with Vietnam. One camp went to college and did not serve (engaged in protests, drugs, and a me-first mentality), while the other camp fought an ugly, disabling war and came home to vile threats and demonstrations against them. Still unanswered: We bled and died for what? Today, both Iraq and Afghanistan echo the same question.

Big business, corporations, banking firms, and investment brokerages, must become more introspective and ask themselves, What is our role in society? The answer "Showing a profit for investors" is wrong; this encourages problems such as funding predatory lenders who pick on the poor, gambling with derivatives/takeovers, and bankruptcy for profit or "liar's loans." The better answer is, "A move toward personalization by gearing products, services, and systems to individual customers, clients, or patients" (managing intellectual capital and growth thrives in this climate; performance is "value-added"). Michael J. Sandel, in his book *What Money Can't Buy,* cautions, "In a more and more unequal society, it's more and more difficult to sustain the mutual respect of all citizens for one another."[6]

Capitalism in itself is good . . . as long as some restraint exists to favor basic ethics over engrained corruption. Example: in 2011 an American company sold Egypt Deep Packet Inspection (DPI) equipment that enabled the Egyptian military to track, target, and crush political dissent over the Internet and mobile phones.[7] No regulation existed to prevent this.

THE THIRD INDUSTRIAL REVOLUTION

The free-enterprise system has brought more people out of poverty than any other economic system the world has ever known. As the world's people divest themselves or are pulled away from excessively lenient/fiscally undisciplined governments and/or restrictive, religiously controlled governments (both denying a reasonable life in accord with what could and should be available), the free-enterprise system will grow exponentially worldwide. Power is moving from New York City to Washington, D.C., as global clout shifts toward Singapore, Hong Kong, and Shanghai. The weak link in this shift is the Earth's resources.

Presently, our planet cannot supply the addition of a burgeoning middle class in either India or China unless adjustments are made. China is already taking action by winning construction, farm, and natural resources bids in Africa and South America and moving in their own people to work and settle there rather than training and hiring mostly locals to handle things. Besides being lucrative business deals, these construction projects appear more like veiled attempts at colonization.[8]

Natural-resource problems are exacerbated by the fuel crisis (even with new oil fields being found, we still need to cut the cord with oil). To make real change, the source of energy must change. Existing technologies must change too. Give them a good "bath" (dirty tech is the name used for converting old to new; investigate doings at the equity firm of Virgin Green Fund, www.virgingreenfund.com; then examine the recent eco-friendly makeover of the Empire State Building in New York City, which reduces energy costs by $4,400 million per year and has created 252 new jobs). Change also applies to predominately Muslim nations that use terrorism as a foreign policy and source of gross national product (apparently not realizing or caring how their actions destroy not only people, but also their own environment and natural resources, blinding them to the real terrorism threatening every spot on earth: *weather extremes*).

Is the world toast?

Enter economist Jeremy Rifkin with a startling observation: *a new industrial revolution is on the horizon and will change everything.* "The conjoining of Internet communications technology and renewable energies," says Rifkin, "is giving rise to a Third Industrial Revolution. In the 21st century, hundreds of millions of human beings will be generating green energy in their homes, offices, and factories and sharing it with one another across intelligent distributed-electricity networks—an Intergrid—just like they now create information and share it on the Internet."[9]

He believes this can be done through:

1. A shift to renewable energy (green sources)
2. The conversion of buildings and homes into micropower plants (new construction must be energy neutral)
3. Green energy made easy to collect and store (by preserving solar energy in batteries, for instance)
4. Connecting the energy Intergrid across continents ("smart networks" merge collected energy via meters and into Internet feeds, thus energy networks and communication networks "fly" together)
5. Plugging in electric cars/appliances to this "smart network" of energy (the European Union's projected date for eliminating cars powered by fossil fuels: 2050). If you haven't read Rifkin's book *The Third Industrial Revolution: How Lateral Power Is Transforming Energy, the Economy, and the World,* consider it a must-read.

Stop a moment. Did you hear what Rifkin said?

+ THE THIRD INDUSTRIAL REVOLUTION. The Rule of Thirds tells us industry as we know it ends with the global revolution now beginning. It also tells us another presence is moving through this shift in a rhythmic timing that accords with natural law and sacred proportion. (The recent growth rate in India and China brings one-third of the human race into the oil era—the perfect ratio to ignite "smart networks.")

+ LATERAL POWER. The side-to-side movement enables the restructuring of human relationships, top to bottom, all around, with profound implications for the future of society and governments. This type of distributed power will create a collaborative age of linked economies. What is trying to emerge through this is the spiritual presence of the larger whole and the capacity of each person to become a change agent in that whole.[10] *This is that sense of meaning the new kids hunger for and know exists.*

THE NEW KIDS' BUSINESS MODEL

True, the new kids are moving into a harsh marketplace without a work ethic to match. Their "we'll do it our way" sense of entitlement slams them into one wall after another: job applications read by computers, not people, that discard the experienced for "young ideas" (a cover for slashed insurance/pension benefits); job skills that don't fit requirements, even if college trained (a cover for whiners and complainers); job wages lower than the debts they are saddled with (a cover for being stuck with the economic mistakes of their elders).

In a very real way, our new kids are lost to the job market—the old one staffed with traditional employers who operate in a management style out of sync with the way the world is changing. Skills of the young wrap around collaboration, teaming up with others to create a renaissance of self-direction and meaning. They do not see themselves as employees or resources. They're partners who direct their own lives

. . . in and through the creative space of a hub—not an office, but a "docking station" where they can plug in, discuss ideas, and do their best work.

Hub space is defined as a center everywhere and a circumference nowhere. These spaces operate on chaos theory: out of disorder comes new order; divergence from random data can spin out wild new patterns and exotic pathways to better solutions. Hubs buzz with activity and endless curiosity amid odd environments where creative thinking is not only allowed but encouraged. The goal: build, invent, create what is useful. In a partnership position, the new kids are able to self-govern/ act with choice, yet work happily interdependently with others.

If hub environments sound like they are made for a whole new breed of folk, know that they are. The young adults of today and tomorrow are optimistic, value diversity, and are civic minded multi-taskers who want to be recognized for their achievements. Although they communicate well electronically, they flounder with personal skills and need a lot of hand holding and encouragement. They require a certain amount of supervision and structure, have short attention spans, and lack patience for menial chores, yet they are absolutely brilliant, clever, and innovative.

No doubt about it: they are the most high-maintenance generation in history, while simultaneously operating as the highest-performing generation in history.

What is their business model? Here's what one told me: "My purpose in life is to be amazed. To join with friends and strangers to enjoy, help, uplift, and protect each other and our world. Money serves me. I do not serve it." Translation: meaning trumps promotions. They truly want to make a difference in the world. Issues are important, not labels nor political parties. They have a fine sense of caring and justice, would rather collaborate with their coworkers than compete, and are unafraid to rebrand themselves and retrain. They are the perfect group to handle lateral power, network broadly, and utilize intuitive guidance. Businesses like Hewlett Packard and Southwest Airlines have caught on.

Using what they call "swarm intelligence," they now encourage employees to self-organize on the spot, without a manager's authorization, and pool their intelligence and creativity to find the best response to rapidly changing markets. This is the perfect business model for them.

NEW LEADERS

There is virtually no president, prime minister, dictator, ruler, or individual in a major leadership role in any country who is prepared for what is happening in the world today. The continuing shift in international economies is challenging the way businesses and institutions organize themselves, create wealth, and present themselves to the world. A manager today must combine East with West and be bilingual. This is hitting Asia, Africa, Latin America, and the Middle East the hardest, as breakneck growth and changes in availability of resources are pushing cultures and governments to the limit. Job recruiters worldwide are desperate for top talent. Myopic tribal leaders are just as desperate to hold back the tsunami of technologies that are flooding their countries, nullifying the effectiveness of force and slaughter. Hatred has become too expensive to continue!

Some suggestions for tackling runaway change and the lack of leadership:

+ Redesign the way you think: observe, watch, experience to build confidence. Remember, no one is a victim of their genes or hereditary traits.[11]
+ Use your intuition as a business advantage, a tool for core creativity.[12]
+ Share products and services, and emphasize experience over excess, community over commerce.[13]
+ Overcome obstacles by developing the "learning organization" structured around personal mastery, mental models, shared vision, team growth.[14]

+ Build bridges across disciplines, sectors, with a vision/systems perspective.
+ Regard anger on the job as an opportunity to make something better.[15]
+ Bring your compassion as well as your intellect to work.[16]
+ Light up when you think about giving; become a "thrillionaire."[17]
+ Subscribe to *The Optimist* magazine (formerly *Ode*), the international magazine for innovative and creative thinkers.[18]

The best leadership trainers are individuals who have previously undergone either a near-death experience or a spiritual transformation of some kind. What they went through "redesigned" their mind in the sense that they return as clustered thinkers (as opposed to sequential/selective thinkers)—a sign of genius[19]—with the ability to abstract and be comfortable with ambiguity. Thinking outside the box no longer applies; to them, boxes don't exist (they see beyond what limits). Most rely on the sacred silence of meditation/contemplation to guide their decisions and their lives. An example of this type of trainer is Doug Krug. At home within any group, he specializes in the challenges of government, medicine, and law enforcement.[20] "The game of improvement has changed," he notes. "We do not need to solve all the problems to create the future. The answer is where you are. To change the outcome, change the questions." His understanding of the mind in relation to the soul is quite unique, as with any trainer who offers a different perspective. Inquire. Look around. You'll find numerous people like Krug active in the world today.

NEW MONEY

I've spoken earlier in this book about how the young are reconsidering the act of buying and selling, what money is, and how we might change its handling. What follows are some even newer ideas that have real heft to them:

✦ Rent whatever you have. With Facebook, Twitter, e-mail, and blogs, it is easy to advertise stuff and name prices and terms. The extra money is great.

✦ Business in a box (radio charger, LED lamp, solar panel): that's all that's necessary for people in rural/undeveloped areas to advertise their products, communicate with customers, make sales.

✦ Build an entire business ecosystem that provides products and services through sharing, community participation, and a culture of trust.[21]

✦ Bring about the Third Industrial Revolution with a new breed of business students who go green as a way to wealth.[22]

✦ Dare to Care shows individuals how to use money to serve personal values and the well-being of others in a love-based way.[23]

Downscale or eliminate credit cards, reconsider cash, and invest long-term where your values are. The Fed, by printing more money, devalues the money we have, which is the hidden tax we pay against our net worth. This flawed system is changing as individuals create their own economies and help others to do the same through microloans (www.microplace.com).

NEW ANGER

There's a flip side to where we're headed as a people. Allow me to wave a few red flags highlighting other issues that affect business and politics/government.

The digital age concentrates wealth in fewer hands, exploits personal information, and makes possible undeclared cyberwars where hackers use malicious codes to enact physical damage (like what happened in late 2010, when Iran's nuclear facility was digitally attacked). Al-Qaeda has been running this type of hacker school for more than a decade; so has the Blue Army in China and just about any other computer school in the world (including in the United States). Social activism operates in a similar manner called hacktivism. Innovators are now experimenting with putting implants in contact lenses so a person's eyes can access the Internet at will.

"Ants"—white-collar workers who can't find decent work or a place to live—are China's newest underclass. China's men without women are becoming more strident, cocky—the forerunners of major social problems in fifteen to twenty years.

Female abuse has exploded in Arab and Muslim countries. The Arab Spring is quickly devolving into voter's remorse (the better-organized and -funded Muslim Brotherhood is gaining converts). If there ever was proof that Muslim clerics have perverted Islam, it is now. Outright butchery and torture has far exceeded any interpretation of what is permissible in the Qur'an. A Pakistani journalist, for instance, must consider on a daily basis whether to report the news as it really happened, or stay alive.

"Afghanistan's Last Locavores," a shocking article by Patricia McArdle, published in the *New York Times,* on June 19, 2011, reveals that the most promising model for sustainable living is not found on organic farms in the United States, but in Afghanistan. Afghan homes are built to be warm in winter and cool in summer, yet we are pushing them into cement and cinderblocks—more modern, but less efficient. Renewable energy resources that could be inexpensively harnessed are abundant in this country; still, we are building a twentieth-century power grid for them that will force Afghans to purchase the bulk of their electricity needs from the Soviet Republics for decades to come. What disaster are we trying to free these people from—the Taliban? Even they are reconsidering their future in this country.

Every year since the 1960s there has been a massive oil spill in the Niger Delta. Locals complain of sore eyes, breathing problems, and lesions on their skin. It's sickening stuff. Many Nigerians watched Americans berate British Petroleum for what happened in the Gulf of Mexico, while no one has done a thing to help the Nigerians.[24] Cleanup has been halfhearted; compensation paltry. The "black tide" of gooey oil continues to benefit oil companies and corrupt officials, while most Nigerians live in poverty.

A *Huffington Post* headline from October 12, 2011, read "More Black Men in Prison Today than Were Enslaved in 1850." "Warehouse prisons" fail to correct anything. *Beyond Vengeance, Beyond Duality* is a how-to-correct-this-nightmare book by Sylvia Clute that could make a real difference.[25]

There is no cause that can justify terrorism. There is no scandal that cannot be broken by an electorate that refuses to be silent.

18   THE FIFTH WORLD

Let us resolve to be masters, not the victims, of our history, controlling our own destiny without giving way to blind suspicions and emotions.

JOHN F. KENNEDY

Here's a quick scan of a myriad of the world's young—with a tie to elephants (no kidding):

Africa: More than three hundred thousand boys, hopped up on drugs and wielding AK-47s, have been forced by soldiers to commit brutal acts of slaughter. Now devoid of human pity, these children were once gentle boys trapped by war.[1] Human sacrifice is on the rise in Uganda—mostly of children (in the belief that drugs made from their organs will bring riches). More than 40 percent of the continent's people are under the age of fifteen, and they are ready to change the way Africa works. These kids are standing up and fighting back through education and by demanding democracy, transparency, and an end to the corruption that poisons their governments. They call themselves Cheetahs.

Iran: Roughly 75 percent of Iranians are under the age of thirty. They are actively taking to the streets to protest what they believe is a corrupt government. A large number of them were born in the 1980s, when, by law, children were wanted, protected, and

well cared for. This enabled the widespread growth of the prefrontal lobes (the wings of the brain). Hence, they refused to be
silenced.

North Korea: This saber-rattling dictatorship is now led by the
youngest son of "Dear Leader." He is twenty-six, shy, overweight,
and a heavy drinker. He is capable (as were the African boy soldiers) of doing whatever he has to—for a while.

India: More than half of India's population is under the age of
thirty, upwardly mobile, ambitious, and education-minded, while
at the same time actively participating in volunteer efforts, envi-
ronmentalism, and making a positive difference.

China: Although the world is their oyster, typical Chinese
Millennials are sent to "reeducation camps" so they will become
more nationalistic, less ideological, and more market-savvy. They
are China's sixth generation from Mao.

Ukraine: Chernobyl's children have shown a mental agility and
health superior to those in unaffected areas, leading to claims
that the radiation created a superior breed.

Russia: Young militants act like the Brown Shirts of former Nazi
Germany—belligerent and prone to mob rule. Rappers are now
the rage.

United States: White-supremacy groups are on the rise and are
angry at the election of a black president. Called skinheads or
Sons of Anarchy, they mimic the young militants of Europe.
Almost a quarter of U.S. kids now live in poverty;[2] many of the
rest volunteer to help feed those who are hungry.

Arabic countries: The majority of young Muslims are more conservative than their parents, preferring to die in jihad than grow old;
60 percent of the Taliban are uneducated youth. The younger
the child, the more strident. More than half the population is
under the age of twenty-five. Muslim children are the first to be
tortured in war.

Being positive or negative is not my intent here, but being honest is. There was some research done on young elephants that will demonstrate the point I am trying to make. When in a group and left to themselves, young male elephants invariably turn rogue. If a few older male elephants enter, the young calm down and cease rogue behavior. The pattern of young elephants turning rogue without the calming, steady presence and guidance of parents and elders applies to every grouping of young in the world. Research with elephants mirrors the human family exactly.

The focus of this book is to shine a bright light on evolution's children, our new kids, to show how different they are from previous generations, what they face as they mature, and how they fit into the larger cycles of the Great Shifting currently underway. The coming of the Fifth Root Race was predicted thousands of years ago. Leaders in the theosophical movement gave us this baseline: *"Consciousness separated into two hemispheres—East and West—is now fusing back together, a global leap in species refinement"* (see chapter 3). Gifted artists, psychotic killers, exceptional geniuses, enraged bullies, spirit-led cripples—these are our new kids, each possessing the same overall pattern of traits. Forget categories and labels. "When the tide comes in, *all* boats rise."

With that quick scan I just gave you of kids around the world, let's remember that what makes the crucial difference in what becomes of them is parents, elders, mentors.

Remember the elephants!

WE WERE WARNED—BUT NOT BY A PSYCHIC

Yes, many psychics predicated the Fifth World, but not with the same specifics as did generational researchers William Strauss and Neil Howe in their seminal book, *Generations: The History of America's Future, 1584 to 2069.* They wrote the following: "Based on historical patterns, America will hit a once-in-a-century national crisis within the decade, . . . 'Like winter,' the crisis or 'fourth turning' cannot be averted. It will last 20 years or so and bring hardship and upheavals similar to previous fourth turnings, such as the American Revolution, the Civil War, the Great Depression, and World War II. The fourth turning is a perilous time because the result could be a new 'golden age' for America or the beginning of the end."[3]

They chart four turnings to generational cycles, each a shift, the first from a high period of confidence and new order, to the second of rebellious awakenings, then uneasy unraveling, until the fourth is reached—a time of upheaval. Their idea of turnings is very similar to the four levels of economic ups and downs. The timing they offered for when the fourth turning would begin was 2013—after the end date of the Mayan calendar. The Vedic tradition of world ages or yugas also follows a four-level track: Golden Age, Silver Age, Bronze Age, Iron Age—with similar descriptions and understandings of what develops at each level, to the patterns already mentioned. However, Vedic wisdom says that the world cycles or yugas *recycle* through a progressive spiral of ascending energy and descending energy, creating what some call the Grand Spiral of Remembrance (who we are, why we're here, where we're going). The majority of ancient calendars, no matter where in the world, move the same way—through a spiral of ascents and descents.

And they describe five major levels, or turns, not four. The most famous of these five-level tracks is the Mayan calendar.

THE COMING OF THE FIFTH WORLD

Whether you're a Mayan elder or an archaeologist, the Sun Stone of the Mayans is an impressive, almost unbelievable carved disk of evolution at work, calculated with a precision we're only newly capable of appreciating. Yes, you can use the long count of the Calendar as a calendar, but its real value is as a tracking device, laying out the steps of development that consciousness uses in the earth plane. We are the grand experiment, mystics and ministers and shamans tell us, here to see if life forms like us can succeed, not only in our transformational journeys, but also assisting in the greater journey of consciousness awakening to itself. Sounds lofty, doesn't it?

Shown on the Sun Stone are Five Suns or Five Worlds. Interpretations vary, depending on whether you're a scientist, a traditional elder, or a visionary. Only modern worrywarts came up with the notion that the end of the Calendar means the end of the world. No one else is so foolish. Ancient calendars spiral. The Sun Stone is no exception.

The Mayan Calendar begins with the beginning of all things. The worlds it describes can be summarized in this manner:

> **First World:** *Jaguar/Ocelot Sun* (Earth element, feminine energy). Said to be a time when giants walked the earth. It ended in devastating winds, fire, and long periods of darkness.
>
> **Second World:** *Winds Sun* (air element, masculine energy). Said to cover the advance of early humans. Ended when huge forests flattened out because of cyclones. Great winds, hurricanes, darkness.
>
> **Third World:** *Rain of Fire Sun* (fire element, feminine energy). Said to be a time of creative invention, large structures, flourishing societies. Ended in rains of lava and fire, volcanos erupting, darkness, ice.
>
> **Fourth World:** *Water Sun* (water element, masculine energy). Said to stimulate written language, law, cities, metal work, much invention, art, commerce. Ended in great floods, rains, storms. The rise of materialism and the dark side of power.
>
> **Fifth World:** *Quake/Movement Sun* (ether element, fusion of masculine and feminine energies). Said to be the age of modern man and space travel. Due to end in huge shifts, movements, earthquakes, perhaps a pole shift.

Note: There is disagreement about Second and Fourth Suns. Some claim they are opposite of what is shown. Most scholars and folklorists, however, concur with the rendition presented here.

Some "experts" state with absolute assurance that the five-cycle series of worlds ends December 21, 2012, with a Sixth World beginning the next day. They back this up by pointing out that the Sixth Root Race, or indigos, have appeared. With the same absolute assurance, others claim that the last of the five, or Fifth World, begins on that date. What no one seems to notice in this banter is that the Mayan Calendar spirals; the movement it tracks is a fluid wave form. That means that both versions of stop and start dates could be true, depending on the spiral's tilt. If I'm right—and I believe that I am—then what changes on December 21, 2012, *is the flow of energy to one of accelerating, ascending wave forms.* We're talking about potential here that is off the charts.

And does the Sun Stone really point to 12-21-12 at all? No! This date was found elsewhere; in 2010 on a stairway carved with hieroglyphs, found in the Mayan ruins of La Corona, Guatemala. Marcello Canuto, the director of Tulane University Middle America Research Institute said in a statement, "This text talks about ancient political history rather than prophecy."[4] It was modern researchers who connected an end date with the Sun Stone, using the Mayan 13-bak'tun cycle of measuring time—without realizing these astronomer priests actually used systems far in advance of such dating. Proof came in the May 11, 2012, blockbuster: "The Oldest-Known Version of the Ancient Maya Calendar Has Been Discovered—Deep in the Guatemalan Rainforest." Found in ruins missed by others were room-sized murals, lavishly adorned, that shocked everyone. "The Mayan Calendar is going to keep going for billions, trillions, octillions of years into the future," said archaeologist David Stuart of the University of Texas who worked to decipher the glyphs. "Numbers we can't even wrap our heads around."[5]

This discovery establishes that we haven't even begun to understand Mayan mathematics. But we can recognize something odd signaled by the Calendar that coincides with the same oddity in the astrological pattern of the Great Shifting. And that is, there's a swing time or null space between 1980 and 2018 when the shift moves into space (and when the Millennials and 9/11s gain entry). This swing time is rather peculiar in that the accelerating energies do not and will not follow any particular course . . . they are undefinable and without apparent direction, or null. It's a manic period, where everything seems to happen at once or in rapid-fire succession, and nothing is really clear as to whether it's positive or negative or even aimed any particular way. Predictions seldom hold true and plans often go awry. What was once constant and dependable is now on the skids. The formerly ridiculous is what suddenly makes sense. It's chaos in full swing . . . and out of chaos *always comes a new and better order.* Our new kids are made for this. They can find directions intuitively and improve on things as they go along, thanks to group power.

However you call it, the Fifth World isn't just coming or going; it's here. So let's take a gander at the incredible fives Fifth World energy is unleashing. This may seem a little strange at first, but keep reading. It will make sense later on.

THE INCREDIBLE FIVES

Fifth World: A time when polarities shift on every level, and that includes gender issues, genetics, the two brain hemispheres, religious factions, wealth, relationships, governments, business-politics. A time of fusion, merging.

Fifth Root Race: Children as volunteers, here to establish a new Earth and possessing the attributes, skills, weaknesses, and strengths needed to do the job. Coming in waves. Can harness challenges and disasters if mentored when young. To them, the universe is alive and intelligent and stuffed full of potential.

Fifth Element: Ether (also spelled *aether*) is the substance of space, an invisible, interconnecting, threaded fabric or webbing that constitutes the matrix time-and-space collapse into when energy expands. Ether is not an Earth element; rather, it is a realm of patterns and causality. All manifests from here. All thoughts, feelings, actions are recorded here. The akashic records (the record of all things, all people, all life), written upon the skeins of time, are found in the ether.

Note: I'll be sharing some personal observations when appropriate. This one from what I witnessed during my three death/near-death experiences of 1977, and afterward, when I interacted with the ether.

What I saw was a pliable, closely-woven, preatomic web of interlacing, interacting, circular logic units (airy threads of bubblelike components), which made up the fabric of information (intelligence) that allowed thought and the flow or movement of thought to expand, contract, stabilize. These circular logic units composed the ether, and they appeared as sparkling or twinkling particles or sparks, or, somehow inert and dark (depending on whether they were "on" or "off," visible or invisible). The ether I saw varied in contour: thinner near objects of mass, and thicker farther out in space, where its denseness constituted what I believe to be zero-point energy. It was weightless, transparent, frictionless, and permeated all time/space/ matter; and functioned as the medium by which light can be transmitted in a vacuum. The microwave background of its circular logic units was even throughout, suggestive to me of order, purpose. I witnessed tides and flows in the ether matrix as if its fabric threading were "floating" in a type of plasma, a primordial "soup." The power of zero-point energy seemed to be its major "ingredient," along with dark (invisible) and luminous (visible) matter.[6]

Fifth Dimension: The first through third dimensions have to do with the laws of time and space. The fourth dimension includes the astral and etheric planes. The fifth dimension frees us from time/ space dynamics altogether, while enabling us to weave our intentions directly into the fabric of what we want to manifest. Nothing is hidden in the fifth dimension; all is revealed. Intention directs movement and manifestation in this dimension. Consciousness exists here as a resonance pattern, a harmony. Says physicist James E. Beichler, Ph.D.: "Through the fifth dimension, all particles in existence link to all other particles. We can detect the fifth dimension through emotions, intuitions, intangibles. It is a single field— wave function is actually a volume in the fifth dimension."[7]

Fifth Chakra: Various mystery school traditions tell us that as each Root Race advances, challenges specific to the wave of energy that group represents will accompany it. These energy waves correspond to certain chakras (or spinning wheels of light) located at each of the major endocrine centers in the body. The job of each Root Race is to fully develop the power of its corresponding chakra throughout the populace, thus energizing those particular qualities, activities, and challenges within the social structures of the time. The fifth chakra (willpower) is associated with the throat, thyroid, neck, mouth, and nervous system, and has to do with the world of ideas. Fifth-chakra energy wraps around issues of will and domination, and the question of power over or power to.

Fifth Brain: The science of neurocardiology has established that 60 to 65 percent of heart cells are actually the same type of neural cells as those located in the brain. Thus the heart is now considered our fifth "brain" (the other four are the reptilian or old brain, the limbic system, neocortex, and prefrontal lobes). Science has also shown that the heart produces an electromagnetic field in the shape of a torus five thousand times more powerful than that of the brain and is the major glandular center in the body. It converts energy to create infinite numbers of wave harmonics, and *reacts to conditions four to five seconds, sometimes minutes, before occurrence.* Literally, our heart is our first responder, alerting the brain to what is about to happen before it does. The heart corresponds with higher energy fields when one feels good and when in love.

Fifth Basic Force: Torsion waves (chi, prana, ki) are the information carriers, ensuring that nothing is ever lost. Transmits order; preserves information within a system to prevent the increase of entropy. Torsion waves warp and modify space and time. They are associated with psychic phenomena, sacred sites, crop circles, and with dark matter and dark energy. Russian scientists refer to torsion waves as "biogravity." Other terms: orgone, bioplasma, bioenergy. Torsion waves can be influenced by consciousness, pass through all shielding, and are not weakened by distance. Used for energy healing, these waves have a role in the life process as the spin of elementary particles. They exist in two forms: one spins to the left, the other to the right; one slows time, the other speeds it up; one increases order in a system, the other decreases order.

Fifth Brain Wave Frequency: A fifth brain wave has been verified: gamma waves. Gamma operates at 25 to 60 hertz. It modulates perception and consciousness, and relates to simultaneous processing of information from different brain areas (i.e., involves memory, learning abilities, integrated thoughts, and information-rich task processing). The other brain waves are beta (12–25 Hz), alpha (7–12 Hz), theta (4–7 Hz), and delta (0–4 Hz). A dowser, when in the dowsing "mode," can register both gamma and delta waves simultaneously (a sign of being wide awake while fast asleep). The new kids do this often—making it difficult to measure the true range of their intelligence.

Five Types of Intelligence: Intelligence IQ measures processes of thought and rational analysis. Emotional EQ measures intuitive, emotional understandings of the heart. Spiritual SQ measures wisdom in connecting with the higher self. Wholistic WQ measures profound connections to potential, knowing, and others. Quantum QQ measures superspeed creativity and connections to Allness.[8] Science does not recognize anything it cannot physically measure; thus SQ to QQ is considered fiction. It is at QQ levels that many of our young function.

Fifth Ray of Destiny: As the human family advances in a quest to fulfill its destiny on the Earth plane, various rays of light are said to be beacons or guiding lights to make easier the way. Not to be confused with personal rays that may color one's aura or signify his or her life's work, these destiny rays overspread evolutionary movements. The Fifth Destiny Ray can best be understood through its symbolic connection to the planet Venus and the qualities of mercy, compassion, and unconditional love. It signals a time of embracing the Divine Feminine, the power of women, the joy of consensual sex, and the healing that is possible when we honor and care about each other.

Fifth Communication Wave: The first was sign language. The second was the use of stelae—inscriptions on markers, stones, pillars, flat surfaces, walls. The third concerned the invention of papyrus as a paperlike material for writing scrolls and ancient documents. The fourth heralded the printing press and movable type—the first published book was the Gutenberg Bible. The fifth communication wave was the personal computer, introduced in 1982—the very year when the new children began to enter the earth plane in mass (the primary start of the Millennial Generation). Our new kids understand computers because they bear the "mark" or energy frequency of the computers' entry into the world at large.

Fifth Discipline: This heralds the development of organizations, corporations, and businesses as learning centers—able to go beyond adversarial approaches and endless debates of head versus heart, left versus right, science versus religion, business versus government, altruism versus self-interest, vision versus practicality. They mark a new synthesis for combining the desire for profit with the dedication of seeking a higher road to the future and better ways of operating—the discipline to overcome obstacles using a structured framework of personal mastery, mental models, shared vision, and team learning.[9]

Fifth Agreement: Don Miguel Ruiz gave us *The Four Agreements,* which are: be impeccable with your word; don't take things personally; don't make assumptions; always do your best. *The Fifth Agreement* is: be skeptical; learn to listen.[10] Ruiz reached back to the Toltec wisdoms of his heritage and brought forth the essence of truth found within them. The guidance to do this came from his near-death experience. The world's people say, "Thank you." There is another way to look at that Fifth Agreement, though. It goes like this: "Show up. Tell the truth. And don't be attached to the outcome." Both versions of that Fifth Agreement speak directly to the heart of the Fifth Root Race and the Fifth World.

AN EXTENSION OF FIVES

There are other fives of mystical note that have meaning appropriate to this primer. So let's include them too.

Five Races/Five Senses: The five races of the human family are already known (although some scientists point out that there are technically only four). Edgar Cayce, one of the most famous psychics ever to have lived, said that each of our five sense faculties correspond to each of the races, as if that race had a major or dominant way of sensing that was recognizably unique in its strength. Certainly all peoples have the use of all faculties of perception and sensing (unless hampered individually); still, according to Cayce, there are standouts, depending on one's race. His revelations follow:

White Race	Vision and sight
Red Race	Sensitivity and touch
Black Race	Emotions and taste
Yellow Race	Sound and hearing
Brown Race	Earthiness/the physical and smell

Five: it's the number of humankind—two legs, two arms, one head, in spread-eagle stance, forming the five-pointed star . . . the biblical star of the Magi.

Five: in the art of numerology, where each number has symbolic meaning, it refers to progress; change; sexuality; moving forward; curiosity; ideas; travel; communication; nervous energy; the physical need to move, exercise, experiment.

Generation 14 (1 + 4 adding up to 5): The Millennials, the nation's fourteenth generation . . . the shift generation in the age of shift. Born during that null space when the Great Shifting moved into place, readying the earth's energy waves for rapid accelerations to come. There's never been a generation before like the Millennials, at least not that we know of. Although they possess the strengths and weaknesses covered at length in this book, no one can ever really know what or who they are, as they can alter in a flash. They come from null space, and its energy signature is the same as theirs—as with the 9/11s too—as it is they who bear the burden and the call of the deep truth of September 11: it is time to rend the three-thousand-year-old curtain of distrust and pain held in the ethers, so the old wounds can be healed. Rumi, the great mystical poet, once said what the new kids are born knowing: "Out beyond ideas of wrongdoing and rightdoing, there is a field. I'll meet you there."

It is obvious to me that we are still in Fifth World energy, and I predict we will remain so until 2132 or 2133, with the thirty-third passage of Halley's Comet. As that comet once again streaks across earth's skies, Aquarian energies will ascend like never before, revealing the results of our efforts now and during the years to come. We have another chance to remake this world and self-correct. Let's not muff it.

19

TIMELINES
AND VARIATIONS

*There is a science that runs like a river of light above
all the sciences. It never changes its assurances. It is the
Mystical Science.*

EMMA CURTIS HOPKINS

Older mystical and religious traditions from around the world believed in seven great turnings or evolutionary cycles to the ascending energy wave form now underway before it completes itself and reverses motion (in the far-distant future). Accompanying each turning or world is a Root Race, a genetic "redo" necessary for human form to adjust and acclimate to new evolutionary energies and pressures.

The Fifth World or Movement Sun is here and accelerating. Following it is said to come the Sixth World, or Spirits of All Living Things Sun, and the Seventh World, or Melting Back into Oneness Sun (neither of these last two show on the Mayan Sun Stone but are readily acknowledged by most traditional elders/mystics).

Seven worlds, seven Root Races. Ascending and descending energy moving along a grand spiral that, through phases of evolution and devolution, frees the spirit.

If you think about it, carvings on the Sun Stone never could have shown more than they did, as the element for the Fifth World is ether and ether cannot be charted. In the ether, intention occupies the "driver's seat" and minds cohere. Knowing this enables us to recognize that space, all-around-us space, is actually a field of interconnecting/interacting intelligence "logic units" and memory storage that we use and reside in 24/7. What once seemed the product of imagination or anomalous is being reconsidered as very possibly scientific fact. The old mystics were right: the dark reaches of the silent vacuum shimmer with potential.

Recognizing ether's presence requires that we reconsider what we think we know about a lot of things, especially time. Science has established that solid objects are mostly space, the experience of time is a function of speed in a memory sequence, and gravity bends light. This indicates that time is not static; it can physically slow down or speed up or hiccup. Time can also collapse or leap or slip into discontinuity (nontime: a condition in which time and space are said to converge, which may explain why plants *suddenly* produced flowers, rocks *suddenly* formed crystals, reptiles *suddenly* became birds—all of which happened during conditions of intense pressure where longing, desire, and need could have deviated and shifted time). Reality, not just time, is fluid in the sense of being mutable and open to influence (molecular changes, our choices). Time dilation—when independent observers simultaneously perceive noticeable differences in objective reality as viewed from their different vantage points and rates of travel; the twin paradox—is real. A massive release of nuclear radiation is known to cause such dilatory effects. So does space travel.

Take a breath. Now ready yourself for another volley.

There are elastic time, warped time, variations in time from one locale to another, time ripples caused by earthquakes or violent events that affect the Earth's wobble. Of course you already know about objective and subjective time: Chronos (numeric/chronological, linear/external time) and Kairos (right moment, natural, or divine, cyclic/internal time). And because of this transitional period or null space we are in that precedes our solar system entering the Photon Belt, we are speeding into a type of superluminous brightness (photon particles) said to enable instant access to existent and preexistent information with a simultaneous-everywhere type of consciousness, and an instantaneous type of telepathic communication (thoughts from various sources overlaying and overlapping each other).

What I just said was a mouthful, so let's take another breath.

I'm not a scientist, so I can't explain specifics, but I can give you the basis of how and why time variations occur. Before I do, though, I want you to know why I'm doing this: our new kids are born knowing how to jump time.

Example: A seven-year-old boy told his music teacher, "There's a tear in time. Kids like me can go back and forth whenever we want. Older people can't, though. From nine on it's harder to do. But for a seven-year-old like me, it's easy."

Wake up, parents. Your children are familiar with aspects of time that you are not. Don't be surprised if they "ride" wave forms in the in-between.

THE IDEAS OF ITZHAK BENTOV

I know of no one who gave us a better guide to understand time deviations than the late Itzhak Bentov. He was a biomedical engineer turned cosmologist who, while soaking in a tub, tripped across the limitless boundaries of time and space. His ever-popular *Stalking the Wild Pendulum: On the Mechanics of Consciousness* outlines his discoveries.[1] The diagram on the following page illustrates his view of objective, subjective, and beyond time-space relationships (how time deviates).

Bentov felt there were two kinds of time and space: *objective* (conscious), existing in verifiable units that could be scientifically measured, and *subjective* (subconscious), more flexible and capable of being stretched or compressed according to one's own state of mind. He said:

ITZHAK BENTOV'S VERSION OF OBJECTIVE, SUBJECTIVE, AND BEYOND

Normal State

Both versions of time parallel each other; both versions of space parallel each other. Time appears as sequential and orderly, while space appears as air filled with solid objects. Our environment and all that we perceive are normal, ordinary, and what we are used to. Nothing changes. The integrity of perception is unchallenged.

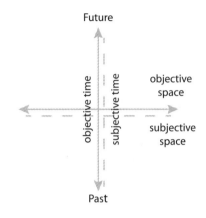

Altered State

Subjective time begins to separate from objective time. The same separation occurs with subjective and objective space. Time is no longer sequential and orderly. Space changes and objects appear less solid and dependable. The space-time coordinates we are used to lose their relevance. Our perceptual modes of awareness are freed to expand and enhance, while sensory feedback either decelerates or accelerates.

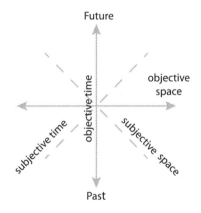

Convergence

Subjective space overlaps with objective time; objective space overlaps with subjective time. Everything converges, making it possible to be everywhere at once, all at the same time. There are no longer any separations. Nothing divides. Normal coordinates and definitions disappear altogether. Limitations of any kind no longer exist.

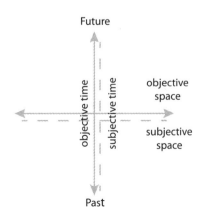

We know that in an altered state of consciousness, such as a dream, we can experience an enormous amount of events in only a few minutes. Time seems to expand, and for every objective second one has hundreds of subjective seconds. Now imagine a situation in which the subjective time axis deviates so far that it becomes parallel to and overlaps objective space. This would imply that our subjective time fills all objective space—it takes no time to go anywhere. This is what happens in expansion of consciousness. We can fill the entire universe with our consciousness at infinite speed and be everywhere at once—in other words, become omnipresent.

The concept of omnipresence, as expressed by Bentov, is a condition whereby all forms of existence, time and space as well as objective and subjective, overlap and then converge. Consciousness is not only freed when this happens, but it can also expand to fill the whole of creation instantaneously and become what poet Gary Snyder called Everywhen.

FUTURE MEMORY

In my research of near-death states, I found that one of the aftereffects is the ability to live the future *before* it occurs. This is not precognition, the act of knowing or feeling—sensing—the future before it occurs.

What I call future memory is the ability to fully live a given event or sequence of events in subjective reality before living that same episode in objective reality. This is usually, but not always, forgotten by the individual after it occurs, only to be remembered later when some signal triggers memory. Sensory-rich, future memory is so detailed that it includes each movement, thought, smell, taste, decision, sight, and sound of regular physical living. All of this is *actually lived and physically, emotionally, and sensorially experienced*, not merely watched (clairvoyance), heard (clairaudience), predicted (prophesied or forecasted), or known (precognition). The experience of living it is so thorough, there is no way to distinguish it from everyday reality.

Many of the people I interviewed during my work in researching not only near-death states but also transformations of conscious (no matter how they were caused), talked about future memory as if it were already known and already lived, as if what they are now doing is but an afterthought or perhaps a rehearsal, the acting out of a previously written script. For them, *the present moment is past tense.* This awareness, regardless of duration, is intense and may appear as precognition or clairvoyance when neither is the case. For them, it is more a process of memory than anything psychic. They actually *remember the future* as they remember the past. They are not seers. They do not predict. They are just people who now live in a different reality system than before, where the understanding of time and space has shifted from the norm.[2]

I think you get the gist from this that time, either objective or subjective, can alter and vary and deviate in ways few imagine. Time begins to change for anyone who has gone through an impactful transformation of consciousness, such as kundalini breakthroughs, vision quests, near-death states, baptism of the Holy Spirit, mountaintop or unity experiences, spiritual breakthroughs, deep states of prayer, certain spiritual disciplines, and so forth. When we pass through the threshold between life and death, sanity and insanity, reality and fiction, we come back changed. Today's children, however, are being born as if "thresholders." And that means *they often know things their parents don't, and can experience life on multiple levels simultaneously.* They are the new normal!

BEFORE TIMES

Societies throughout the world steadfastly deny the existence of anything that defies their mutually accepted view of time (as established by experts, of course). Take, for instance, the modern-day island/country of New Zealand. They cling to the idea that populations have been there for about four hundred years, even though a wall exists that was built two thousand years ago, with evidence of habitation going back at least four thousand years. The reason this evidence is ignored? They would have to rewrite the history of New Zealand, and their politicians say no. Thus the wall is deemed "natural" and not man-made.[3]

Thanks to satellite photos and new archaeological tools, what was once accepted as historical fact is subject to revision. Of what we know, modern humans descended independently from common ancestors that lived on nearly every continent and mingled with earlier human types (Associated Press, January 12, 2001). Lost civilizations are everywhere . . . along the Gulf Coasts of Florida, around Japan, New Zealand, the Yucatán, Sahara and Gobi deserts, to mention but a few. Disasters in the distant past could account for the hidden or buried, but they could also account for a whole lot more.

Our earth was rocked 11,500 years ago by a cataclysm that so scarred humankind, according to Barbara Hand Clow, that "we are a wounded species." Her book, *Catastrophobia* goes in-depth about the truth behind Earth changes and how people are affected by them.[4] Her point, that there is more to disasters than destroyed civilizations, calls to mind what happened August 27, 1883, when the supervolcano Krakatoa exploded. Nearly forty thousand people were killed and swirling dust caused temperatures to plummet with lurid, unsettling displays of light. Like Clow, foreign correspondent Simon Winchester noticed something else rising from the horrors . . . the eruption triggered a wave of murderous anti-Western militancy (Brits failed to help affected Muslims), which became one of the first outbreaks of Islamic violence anywhere.[5] Massive change can release a type of fear and anger that can imprint the collective consciousness of the human family in ways similar to shell shock. Our new kids are coming in with the flip side of their energy signatures as *anger* (Millennials) and *fear* (9/11s). This underscores one of their tasks: to heal the old wounds as they readjust their own energy fields.

Something else—evidence of advanced civilizations existing before time as we know it existed, are tossed off as fiction and sold as "junk" by institutions and universities. Footprints in stone, objects in ancient strata; humanoids in the time of dinosaurs; unknown builders of

prehistoric mounds, observatories, cities; ancient art and medicine—
these remnants still exist. There are simply too many of them to ignore,
but we do.[6] Why? Because anomalies such as these suggest that humans
came here from off-planet. Like the New Zealanders, we don't want
anyone messing with the histories we prefer.

Enter Maurice Chatelain, director of communications for NASA's
Apollo Program, who, while studying the Sumerian clay tablets apparently written in 700 BCE, discovered a fifteen-digit number that is
turning out to be the great constant of the solar system. The number
is 195,955,200,000,000. "Sumerians . . . used calculations based on
multiples of sixty, more than three thousand years ago. We still do not
know for sure who the Sumerians were and where they came from, but
we have found out that they were truly great astronomers who knew
the revolution periods of all the planets in the solar system, including Uranus and Neptune. They were the ones who divided the day of
86,400 seconds into 24 hours of 60 minutes with 60 seconds each."[7]

David Wilcock in his book *The Source Field Investigations,* talked a
lot about Chatelain's Nineveh Constant and about the Sumerian cycle
of 6.2 million years, with ten of those cycles being 62 million years (the
cycle of sudden species evolution in the fossil record), and about how you
can subdivide the number into the precession of the equinoxes.[8] He also
mentions how the Nineveh Constant is truly the master number of all
other cycles, including the orbit of every planet. His discussion is breathtaking, and what Chatelain found is a game changer, for it indicates that
we as humans did indeed come from another place besides planet Earth.

Before time? Children talk about things like this and about previous incarnations in other bodies in other worlds on other planets, and
even once existing as standing waves, comets, bits and pieces of planets
and stars—as if everything in the universe is alive and has memory and
volition. If you think this is no more than crazy fiction, just wait until
children of the Aquarian Generation arrive.

TIMELINES—SOCIAL CYCLES

Astrology can be an appropriate and helpful lens with which to view timelines. Its mathematical and mythological systems create road maps we can use for this journey we call life. However destined something might appear, our choices can influence and alter how things happen—the outcome. It is possible through tracking the various planetary orbits to ascertain certain cycles. Take the planet Uranus, for instance. Its seven-year passage through each zodiac sign heralds the changing of social cycles. Symbolically understood as an awakener/reformer, the "heavenly flashlight" Uranus illuminates whatever needs changing within what that sign described so action can be taken. Take a look at what follows to see what I mean:

1975	**Uranus entered Scorpio:** Sexual revolution, rise of counterculture, psychotherapies, drug use more common than realized, misdirected wars, secrets/crimes revealed.
1981	**Uranus entered Sagittarius:** New Age movement, "Jesus saves," merger mania, foreign exchanges, unparalleled desire for higher knowledge/global travel, all-time high in sports money and gambling.
1988	**Uranus entered Capricorn:** Political revolutions, death of Communism, earthquakes on all levels (whether physical, cultural, or personal), "greed is good" mentality, excesses, business takeovers, middle-class pain.
1995	**Uranus entered Aquarius:** Information explosion, global Internet, high technology, the quick fix, U.S. jobs shipped overseas, nervous breakdowns, media rule, new hope, a flood of inventions.
2003	**Uranus entered Pisces:** Rise of the need for

meaning-making, spiritual technologies, clash of religions, imagination explosion, innovative usages of entertainment/fantasy and drugs, alternatives in medical treatment.

2010   **Uranus entered Aries:** Digital rant, bullying, worldviews clash, pioneering discoveries, global freedom cry, overthrows/revolutions, warriors/fighters, courage, weather extremes/quakes, male power versus female.

2018   **Uranus enters Taurus:** Security/safety issues, fortunes alter, power changes hands, fertility problems, Earth changes, farming/sustainability revolution, rebuilding infrastructure, usage of plant/animal intelligence.

2025   **Uranus enters Gemini:** (Pluto enters Aquarius, the sign ruled by Uranus.) Lightning bolts of change and transformation on every level, new forms of global and outer-space communication/travel/exchange, new innovations.

TIMELINES—GENERAL

Now that you have an idea of how this works, consider the brief tour that follows as an informative romp. Remember, Pluto addresses the larger scale, like generations of people and mass movements. Cycles can and do overlap each other, which increases pressure/stress at the same time that opportunities skyrocket.

1840s   New Thought movement began, with spiritual trends that culminate in 2024 (184-year-phase of spiritual discovery and holistic development).

1980–2018   Null or undefined space when the Great Shifting moves into place (entry of Millennials and 9/11s), a maniac period where everything happens at once or in rapid-fire succession, nothing is clear, chaos is in full swing.

2006–2076 Mars goes "off-stride" (retrograde) in the U.S. astrological chart for the first time in the nation's history (by progression). U.S. energy, power, and influence wane. A time to reconsider America's aggressive tendencies before trying to "correct" others. Cycle lasts seventy years (until 2076).

2009–2023 Pluto in Capricorn, corrupt politicians, corporate imperialism, the great global contraction, shifting of wealth, rethinking growth, the three Rs (reduce, reuse, recycle), practicality/responsibility emphasized, a return to fundamentals, wealth excesses, possible class war, food and water scarce.

2010–2018/19 Uranus in Aries, decision time: do we head toward the Third Industrial Revolution or a debt crisis? Arab Spring may become Arab Fall, life/death challenges, authority conflicts, shootings on the rise, portal into the Great Shifting (completes what began at 1987 Harmonic Convergence).

2010–2018/19 Uranus and Pluto square each other seven times—during June 2012, September 2012, May 2013, November 2013, April 2014, December 2014, and March 2015. Times of great pressure and stress, meltdowns, collapse of major institutions (think of the state of the European Union), energy comparable to what set up the earliest portion of the American Revolution (1754–1758) and Columbus and other Europeans colonizing Western Hemisphere (1493–1500), triggers in place for a major depression and/or rebirth. Major innovations possible.

2011–2025   Neptune moves into its own sign of Pisces, "lifting of the veil," hidden truths revealed, borders dissolve, consciousness of true self, dreams important, compassion (only 5 percent of people are ready for higher states of consciousness), nation almost bankrupt, drastic change in Iraq, Egypt, Russia, and throughout Europe.

2012–2122   The foundation years, preparation for the Sixth World and Sixth Root Race due to begin a century or two following.

2013–2015   One massive square after another. Relentless pressure between Uranus in Aries square Pluto in Capricorn (detailed on page 189). Direct effect on economies everywhere.

2013   Giant solar flare predicted (protect computers and data storage). The National Security Agency Utah Data Center comes online (said to be the world's largest interceptor and data collector of all forms of communication—top secret).

2018–2025   Uranus in Taurus, a time of Earth concerns/Earth changes; fortunes change hands; global economies switch; security, safety, food issues; different forms of housing, farming, doing business. Water shortages.

2019–2020   The year when Saturn (the disciplinarian) "sits atop" Pluto in Capricorn, could experience serious climate and cultural changes/die-offs, caution.

2020   China is projected to build the world's first exascale supercomputer. If they succeed, they become the number one superpower in the world.

2020s   Asia's middle class is slated to double during this decade, and will dwarf all other markets and account for 40 percent of global consumer spending. Leads up to China in the 2030s reaching its greatest growth.

2022	Pluto returns to its "birth" place in the chart of the United States. People do not have Pluto returns but countries can, as it is a 248-year cycle. Corporate America could implode during this time, with unprecedented challenges to government, banking, investments, marketing, buying/selling. Exceptional, perhaps radical changes, for good or ill. Look for incredible steps forward in science, medicine, and food production. Impact begins in 2020 and extends through 2024. Death of the old, birth of the new.

NOTE: **2023–2060**	Turbulent stressors emerge that could lead to World War III.

2024–2043	Pluto in Aquarius, entry of Aquarian Generation; genetics change; massive resource challenges; unparalleled advances in medicine, chemicals, technology; makeup of societies alter; beginnings of Islamic reformation and the rethinking of strict sharia laws by Muslims.
2025–2033	Pluto in Aquarius, Uranus in Gemini; healing of opposing views possible; new ways to communicate, travel, and entertain; outer-space issues; struggle for liberty and social justice; determined, independent, revolutionary character. Exceptional growth and harmony possible in the U.S.
2029	Asteriod predicted to come very close to Earth.
2034–2036	Time frame when potential for World War III is the strongest; critical stressors worldwide, especially in food, water, and ecology.
2035	China is projected to use 4/5 of the world's paper, 70 percent of the world's grain, and have more cars than in all the other countries combined.

2036   Russian scientists warn of asteroid hitting Earth. NASA disagrees.

2040   Half the U.S. population will be brown or black; educators must determine how to prepare children of color to do better in school and improve language skills.

2040–2050   Battles with Muslim extremists at its peak.

2043–2067   Pluto in Pisces, illusions/delusions of the past disappear, as do religious persecutions, regrets faced, acceptance of Christ as a state of consciousness possible to attain (the true Second Coming), messiah figures emerge, female and child abuse and denying women equal status a major global issue, alternative/complementary healing procedures now standard.

2045   Uranus opposite Pluto in the United States chart. What we missed during the Pluto return will surface here, with sweeping changes for the working class. Effects global collective. Tied somehow to climate/planetary reversals. Changes will tend to come one right after another. Will make itself known several years before and several years after 2045.

2048   Hundredth anniversary of Universal Declaration of Human Rights, a set of fundamental human rights for all people adopted in 1948 by all countries of the United Nations. Its five basic freedoms: speech, environment, religion, from want, from fear. (*2048: Humanity's Agreement to Live Together* by Kirk Boyd [San Francisco: Berrett-Koehler, 2010] dispels the myth that peace and prosperity are unattainable.)

2050   World population expected to peak; 300-year population boom ends. Empty buildings, fallow fields, extremely low births (some countries already below replacement rate). Projected date of European Union switching to all electric cars and running on smart networks of green-energy electric power. Power will reside with nations able to attract immigrants.

2060   Isaac Newton predicted this year would end the world as we know it. *NOTE:* End of turbulent stressors that could cause World War III (that begin in 2023).

2076   U.S. energy back to full potential. The nation could become the "wounded healer," a true humanitarian for the world.

2132– 2133   Aquarian energies now measurable, thirty-third passage of Halley's Comet, energy on planet alters, consciousness accelerates.

2375–4535   Age of Aquarius according to star charts. Pisces energy continues early on, Christ spirit heightens, rise of Seventh World/Seventh Root Race in latter years.

2948   Predicted beginning of the fabled Thousand Years of Peace. Solar energy wave form begins its descent afterward.

If you are expecting the magic of a golden age to begin December 21, 2012, think again. Dazzling and dramatic improvements are indeed ahead of us; still, contractions, although painful, continue. They remind us to clean up our messes as we go along. In truth, the future can be fickle. Anything can change . . . in the twinkling of an eye.

20 THE GREAT SHIFTING

*Evolution is the awakening of the soul to recognition of its
unity with the Whole. Material evolution is an effect, not
a cause.*

SRI AUROBINDO

The Age of Pisces has been dubbed "the age of suffering." What's coming is the age of awakening and restoration, alias the Aquarian Age. Each age spans about 2,160 years, a cosmic month in the great Cosmic Wheel of 25,920 years. As one age ends and another is about to begin, the two overlap, and for around two hundred years or so. Overlaps accelerate energy (after all, you're getting two for the price of one), with the opposite of the incoming sign the first to move in. In this case that means Leo (the opposite of Aquarius). When you think Leo, think big and bigger, control, drama, money, and the heart. So what have we been dealing with for a while? Big, dramatic stuff: huge ventures, massive failures, large profits, high stakes, pop-star royalty, unbelievable corruption, billions lost with nary a blink, biblical storms, genocide on a scale beyond what the human heart can bear. Can we forgive? Can we love each other? The kids say yes. Adults aren't so sure.

The Great Shifting refers to the cosmic year, not just the shuffle of ages. I know we've been singing about "The Age of Aquarius" for decades, but, as you saw previously, it will be some time before the Aquarian Age actually gets here. We get a good taste of those energies,

194

though, when Pluto moves into the sign in 2024. Still, it's the entire span of those foundation years (2012–2122) that enable us to "make ready" as we go along—so we can adjust to the future Sixth World, Sixth Root Race, and Aquarian Age, as well as the continuous over-the-top flip-flops of the Great Shifting. We've been clinging to old stuff: old energy, old medicine, old agriculture, old governments, old leaders . . . under the guise of "Save our jobs." Won't work. And the kids know it. That's why Occupy movements are worldwide.

What kick-starts real action? Aries. Uranus rules Aquarius, but right now Uranus is in the sign of Aries. As the zodiac's first sign, Aries energy is that of a fiery pioneer and go-getter: the birther of courage, initiation, beginnings, sports, revolutions, the dare (like Dare to Care, a new way to regard money mentioned in chapter 17). The fearlessness of Aries energy will tackle anything, with one goal: triumph. But Aries energy is also associated with an increase in earthquakes and weather extremes. The Great Shifting says, "Change." Aries hollers, "Right on."

OUR SURPRISING UNIVERSE

Our universe is alive. It has nurseries complete with umbilical cords to send nutrition into wombs filled with embryos. It has at least a dozen dimensions and spinning black holes that function like subways, enabling energy forms and quasars to tunnel through—shorten the distance from here to there. Galaxies speed across the heavens like Frisbees. Something is attracting them to form patterns as they speed along, and that something is called the Great Attractor. Science tells us we live in a bubble universe where 95 percent of the energy is dark (at zero point).

Thanks to science, we also know—as of 2008—that all the planets in our solar system are expanding and warming up. And that's not all they're doing.

+ **Sun:** Magnetic field more than 230 percent stronger than in 1900. Frenzy of activity.

+ **Venus:** Now glowing in the dark, as is Jupiter's moon, Io.

+ **Mars:** Atmospheric density up 200 percent since 1997, ice-cap melt changes surface features, official photos of face on Mars show signs of "airbrushing" (standard NASA response for questionable or mistaken features).

+ **Jupiter:** Highly energized, surrounded by glowing doughnut-shaped tube of energy in relation to path of Io, magnetic field doubled since 1992.

+ **Saturn:** Polar regions brighter, magnetic field strength increasing.

+ **Uranus:** Appears to have had recent magnetic pole shift of 60 degrees.

+ **Neptune:** Appears to have had recent magnetic pole shift of 50 degrees, 40 percent brighter in infrared since 1996, increase in atmospheric pressure and temperature on moon Triton.

+ **Pluto:** 300 percent increase in atmospheric pressure in last decade, Hubble Space Telescope observes color changes as if it had seasons, 20 percent increase in red color.

Human physiology resonates with the same pulse as Earth, which resonates with the sun, and the sun resonates with the solar system, the galaxy core, and the universe. We are bound together as if in a sacred circuit. The electromagnetic plasma field enveloping us has become measurably thicker of late, perhaps to hold us together as speeds increase. The Great Attractor calls.

ON OUR DEAR PLANET

Earth's ice caps have dramatically thinned out. The structure of Earth's gravity field since 1997 has shifted from an egg shape, elongated at the poles, to a more pumpkinlike shape that is flattened at the poles. NASA cannot explain this. The base frequency of cavity resonance (Earth's heartbeat), having hovered around 7.8 hertz for a long time, is now rising and expected to reach 12 hertz after 2012. This is the trigger most feel will accelerate widespread evolutionary changes and could lead to a full-blown magnetic pole shift.

Oops—it's already happening. A headline on January 7, 2011, read "Earth's Magnetic Pole Shifts, Screws Up Runway at Florida Airport."[1] That drift of magnetic north toward Russia *is* noticeably speeding up. It won't take long before all compasses must be readjusted, not just for airlines and runways. Scientifically established is the fact that there have been thousands of magnetic pole shifts in the Earth's past. Uranus and Neptune show evidence of a recently occurring one. A magnetic pole shift mostly messes with growing things and transportation, but a geophysical pole shift is quite another story. That kind of shift affects the position of the Earth's axis and could move our planet enough to change our pole star, which now is Polaris. If you think we're having environmental challenges now, imagine what could occur if our planet twists around just enough that a different pole star reigns. Yup, it has happened before. Again? Just look at Japan. On March 11, 2011, an 8.9-magnitude earthquake *moved the entire country 8 feet to the east.*

Speaking of climate change, during 2011 nine nations scorched under record-breaking temperatures: Russia, 111 degrees; Niger, 118 degrees; Sudan, 121 degrees; Saudi Arabia and Iraq, 126 degrees; and Pakistan, a hair under 130 degrees. There is way too much carbon in the air for a healthy planet. Freak storms have almost disseminated parts of Thailand and Pakistan. Joplin, Missouri, was nearly wiped off the map by a giant tornado. Ten disastrous weather events hit the U.S. in 2011, causing more than a billion dollars in damage, along with loss of life and property. Rare? Not anymore. Weather extremes are the new normal—for at least the next six years, and probably longer.

Earth changes? Plenty ahead, and we're just getting started. Besides what happened to Japan, Africa and Asia are splitting apart in the Great Rift Valley, creating a new ocean floor. A vast magma pool has been discovered under the southwestern part of Washington State that "feeds" the three volcanos of Mount Saint Helens, Mount Rainier, and Mount Adams. Supervolcanos are the larger threat. We know about Krakatoa (its "daughter" is busily growing alongside the previous eruption). The second has been located beneath Naples, Italy, and the third is in Yellowstone National Park (although scientists currently dispute this). Reread your history of Krakatoa to get a better idea of what can happen when a supervolcano goes off. Scary. And then there's that massive lava ridge alongside the Canary Islands. Looks like it may split off. If it does, huge tsunamis could obliterate the U.S. Atlantic Coast. Even scarier.

Some scientists claim we're experiencing global warming. Others say a new ice age is underway. Government theorists claim that the High Frequency Active Auroral Research Program (HAARP microwave towers) installation in Alaska is a contributing factor to the increasing number of earthquakes worldwide. A rare earthquake in Virginia (35 miles from my home) was supposedly caused by fracking in West Virginia, in line with the quake zone in Mineral County.

Here's the real scoop: The Great Shifting is a time when Earth and its many life forms (including us) undergo profound changes. Some species die out; new ones appear. Climate zones alter, as does our pole star. Yet humans survive and will continue to. The modern age accelerates the shifting but does not cause it. Geoengineering, an attempt to "cure" the climate through blocking sunlight, spraying chem trails, and horsing around with water and wind, is causing a huge backlash by intensifying greenhouse-induced drying, threatening species, and causing more severe weather than before. Either we don't know what we're doing, or this type of engineering was never a good idea to begin with. Nix to the geos.

Believe it or not, there's actually a good side to disasters. Wildfires help our forests by removing dead "fuel," pumping nutrients into the soil that are crucial for plant growth. Volcanic eruptions are essential for development of life and healthy environments, with the added benefit of geothermal power. Landslides serve an aesthetic purpose on landscapes, create habitats in streams for fish, and break up stream flow. Hurricanes push up sea sediment (good soil), nourish marsh vegetation, build land higher, and are a major source of needed rain far inland.

Earthquakes, the very forces that cause them, produce oil and gas and spread them far and wide, concentrate other resources, split continents, form great oceans, and build mountains.[2]

Because of the extent of change we are undergoing, borders of countries and regions will alter along the lines of race, ethnicity, and religion. Alliances of tribe and culture will define trading partners, not politics. The real uniter, though, will be the human outreach from our various affinities. Contrast this: in 2010, victims of Pakistan's massive flood were mostly ignored, even by fellow Pakistanis, because of a half-hearted request for and finally a shunning of aid (cultural pride); in the same year, the thirty-three miners in Chile, trapped by a cave-in, became global superstars when their families and mine officials gladly shared both fear and hope as they welcomed prayers and whatever help anyone could give. Their rescue became our rescue. Borders dissolve once we connect on the human level and express from the heart.

OUR GENETICS ARE CHANGING TOO

Did you know that the dying process of cells is virtually identical to the dying process of stars? DNA came from outer space, science says, perhaps meteorites. The DNA molecule is structured on phi or the Golden Mean (the core base of sacred geometry). The Golden Mean and Fibonacci sequence (harmonic variations of phi) inform the very fabric of space-time. No transitional fossils exist to counter the idea of spontaneity, the leaps and bounds species development took as if affected by some type of torsion energy (the concept of a universal creative consciousness or higher-dimensional radiation from the galactic center). The greater the density of torsion waves, the more spectacular the result—like the living organism we call Earth, us, and everything else.[3]

That makes us "star born," with a genetic history that reads like a science-fiction novel where mutants rise up and displace "normals," first one way and then another. To prove my point, I invite you to explore with me "things weird."

Claudia Kalb in her incredible article, "In Our Blood," focuses on DNA testing results that are shocking. Get this: "Scientists say that by using Y and mitochondrial DNA, they can date the earliest female to 150,000 to 250,000 years ago and the earliest male to 60,000 to 100,000 years ago."[4] Within this finding is the question, How did we reproduce without males? Do we even need males? She also showed that our ancestors are not necessarily who we thought they were. Genes from China, for instance, sweep throughout South and Central America, the Mayan culture, and other groups in the Americas. European genes pop up in Native Alaskans and in various Canadian and Native American tribal nations too. Lots of African-Americans have no genetic link to the black race in Africa.

Edgar Cayce, in his psychic readings, stretched out everything by saying we began on Earth with a "thought body" that gradually took on form and density. Over time, we supposedly mixed with species already present to form mythical creatures like centaurs (horse men), gorgons (winged female creatures with snakes as hair), furies (snake-haired bird women), sirens (bird women with enchanting voices), satyrs (goat men), harpies (pesky bird women), cyclops (giant single-eyed men), mermaids and mermen (fish people), Nephilim (giants, as per Genesis 6), and so on.[5] It took centuries for genetic mix-ups to be healed, according to his readings, and produce bodies similar to what we have now.

If you think Cayce's readings are utterly ridiculous, consider these anomalies and fresh finds:

+ A race of Hobbits, similar to what J. R. R. Tolkien described in his famous Ring trilogy, *actually existed in Indonesia.*[6]
+ Early humans were more prey than predators. They relied on their wits and social skills to survive. Cooperation determined survival, *not aggression or warfare* as misstated in history books.[7]
+ Giants lived, some measuring over 23 feet tall. Skeletal remains have been found in Egypt, Greece, India, South America, and Mexico. Organizations like the Smithsonian Institute have a

history of investigating such finds, then having the artifacts mysteriously disappear once they leave. *Hundreds of misplaced and ignored giant bones still exist.*[8]

+ The true founders of the Egyptian civilization, supposedly "star people," were black. This Black Genesis challenges existing histories.[9]

+ Research on haplotypes (blood types) has *revealed an X haplotype that cannot be traced* (it may be a mixture, but so far it appears to be unique on the planet). Predominant carriers are Basques, Berbers, Great Lakes Mound builders, Iroquois, Algonquin, and Picts (Scythian/Iranian). It emerged around 11,500 years ago, when Cayce said Atlantis sank and the survivors fled to the very areas where the bloodline exists today.[10] (Barbara Hand Clow gives the same date for the cataclysm that wounded humankind, the same time frame when there was a sudden change in the fossil record.) Is this haplotype proof of Atlantis and of a unique people?

+ *Y is the quickest-evolving chromosome* in the whole human genetic code. Good thing, because pollution is weakening male genes, boys are far more at risk than girls for learning disorders, some male fish are born feminized (have eggs in their gonads), and there are sharks getting pregnant without a male sperm. Science tells us that the male gender emerged long after the female. Is the sudden rise in risk factors why the Y suddenly turned on?

+ Any mutation entering the gene pool, if not subsequently reinforced, will be *diluted and disappear in seven generations.* Is this the explanation for the biblical phrase "The sins of the fathers shall be visited on the sons, even unto the seventh generation"?

Claims galore are flooding news outlets and blogs, intensifying talk about the new human now emerging (to be called Homo luminous). These claims focus on the small electrical field around DNA—as it is arcing, skipping around, and emitting a larger field than usual. We know from the work of Nobel Prize winner Barbara McClintock that genes can jump around, but what a few psychics are predicting goes beyond that. They believe that the functional pattern or codons of genes are "waking up" and becoming more active, making kids who have this gene mutation resistant to disease. So far this particular codon prediction has proved false.

What has proven to be true, however, is this: 7 percent of our genes are undergoing rapid-fire acceleration. Scientists admit they haven't got a clue as to what this mutation means or what the next generation will be like with the mutation. They just know something big is happening to the human species and it is happening right now.

Allow me to venture past psychic findings and anomalous histories to make good on the cliffhanger promised in chapter fifteen. It concerns a "homogenocene." Christopher Columbus caused the first one five hundred years ago. The next has already begun.

THE FIFTH CENTURY AFTER COLUMBUS

Geological forces split continents apart more than two hundred million years ago. Each of the two halves created by the split developed totally different plants and animals. Charles C. Mann in his book *1493: Uncovering the New World Columbus Created,* paints a graphic picture of what happened after Christopher Columbus set foot in the Americas.[11] The separation of continents ended with that one footprint, followed by the most momentous biological event our planet had undergone since the death of the dinosaurs. Why? Mann explains it this way: "The Columbian Exchange, as researchers call it, is the reason there are tomatoes in Italy, oranges in Florida, chocolates in Switzerland, and chili peppers in Thailand. More important, creatures the colonists knew nothing about hitched along for the ride. Earthworms, mosquitoes, and cockroaches; honeybees, dandelions, and African grasses; bacteria, fungi, and viruses; rats of every description—all of them rushed like eager tourists into lands that had never seen their like before, changing lives and landscapes across the planet." A homogenocene, the mixing of unlike substances to create a uniform blend, resulted.

The modern age birthed in that one event. Any goal of finding a quick route to China was tossed in a mad scramble for profits. The result: a worldwide network of ecological and economic exchange that fostered the rise of Europe, devastated imperial China, disrupted Africa, and for two centuries made Mexico City the center of Asian and European interactions with the Americas.

The impact of Columbus influenced a variety of activities and events:

+ The silver trade in China and a huge loss of trees because of it
+ The rise of rice, maize, wheat, sugarcane, and potatoes as the largest food crops in the world
+ The agro-business complex that became the template for modern agriculture
+ Tobacco from China used as snuff in England and smoked in the Americas (which protected against malaria-laden mosquitoes)
+ Rubber trees in Asia sucking up water and drying out entire water systems (rubber was the third prong for industrialization; steel and fossil fuels were the other two)
+ Unprecedented reshuffling of people and traditions
+ The first wave of slavery, mostly of Europeans, criminals, castaways (many died in fields because of the malaria Columbus brought over)
+ The second wave of slavery, of Africans (immune to malaria, plus skilled at ironworking and horsemanship)

Factually, America, already heavily populated by Indians, became an extension of Africa, not Europe. It was the Africans themselves who controlled the supply of African slaves, as slavery was the only form of private revenue-sharing property recognized in African law. Within a hundred years, one in five people across the world died because of the Columbus homogenocene (from diseases, multiple types of slaveries, brutal working conditions, industrialization, hunger, environmental destruction, etc.).

The modern world as we know it today started because of a trade-route miscalculation. The "afterward," what followed the extremes of convolution and change, produced enormous and profound benefit.

I said a new homogenocene the likes of the one caused by Columbus is currently under way—five centuries after the first one—because the world's largest biotech firms, companies like Monsanto, DuPont, BASF, and Syngenta, are in a rush to take full advantage of another miscalculation, a law that allows "improvements" in seed stock to be patented. Billed as a move to alleviate the world's hunger and raise better crops, these biotech giants are investing vast sums in genetically modified organisms, or GMOs. The result of their genetic manipulation has already created nightmare convolutions—superweeds, pesticides engineered into grain heads, genetically altered nutraceuticals in "organic" baby food, and unfair trading and economic policies that place undue burden on farmers. France and Germany have outlawed GMOs, but here and in other countries, biotech companies are praised and favored, their modifications unlabeled (see chapter 15).

Genetic alterations, along with excessive hormone use in livestock, has invited all sorts of questionable practices—among them changing the lignin content in plants and trees (the substance that protects them from insects, disease, animal browsing, wind, and other environmental stressors). Mountaintop removal, still another legal miscalculation, is destroying forest ecosystems while spreading cancer—especially among Appalachia's children.

Mann would argue that any more genetic and hormone changes in nature are, in reality, the final drawdown of the Columbian Exchange—that what was given is being taken away, that the protections diversity affords are disappearing in a rush for "controlled blends." This may be so, but more is at stake this time than any global compatibility of plants and animals, international business affairs, laws, and profits.

Genetic modification is the specific goal—a goal that affects the chemical codes of every living thing. There is no biotech company, no business plan, no medical facility, no government that can predict the outcome of this. Pandora's box is open wide. Christopher Columbus never meant to cause a homogenocene. Nor has Monsanto, or any of the other companies trying to climb aboard the genetic gravy train. What they seem to have forgotten is how what they do affects all of us, their children, our children, and the "drippy" chem line of cells and genes.

I believe that GMOs, along with brain changes caused by digital excesses, planetary geoengineering, skyrocketing drug and alcohol addiction, and too much ionizing radiation are propelling the second-most-momentous biological event since the death of the dinosaurs. It is the time of the Great Shifting. A revolution in genetics is to be expected—and it will be huge. After the extremes of convolution, unimaginable benefits could eventually follow.

LEARNING WEBS

Back in 1979, James Burke introduced his theory of "learning webs" in a ten-week series titled *Connections* that was carried on several television channels. "Imagine knowledge and history as being rather like a three-dimensional globe made up of millions and millions of threads interacting across it," he told us. "The center of the globe is the beginning, and the edge of the globe is the modern world." He continued: "What I am doing is traveling through this web, sometimes starting in the past, coming to the edge—which is now; sometimes starting at the edge, going in and coming back out again, looking more at the nature of how knowledge occurs than to say, 'This is why the modern world is the way it is.'"

Burke's series linked seemingly unrelated people, events, and ideas, similar to what Charles Mann did in his book. "Those unexpected linkages showed us a broader pattern—one that explained how our world got the way it is." Burke said his job is trying to teach people to start looking for patterns in the way that technology and science affect society. Recognize the patterns, the learning webs, and then what follows can be influenced or changed.

The Great Shifting has been the herald for cataclysms in the past; several have already occurred of late. What I see as more important, however, are adjustments in the learning webs, what spreads from our second homogenocene. We humans have such short memories. Reflecting back five hundred years shows us that the actions we take today, our choices, our decisions, are far more important than worrying about any cataclysm. We *can* make a difference.

21 A Grand Plan

*And God said to the soul: I desired you before the world
began.*

MECHTHILD OF MAGDEBURG

Mark my words: this second homogenocene will be as dangerous as it is
wondrous. If we can rein back the corporate rush to "own" the world's
plants, cells, and genes, and preserve as much diversity as possible, the
early convolutions we face will not be as deadly as during the first hundred years after Columbus.

Human size, shape, density factors, behavior, and brain development are slated for a makeover during this homogenocene. The new
science of epigenetics offers proof that we really can change that much
and benefit greatly. Bruce H. Lipton, Ph.D., a cellular biologist, explains
the situation this way: "Recently, results of the Human Genome Project
have shattered one of science's fundamental core beliefs, the concept of
genetic determinism. We have been led to believe that our genes determine the character of our lives, yet new research surprisingly reveals
that it is the character of our lives that controls our genes."[1] Epigenetics
demonstrates that the cell's nucleus is a "read/write hard disk," literally
genetic software that is programmed by the membrane's response to
environmental perceptions. The cell membrane is "not like a chip, the
membrane IS the chip."

ALIEN EXISTENCE

Some scientists in China have an interesting idea about "junk DNA," those mysterious noncoding sequences in human DNA that appear without purpose. Hold on to your hat: they believe the "infamous" 97 percent whose function is unknown comprise the genetic code of extraterrestrial life forms. Our science-fiction past does indeed affirm that the human species "skip-scattered" throughout early history, and that there are serious holes in all our various spiritual/mystical/religious/scientific creation stories.

Enter the Intervention Theory, a popular one that states that humankind is the end product of extraterrestrial genetic manipulation. Chief among such claimants is Zecharia Sitchin, a historian and linguist, with his blockbuster *The 12th Planet*.[2] Sitchin believed that the first peoples were created by the Anunnaki, "Those who to Earth came from the heavens" (supposedly a race from Nibiru, a planet in our own solar system with an extended orbit of 3,600 years). His translation of Sumerian texts inscribed on clay tablets suggests that these Anunnaki took their own genes and implanted them into primitive hominids already here to attain the genesis of *Homo sapiens*. Paul Von Ward in *We've Never Been Alone: A History of Extraterrestrial Intervention*, shows how human history is intertwined with the activities of advanced beings on the earth and beyond—as well as in other dimensions.[3] He, among numerous others, is challenging the beginnings of modern civilization and its religions, governments, and cultures.

But, hey, evidence is mounting that there once was life on Mars. Microbes? If that's all our scientists believe is there, then why do they keep airbrushing photos of the face on Mars? And why do they turn a deaf ear to hundreds of thousands of people, including the testimony of military officers and no-nonsense professionals, who say, "There are aliens among us"?

I have a chapter on alien existence in my book *The New Children and Near-Death Experiences*.[4] If you're going to work with kids, as I have, you must be prepared for the stories they tell after their near-death episode—about alien visitations, being from another planet, and attending night "school" with all manner of strange folk besides those of human form. Imagination? Some of it clearly is; still, the bulk of their testimony, and I believe their telling is indeed testimony, is grounded in memory.

With adult experiencers of near-death states (based on three thousand, cases), I found that 20 percent identified with being from another planet, and 9 percent claimed to have been abducted by a UFO. Child experiencers were somewhat different. Based on 277 cases, only 9 percent identified with being from another planet, 14 percent said they had been abducted by a UFO, and 39 percent said they were from another dimension. I didn't find this sense of interdimensionality with adults.

There were two camps to interdimensionality, though. The largest centered on *an orientation to the life continuum*. Kids with this orientation were concerned with life embodiments and the progression and grouping of souls. Their memories embraced prebirth and after-death realms as exit and entrance points to a single life stream or life continuum inhabited by the type of spirits they once were and will be again—their true home. (The majority—about three-quarters of the 39 percent total—recalled this.)

The lesser numbers *were oriented to the cosmos*. Children with this orientation were concerned with the universe's inner workings and the progression of Creation. They identified with formlessness: gases, attractors, particle sparks, waves, energy pulses, plasma, and so forth, as if the substance of their being and their place of residence were one in the same—part of the mechanism and structure that holds together and maintains Creation itself. (Fewer respondents—about one-quarter of the 39 percent total—claimed this orientation.)

Although of lesser number, those oriented to the cosmos challenged the very notion we have of soul and how life is identified. They seemed possessed of almost pure intellect, and they spouted advanced concepts about things like wave forms, energy sources, and power grids in the same manner as the average child might quote football scores. And they were explicit about their origins: "Not here; not there. Elsewhere." Just because these kids occasionally mentioned other planets does not mean they considered themselves from them.

Don't confuse these children with those who remember past lives (the life continuum). These kids acted as if they have never been on this or any other planet before and, frankly, considered the human body, any body, a useless, clumsy appendage. They appeared utterly unconcerned with family issues or personal relationships. Creation to them was alive and conscious; the very gases we breathe, living intelligences. Often they referred to themselves as stewards, guardians, or keepers of that which enables cells and molecules to exist, rather than as evolving souls. True, their memories could be interpreted as awareness in the womb (plasma, waves); still, they were adamant about being here for the "changes." Most stated that they were called here by a signal from the Earth for help.

Dates given in most near-death narratives are useless, so I asked each child to describe what he or she would look like when the changes arrived. Matching their present age against their image projections, I arrived *at the same time frame with each one*: *between the years of 2013 and 2029*. No exceptions.

The majority of adult and child near-death experiencers I had sessions with spoke of the solar system as the university of the soul. They said we are each here for a reason, and that God/Allah/The Divine (Supreme Intelligence) has a Grand Plan and we are part of that plan. You get the sense from them that reincarnation and those intriguing stories of "life after life" are just window dressing for something larger.

ANOTHER LOOK AT BEFORE

Go back to Brad Steiger's *Worlds Before Our Own*.[5] He shows that *scientific knowledge has been known to every culture*. Some of his examples: rock engravings, which may be as old as sixty million years, depicting step-by-step procedures for entire heart-transplant operations and for a

Caesarean section; ancient Egyptians using the equivalent of contraceptive jelly and urine pregnancy tests; the cement used in Mayan dental fillings still holds after 1,500 years; and ancient Babylonians appeared to use what we would call sulfur matches, and had complex electrochemical battery cells with wiring.

Only recently has news been released of the biggest stunner of all: Göbekli Tepe (ruins located near Mount Aarat in southeastern Turkey). This was once a flourishing city and temple complex in a urban setting, replete with evidence of agriculture, animal husbandry, art, pottery, sculpture, architecture, and specialized labor . . . dating back 11,500 years. . . *seven thousand years before the pyramids, before Stonehenge, even before the Neolithic breakout.*

Only 5 percent uncovered (buried gently in sand, as if on purpose), Göbekli Tepe is proof that an advanced society once lived on this planet, and one who knew how to build 19-foot-tall, perfectly constructed and sculpted columns *with no evidence that they used tools,* and showing animals on them *that do not and never have existed—that we know of.* Still buried yet "visible" via electronic equipment are endless circles upon circles upon circles with the enigmatic 19-foot columns placed in the same relation along each circular wall of each structure. Temples? No one knows. The various buildings are massive . . . presenting us with an equally massive puzzle: who were these people, where did they come from, and why did they leave?

Add to that puzzle this one: all of the world's earliest religions venerated the constellation of Cygnus (the Swan), which is located at the Great Rift of the Milky Way. Andrew Collins, author of *The Cygnus Mystery,* discovered that in ancient worship this one point in the sky was considered the gateway of life, death, and rebirth.[6] Cygnus was seen as the portal of souls to and from the sky world. The three center stars of Cygnus fit precisely over the three pyramids of Giza, and are the source of unique subatomic particles (cosmic rays) hitting Earth. Did we come from there? Is the relationship between us more involved than we know?

One more: our globe is a single planetary energy system, with energy pathways that prehistoric civilizations tapped into for power. In a report entitled "The Earth's Crystal Grid," Joseph Robert Jochmans, one of the finest researchers and historians I know, presented a strong case for a dual crystal structure of the earth itself, consisting of a combination of icosahedrons (twenty faces of a three-dimensional polyhedron) and of dodecahedrons (twelve faces).[7] He illustrates in his report how the lines and nodal points of the earth's crystal grid closely delineate every major activity, fracture zone, deposit, migration route, and ancient monument—plus the birthplaces where each of world's religions, philosophies, sciences, art, and architecture formed. And the grid is malleable. When we shift, the grid shifts. Indicated here is that the Earth responds to our care or neglect, our hatred or peace, and possesses its own consciousness.

We already know that the Mayan Calendar is not a calendar like the ones we pin on our walls. It is actually a device for tracking the development of consciousness on planet Earth, and it continues for years past what we can fathom.

We already know, or at least it should be plainly obvious, that it is no accident that the Earth exists as it does. Had the birth of our cosmos been slightly less violent, the universe's expansion would have been too slow to sustain itself. Had it been slightly more violent, the universe would have dispersed into a thin soup. If the ratio of matter and energy to the volume of space at that moment of the big bang had been one quadrillionth of one percent less than ideal, creation wouldn't have happened. We wouldn't be here. It's as if the universe consciously desired the life it would one day cradle. The eminent French scientist Pierre Lecomte du Noüy observed, "From the very beginning, life has evolved as if there were a goal to attain, and as if this goal were the advent of the human conscience."[8]

No matter the question asked, the same answer echoes back: the entire universe was designed for the purpose of creating and expanding a consciousness capable of observing and understanding itself.

CONSCIOUSNESS

Consciousness is more than active awareness. I have noticed that it operates as if an ordering principle that processes, connects, and organizes the full spectrum of visible and invisible realities, and time-space potentials existent in and beyond vibrational frequencies. It is that font of knowingness that is intelligent and forever awake (even if we may be sleeping or brain dead). It is *supramental* in that it extends beyond mind and feelings and functions best via intuition, and *supraluminal* in its ability to move past time-space potentials in its role as the container where creation resides.

We tend to identify consciousness in how we see it operate, yet scientists Harold Saxon Burr and Rupert Sheldrake, through their work with husbandry and reproduction, discovered that there are primary fields of consciousness that envelop and direct forming fetuses and embryos and seedlings. These fields can "cross-reference" and "communicate" with other fields, enabling the life forms within each genesis to reach and teach each other. They found that all that exists is aware of everything else that exists, through interconnecting fields. These findings have been replicated by other scientists.

Our experience of consciousness greatly expands through prayer, meditation, and contemplation, and through the depth achieved when you become whatever you focus on, when you zone out.[9] But here's something you may not know: all breakthroughs that occur during a transformation of consciousness permanently change the experiencer, child or adult, along the lines of a pattern of physiological and psychological aftereffects similar to that of near-death experiences.

These breakthroughs, or what mystics and shamans call threshold experiences, are endemic to near-death experiences and near-death-like experiences. But, more important, that pattern can also be applied to kundalini breakthroughs, baptisms of the Holy Spirit, shamanic vision quests, unity experiences, spiritual transformations, religious conversions, and deep prayerful states. Threshold experiences straddle the boundary between this world and other worlds, between brain and that which lies beyond what the brain can access, between reality and miracles, mind and spirit, life and death, heaven and hell, sanity and insanity. If you make it through the boundary (the threshold), you expand into higher states of consciousness that always lead to the same place . . . Oneness.

Go back in history and trace such spiritual breakthroughs. If enough people became "thresholders," an overall leap in consciousness occurred, as if such episodes (spiritual experiences) *were a biological imperative for the evolution of the human race.*[10]

The conservative figure globally for people in the general population who have had a near-death experience is between 4 and 5 percent. The figure for those who have had other types of threshold episodes triples or quadruples. The science of fluid dynamics tells us that it only takes 4 to 5 percent of any group, condition, or situation to change, for the entire unit to follow. Once flow patterns exceed that tipping point, energy excites or becomes highly charged. When that happens superfluidity is reached and the least-expected thing occurs—*the newly created wave form of consciousness CAN NO LONGER BE CONTAINED.*

The basic patterning for today's children duplicates that of near-death kids. Our youngsters are being born "changed." Now we can see why what is happening is suddenly everywhere. Arab Spring, Occupy movements, Tea Parties, unity consciousness, wisdom of the crowd, flash concerts/mobs—entire populations demanding to be heard, demanding freedom and dignity. The "container" has been breached. Borders are dissolving. Social media and politics aside, a new consciousness has been set free.

GOD/MESSIAH/CHRIST

There's a book called *The Real Name of God* by Rabbi Wayne Dosick, Ph.D.[11] Recognizing that there are many names for God/Allah/The Divine in sacred literature, even beyond the original YHWH (which many pronounce as if spelled *Yahweh*), Rabbi Dosick came across what he believes is God's authentic name, hidden in plain sight in the Bible: Anochi. Isn't that term suspiciously like Anunnaki, the name given by Sitchin to the race of people who supposedly created us? The rabbi makes no such connection. I do, because the majority of those who go through threshold experiences (no matter what type), come back head over heels in love with God.

This love of God is visceral and personal. Thresholders may differ on what to call that presence or what the presence is, but seldom do they differ on its power—like that of a million suns. The goal of any threshold experience is to reconnect the soul with Source, with ONENESS: *one God, one people, one family, one existence, one law (love), one commandment (service), one solution (forgiveness).* Thus, in a very real way, the goal of each spiritual tradition/religion is to release the soul from exile. As threshold experiencer Geoffrey Bullington shares: "Your religion is what you focus on every day. Every thought you have creates. Our contact with God is direct."

Any thought of origins, of a central ordering of mass and consciousness, of creation, brings us to the reality of the greater God/Allah/ The Divine as True Source, as Creator, and our place as co-creators. Throughout what we can know of history, there have been great teachers or messiahs who have come to awaken the populace, to enlighten those willing to listen. Their basic message: there is more to life than what can be seen—a purpose to our lives, a plan undergirding creation, a Central Truth—and to know this truth is to be set free.

The various messianic figures recorded as such in history are:

+ Krishna—world savior who rose from the dead
+ Buddha—also ascended bodily to heaven
+ Lao-Kiun—savior, virgin born, ascended bodily into paradise
+ Zoroaster—world savior, the ancient Persian God, ascended to heaven
+ Mithra—also a Persian deity, whose life and death Jesus the Christ duplicates

+ Aesculapius—the son of God, the savior, who after being put to
  death rose from the dead
+ Savior Adonis—world savior, rose from the dead
+ Osiris—the Egyptian savior, who, similar to Jesus, rose from the
  dead after being put to death
+ Frey—ancient Scandinavian world savior; put to death and rose
  from the dead
+ Quetzalcoatl—the Mexican savior; put to death and then rose
  from the dead
+ Jesus, who became the Christ—the world savior recognized by
  Christianity, virgin born, put to death, arose and bodily ascended
  to heaven

Common to these eleven saviors or world messiahs are unusual
births, spectacular advancements in childhood, teachings given to help
the masses awaken to the truth of their own potential, murder by the
entrenched, rising bodily from the dead, and ascension into a heaven.
And all spoke of a Grand Plan, a Divine Order to all Creation. The
story of Jesus, our present messiah figure, is little different from those
before him—except for one huge variant: he taught about love and forgiveness and modeled the "Christhood" as no one else before him had.
Christ is a state of advanced or higher consciousness that Jesus said anyone can attain. He made plain that, "all these things I have done you
can do and more also." There are several places in the Bible that affirm
"we are gods in the making." The teachings of Jesus summarize all religious thought.[12]

In traditions that describe anything like a Fifth World, a progression of Root Races, changes in body type, and corresponding chakra
qualities developed and refined worldwide were prophesied for each
shift. Also predicted to occur were a new template for Noah, Adam,
and Messiah. These three figures, as archetypes of a grander design, are
the basic models human consciousness has used throughout the ages
to express what saves us (Noah), what establishes new life order and

activity (Adam), and what resurrects to ensure rebirth and continuance (Messiah).

I believe our next Noah template is Nelson Mandela. He exemplifies the highest form of forgiveness and reconciliation. Considering what our world is going through now and the stresses to come, none of us will make it through the Great Shifting unless and until we have learned the lessons forgiveness teaches and can reconcile differences. Mandela truly is a Noah.

And I believe our next Adamic template is Gandhi, the man who not only brought democracy and independence to India, but who created the nonviolent, peaceful protest. This manner of protest was used to free Poland, the Czech Republic, Slovakia, and Ukraine from Soviet domination, topple Jim Crow racism in the United States, and is currently spreading like wildfire across the Arabic states and Russia. Gandhi, through the manner in which he lived his life, taught a better way of how we could live ours. Our next template for Messiah hasn't arrived yet, irrespective of claims.

Special souls have always come to earth to pry open and energize the prevailing mind-set. This is occurring today, as well. What is different this time, however, is that the masses are changing. We're not just seeing advanced beings making an appearance. We're seeing the whole human family rising as a species, evolving to higher states of potential and possibility.

THE THIRD WAY

Did you know that the Fifth Buddha is predicted to appear in this, the Fifth World? He is referred to as Maitreya, the Buddha of Loving Kindness. The line of Catholic popes has one left before the papacy dissolves—this according to a prophesy revealed to the three children who saw Mother Mary at Fatima, Portugal, in 1917, when seventy thousand people witnessed the sun dancing in the sky. Two other time frames have been prophesied: 3797 CE, the last glimpse of the future given to Nostradamus; and October 21, 4772—the final date inscribed on the Tablet of Inscriptions in Palenque, Mexico. The suspicion for what remains is that the new light coming in—the idea of becoming luminous (spiritual)—will occur in stages.

Get this: CERN, the world's leading physics lab in Geneva, Switzerland, has recorded cosmic radiation now intensifying daylight on Earth and providing more light at night. Mum's the word, though, as the lab chief does not want any of the scientists commenting on this; he feels this discovery may involve them in the climate-change controversy.[13]

Did it ever occur to anyone that this new light could be the signal that we are moving from a "dark star" mentality and apocalyptic mindset to an awakening of the planetary mind? The lab chief fears being associated with climate change. How about consciousness change, the real "stargate"?

Evident with global advancements now occurring is the Rule of Thirds, especially with children: ⅓ profoundly gifted, ⅓ quite intelligent and intuitive, ⅓ too violent to handle (some are extremely intelligent but lack frontal-lobe development—entirely "me" centered and without any sense of caring about the results of their actions). The remarkable Rule of Thirds showing up again and again tells us we're on time, the world is progressing on schedule, nothing is lost, a greater hand is at play. And it tells us that the Third Way is a better way.

The Third Way illustrates how people, when faced with life issues, tend to react in one of three ways: (1) we play ostrich and pretend we don't see it; (2) we label it an enemy or a devil and attack; or (3) we confront the situation squarely and honestly, search for the truth behind the appearance, and take decisive steps to initiate a constructive solution. The first way creates victims, the second victors, and the third responsive and responsible participants in life, committed to growth and learning. This Third Way of dealing with life issues is between dualities: between victors and victims, good and evil, darkness and light. The Third Way requires mediation and diplomacy skills, mindfulness, and a willingness to consider *what is appropriate* as a greater priority than self-centered interests. It takes time to learn and patience, and it necessitates cooperation and compromise, but it is the only way of living that shows any promise for a future that is worthwhile for anyone. The Third Way upholds dignity and value and wholeness . . . and *wholeness is spirituality made manifest.*

This way of living is expressed in nature as the Golden Mean. Experiments to record and measure energy wavelengths produced by people who are in love all evidenced the same configuration—the Golden Mean.

Dag Hammarskjöld, second Secretary General of the United Nations, once said, "For all that has been, thank you. For all that is to come, yes!" Let us echo that *YES* to a world of big, bold ideas that can transform lives and countries and bank accounts, and *YES* for the courage to see beyond disasters to recognize a new light coming in.

THE BUTTERFLY PEOPLE

What was once called paranormal is happening so often and everywhere that it is obvious the veil separating dimensions of reality is lifting. Case in point: on December 19, 2011, Todd C. Frankel, staff writer for the *St. Louis Post-Dispatch*, wrote the article "The Butterfly People of Joplin." In the article he quoted some of the children who were caught up in the disastrous May 22 Joplin, Missouri, tornado that nearly wiped out a thriving city. The children spoke of "butterfly people" in and around the tornado itself. The kids said the butterfly people protected them. Some townsfolk claimed they were guardian angels. Others dismissed the whole thing as a child's fanciful imagination. But those who saw the phenomenon never changed their story; they believed there were butterfly people flying around and inside Joplin's terrible tornado, trying to help people.[14]

Conclusion

——◆——

Wrapping Up

I'm one of the few people who understands how producing
technology requires intuition and creativity, and how
producing something artistic takes real discipline.

STEVE JOBS

I have felt that writing this book was an obligation of mine, a way to pass on to those younger than I a framework they could use to measure and understand the challenges they would face just in being alive in the world of today. There's never been a world like this. Inspirations, channeling, predictions from on high; although great for uplifting the soul, they are far too vague to be of much value when pulling up your socks and walking out the door. A primer is what I picked, as a primer is in between regular reading and a handbook. And in-betweens are always more fun, a sock-it-to-ya kind of page-turner.

The 9/11s have never known a homeland that was safe. They are growing up with a depression-era mind-set that will enable them to be more pragmatic and resourceful than their elders. They will be our new inventors and contractors, the likes of Steve Jobs, because they're not afraid of work or of sacrifice. Millennials, the shift generation in the age of shift, were not raised in a manner that would prepare them for what has happened with the economy. They were spoiled and fully expected to find the opportunities they felt entitled to receive. Their anger is palpable, as they continue to fuss and complain. And it is their anger that will drive, push, insist, and demand a better world. Millennial anger can be the stuff of miracles and the fuel behind getting involved, whether in politics, with social structures, or in international concerns. As you have no doubt recognized, the negative aspects of our natures often serve us better than the positive. A quirk of being human, I suppose.

All of today's kids face a unique "wall": unemployment. The younger generations lost to the work ethic of their elders. This is both an opportunity and a nightmare. An opportunity in the sense that our young will reinvent the world to suit new lifestyles and new demands. A nightmare in the sense that they are more likely to cave in to the pressure of drugs, sex, and digital addictions—compromising potential. What will make that all-important difference with our children are mentors, adults willing to guide, teach, test, and give of themselves; to show, not preach.

Everything is coming together now—the Fifth World, the Great Shifting, the second homogenocene, all those fives and thirds—and bringing about massive and profound change. The world will be unrecognizable in less than three decades.

There are several things to remember. A church home of some kind is needed, as are people to pray and share with. These will give kids and their parents a support system like no other.

And this: all major progressive social movements were originated by Quakers—proof that small numbers of dedicated people can accomplish anything. Don't ever think that large sums of money and special interests determine anyone's future. You have that power yourself. Use it.

Afterword

Special Bulletin

During the first week of July 2012, the European Center for Nuclear Research (CERN) announced that the Hadron Collider had uncovered evidence that a new elementary particle exists, predicted by both Satyendra Nath Bose of India and Peter Ware Higgs of England. Dubbed the "God Particle," this tiny spit of a thing is apparently that phase/shift particle or field where light becomes dense enough to take on mass and weight—the initial building block of matter.

A show-stopper, yes, but what does this discovery have to do with this book?

Well, it shows us that the universe is not based on pairs (polarity) but on fours (quadruples)—each with slightly different characteristics. This means that the many-worlds concept is real: what was once just an idea may be a reality of parallel worlds, other universes, different dimensions, unique arrangements of time, space, embodiment—all the elements of a hidden order. This infers that imaginal realms and alien worlds and night school and visionary landscapes and shamanic journeys and the blessed fields of paradise, even of butterfly people, spirits, demons, and angels may have more validity than anyone dared to dream. Our reliable markers for what is real and what is not have just dissolved.

Welcome to the Fifth World. Our children are already tuned in. Now it's our turn. The rules of life, of living and thriving, everything offered in this book, still apply. The existence of a God Particle does not deny the reality of our lives. The discovery actually invites us to open our minds and our hearts . . . a little wider.

NOTES

PREFACE

1. P. M. H. Atwater, L.H.D. *Near-Death Experiences: The Rest of the Story* (Charlottesville, Va.: Hampton Roads, 2011).
2. P. M. H. Atwater, L.H.D. *The New Children and Near-Death Experiences* (Rochester, Vt.: Bear & Co., 2003).
3. P. M. H. Atwater, L.H.D. *Beyond the Indigo Children* (Rochester, Vt: Bear & Co., 2005).

INTRODUCTION. SETTING THE STAGE

1. Refer to the O'Reilly Media website at http://oreilly.com for the full rendering of this influential group's activities, learning opportunities, ideas, and products. Founded by Tim O'Reilly, this company is an innovative leader in creating new electronic "landscapes" for marketing.

CHAPTER 3. THE FIFTH ROOT RACE

1. To read the full article Dr. Alberto Villoldo wrote about this, "Homo Luminous: The New Human," access www.realitysandwich.com/homo_luminous_the_new_human.
2. Contact the American headquarters of the Theosophical Society at P.O. Box 270, Wheaton, IL 60189-0270; (630) 668-1571; info@theosophical.org; website www.theosophical.org.

3. I recommend three books for a more in-depth rendering of the theosophical viewpoint: (1) C. W. Leadbeater. *The Masters and the Path* (Madras, India; Theosophical Publishing House, 1925). This book is still available through the Theosophical Society. (2) Colonel Arthur E. Powell. *The Solar System* (Madras, India: Theosophical Publishing House, 1930). This book is also still available via the Theosophical Society. (3) Phillip Lindsay, *The Hidden History of Humanity: Esoteric Evolution of Planetary Life, vol. 1* (Sydney, Australia: Apollo Publishing, 2007). This more recent volume is available through most online booksellers.

4. To explore the readings of Edgar Cayce and the organization that sprang up around him, visit the Association for Research and Enlightenment (A.R.E.) at www.EdgarCayce.org. This organization offers regular conferences, travel opportunities, study groups, summer camps, library resources, and extensive publishing. Although open to the public, membership is required for services.

CHAPTER 4. BIRTH BUMPS

1. My own books *The New Children and Near-Death Experiences* (noted above) and *The Big Book of Near-Death Experiences* (Charlottesville, Va.: Hampton Roads, 2007).

2. Evidence for transgenerational epigenetics is rapidly growing as our scientists become more adept in genetic research. There are several excellent articles on this. Sharon Begley, "Shaped by Life in the Womb," *Newsweek,* September 27, 1999, pp. 50–57. Sharon Begley, "Sins of the Grandfathers," *Newsweek,* November 8, 2010, pp. 48–50. Daniel K. Morgan and Emma Whitelaw, "The Case for Transgenerational Epigenetic Inheritance in Humans," *Mammalian Genome: Official Journal of the International Mammalian Genome Society* 19, no. 6 (2008): 394–97.

3. Refer to Michel Gauquelin, *Birthtimes: A Scientific Investigation of the Secrets of Astrology* (New York: Farrar, Straus & Giroux, 1984).

CHAPTER 5. OFF AND RUNNING

1. Associated Press, "Study: Half of U.S. Kids on Food Stamps," November 3, 2009, www.cbsnews.com/2100-201_162-5504471.html.

2. David Elkind, Ph.D. *The Hurried Child: Growing up Too Fast Too Soon* (Cambridge, Mass.; DaCapo Press, 2006).

3. Robin Moore, *Awakening the Hidden Storyteller: How to Build a Storytelling Tradition in Your Family* (Boston, Mass: Shambhala, 1991).

4. I was prepared to write eighteen small books featuring animal babies talking about life in the womb and birth issues. Six were finished. Everywhere I shopped samples, I received compliments but no publishing contract. To date, those six finished stories sit in a file.

CHAPTER 6. PIVOT

1. Soleira Green lives in England. Although a gifted intuitive, she is best known for her work with children and young adults and for producing the "Inspiring a World of Social Brilliance" conferences in London. She operates the Visionary Network, offers teleconference opportunities, and issues a free newsletter. Her websites are www.transformingourworld.com and www.theglobalbrillianceproject.com. You may contact her at soleira@transformingourworld.com. The quotes I have used here come from "Visionary Network News," November 6, 2010. Soleira was kind enough to give me permission to quote from her material.

CHAPTER 7. MINEFIELDS

1. Christian Sabyan, Emily Smith, and Manav Tanneeru, "A Profitable Enterprise," July 29, 2011, http://thecnnfreedomproject.blogs.cnn.com/category/the-facts/.

2. There are three well-researched books that cover this. The first, originally published in 1979, was predictive: Christopher Lash, *The Culture of Narcissism: American Life in an Age of Diminishing Expectations* (New York: W. W. Norton & Co., 1991). Also Jean Twenge, *Generation Me: Why Today's Young Americans Are More Confident, Assertive, Entitled—and More Miserable Than Ever Before* (New York: Simon & Schuster, 2007). Jean Twenge, *Narcissism Epidemic: Living in the Age of Entitlement* (New York: Free Press/Simon & Schuster, 2010).

3. Bernard Lietaer, *The Future of Money* (New York: Random House, 2001).

4. Two books: William Poundstone, *Priceless: The Myth of Fair Value (and*

How to Take Advantage of It) (New York: Hill and Wang, 2011). And Dan Ariely, *Predictably Irrational: The Hidden Forces That Shape Our Decisions* (New York: Harper Perennial, 2010).

5. American Academy of Child & Adolescent Psychiatry, "Teens: Alcohol and Other Drugs," March 2011, www.aacap.org/cs/root/facts_for_families/teens_alcohol_and_other_drugs.

6. Thomas R. Collins, "Invasion of the Pill Mills in South Florida," *Time*, April 13, 2010.

CHAPTER 8. QUICKSAND

1. Daniel Lyons, "Facebook's False Contrition," *Newsweek*, June 7, 2010, p. 20.

2. Brian Truitt, "Get 'Smarter' with Twitter, Founder Says," *USA Weekend*, March 25–27, 2011, p. 7.

3. Jessica Bennett, "Privacy Is Dead," *Newsweek*, November 1, 2010, pp. 40–41.

4. "Anti-'Ginger' Violence Leads to 3 Arrests," *The Daily Progress*, December 1, 2009.

5. For a full discussion of this and other changes now happening to a child's brain, read Chris Mercogliano and Kim Debus, "Expressing Life's Wisdom: Nurturing Heart-Brain Development Starting With Infants," *Journal of Family Life* 5, no. 1 (1999).

6. Refer to Roger Ebert, "Why I Hate 3-D (and You Should Too)," *Newsweek*, May 10, 2010, pp. 46–49.

7. George F. Will, "Robert Weissentein's Exhilaration," *Newsweek*, November 15, 2010.

8. Michael M. Osit, *Generation Text: Raising Well-Adjusted Kids in an Age of Instant Everything* (New York: AMACom, 2008).

CHAPTER 9. THE IMAGINAL WORLDS

1. Science is now brimming with such discoveries. Read this book for good information about the latest: Karen Shanor, Ph.D., and Jagmeet Kanwal, Ph.D., *Bats Sing, Mice Giggle: The Surprising Science of Animals' Inner Lives* (London: Icon Books, 2009).

2. J. R. R. Tolkien, *The Lord of the Rings* (London: George Allen and Unwin Ltd., 1954, 1955). The trilogy was published over a two-year period.

Houghton Mifflin in Boston is the American publisher; there have been various editions since the mid-1960s. *The Silmarillion* was published in 1977 by George Allen and Unwin, Ltd.; it is currently available through Houghton Mifflin.

3. Geogory L. Little, Ed.D., *People of the Web: What Indian Mounds, Ancient Rituals, and Stone Circles Tell Us about Modern UFO Abductions, Apparitions, and the Near-Death Experience* (Memphis: White Buffalo Books, 1990).

4. Ibid.

5. David Spangler, *Subtle Worlds: An Explorer's Field Notes* (Everett, Wash.: Lorian Press, 2010). Also Brad Steiger, *Beyond Shadow World: Our Shared World of the Supernatural* (San Antonio: Anomalist Books, 2009).

6. Litany Burns, *The Sixth Sense of Children* (New York: New American Library, 2002).

7. Exceptional books in this regard: Charlotte Reznick, Ph.D., *The Power of Your Child's Imagination* (New York: Perigee Trade, 2009). Caron B. Goode, Ed.D., and Tara Paterson, *Raising Intuitive Children* (Pompton Plains, N.J.: New Page Books, 2009). Sara Wiseman, *Your Psychic Child* (Woodbury, Minn.: Llewellyn Publications, 2010). Robin Marvel, *Awakening Consciousness: A Girl's Guide* (Ann Arbor, Mich.: Loving Healing Press, 2008). Robin Marvel, *Awakening Consciousness: A Boy's Guide* (Ann Arbor, Mich.: Loving Healing Press, 2009).

The summer camp for kids that emphasizes spirituality, nature spirits, and positive ways to use psychic/intuitive abilities is A.R.E. Kids Camp. Held each year, this camp is fully staffed and led by adults who have developed the same skills in themselves. Contact A.R.E., 215 67th Street, Virginia Beach, VA 23451; (800) 333-4499; www.EdgarCayce.org.

Enchanted Forest Intuitive Camp has activities year round. Run by Nancy Baumgarten, MLA, it is one of the best schools around for "parenting and mentoring the PSI senses for families, educators, and YOU." Contact Nancy ahead of time to see what programs are operating: Profound Awareness Alliance, Enchanted Forest Intuitive Camp, 1322 Fisher Branch Road, Marshall, NC 28753; (828) 689-9710; www.PsyKids.org. I also recommend her new book, *The Aware Human: Our Biofield Senses and Mystic Powers* (Asheville, N.C.: Celestial Dynamics, 2013).

The Center for Education, Imagination, and the Natural World has a full, year-round calendar. A little different from the other two, the center operates out of Timberlake Farm, an earth sanctuary, and offers special training for educators, as well as lively and magical programs for children. Center for Education, Imagination, and the Natural World, P.O. Box 41108, Greensboro, NC 27404; beholdnature@aol.com; www.beholdnature.org.

8. Caron B. Goode, Ed.D, NCC, *Kids Who See Ghosts: How to Guide Them through Fear* (Newburyport, Mass.: RedWheel/Weiser, 2010).

9. Louise Ireland-Frey, M.D., *Freeing the Captives: The Emerging Therapy of Spirit Attachment* (Charlottesville, Va.: Hampton Roads, 1999). Books by Irene Hickman, D.O., are also quite good. She has written *Mind Probe-Hypnosis* and *Remote Depossession*. Both were self-published some time ago. With a little searching you might find a copy. One more, geared toward professionals: William J. Baldwin *Spirit Releasement Therapy—A Technique Manual* (Terra Alta, W.V.: Headline Books, 1995).

10. Dr. Ian Stevenson's, *Twenty Cases Suggestive of Reincarnation* (New York: American Society for Psychical Research, 1966) and *Where Reincarnation and Biology Intersect* (Glenview, Ill.; Praeger, 1997), remain unparalleled in their attention to detail and provability of accounts. Tom Shroder, a reporter who accompanied Stevenson on some of his treks, more than validated his work in *Old Souls: Children Who Claim to Remember a Previous Life* (New York: Simon & Schuster, 1999). Jim Tucker, Stevenson's replacement at the Department of Perceptual Studies at the University of Virginia—Charlottesville, wrote a book about his own credible findings called *Life before Life: A Scientific Investigation of Children's Memories* (New York: St. Martin's Press, 2005).

Several other books on reincarnation are worth considering.

Research oriented: Carol Bowman, *Return from Heaven: Beloved Relatives Reincarnated Within Your Family* (New York: Harper Touch, 2001. Robert Schwartz, *Your Soul's Plan: Discovering the Real Meaning of the Life You Planned before You Were Born* (Berkeley, Calif.; Frog Books, 2009). Walter Semkiw, M.D., *Return of the Revolutionaries: The Case for Reincarnation and Soul Groups* (Charlottesville, Va.: Hampton Roads, 2003).

Personal recollections: Bruce and Andrea Leininger, *Soul Survivor: The Reincarnation of a World War II Fighter Pilot* (New York: Grand Central Publishing, 2010). Doris Patterson, *The Man with Nine Lives* (Virginia Beach, Va.: A.R.E. Press, 1994).

CHAPTER 10. A DIFFERENT BRAIN

1. Casey Miner, "This Is Your Brain on Change," *OdeWire* (June 20, 2011), http://odewire.com/82969/this-is-your-brain-on-change-2.html.

2. Ramin Setoodeh, "Gaga's Oprah Moment," *Newsweek,* June 6, 2011, p. 50.

3. Sharon Begley, "Your Child's Brain," *Newsweek,* February 18, 1996.

4. Refer to Ronald Kotulak, "We're Getting Smarter," *Virginian-Pilot,* September 9, 2005.

5. A fascinating read on how rapidly the human race is making progress: Matt Ridley, *The Rational Optimist: How Prosperity Evolves* (New York: Harper Perennial, 2011).

6. One reference for this is a small but jam-packed book: Scott Olsen, *The Golden Section: Nature's Greatest Secret* (New York: Walker & Company, 2006).

7. I have discussed this in three of my books, especially *The New Children and Near-Death Experiences* (Rochester, Vt.; Bear & Co., 2003).

8. Soleira Green published "Quantum Intelligence, Beyond IQ, EQ and SQ: The Evolution of Intelligence" on her website, www.soleiragreen.com. As a visionary, she is actively involved in producing conferences that address "corporate soul" and "global transformations." Her programs change according to demand. I used a chart of her IQ assessments on pages 121–22 of *Beyond the Indigo Children* (Rochester, Vt.: Bear & Co., 2005).

9. Andrew Newberg, M.D., and Mark Robert Waldman, *How God Changes Your Brain: Breakthrough Findings from a Leading Neuroscientist* (New York: Ballantine Books, 2010).

10. Jeremy Narby, *The Cosmic Serpent: DNA and the Origins of Knowledge* (London: Phoenix/Orion, 1999).

11. Joseph Chilton Pearce, *The Biology of Transcendence: A Blueprint of the Human Spirit* (Rochester, Vt., Park Street Press, 2004).
    Also check out www.investigatinghealthyminds.org for the latest in research on the prefrontal lobes and higher brain development.

12. Refer to Stuart L. Kaplan, M.D., "Mommy, Am I Really Bipolar?" *Newsweek,* June 27, 2011, pp. 54–57. Kaplan posits that hundreds of thousands of kids in the United States have been wrongly diagnosed with this disorder, and the results can be tragic.

13. Peter Conrad, *The Medicalization of Society* (New York: Johns Hopkins University Press, 2007).

14. Refer to Christopher Lane, *Shyness: How Normal Behavior Became a Sickness* (New Haven, Conn.: Yale University Press, 2008).

15. A discussion about this appeared in George Will, "Science Tries to Cure Character," *Washington Post Writers Group,* February 28, 2010. See also www.themedicalseries.com.

16. Kaitlin Bell Barnett, *Dosed: The Medication Generation Grows Up* (Boston: Beacon Press, 2012).

17. Michel Habib, "The Neurological Basis of Developing Dyslexia: An Overview and Working Hypothesis," *Brain: A Journal of Neurology* 123, no. 12 (July 27, 2000): 2,373–99.

18. ABC News Health Beat, "Pre-birth Pesticide Exposure May Link to Lower IQ," April 22, 2011.

19. Mike Adams, "The Top Ten Things Food Companies Don't Want You to Know," Healthy News Service, August 14, 2006, www.healthy.net/scr/News .aspx?Id=8590.

20. There is a huge groundswell against excessive installations of electronic equipment and towers. Check out: www.weepinitiative.org, www.alltheones .net/thegalileoproject, www.youtube.com/watch?v=FLeCTaSG2-U, and www.stopsmartmeters.org/2011/04/20/daniel-hirsch-on-ccsts-fuzzy-math.

21. This has long been suspected; now it has been verified. Refer to the work of Deborah Fein, psychology professor at the University of Connecticut. This was covered in an Associated Press news release "Research Suggests Children Can 'Recover' from Autism" (May 9, 2009). Since then, PBS This Morning (January 23, 2012) featured Catherine Lord, director of the Institute for Brain Development, emphasizing that 10 to 20 percent seem to recover naturally as they mature, perhaps even as many as a third (if without any other severe problems). Also see www.integratedlistening.com/ autism-case-study-magie-mcdonough.

22. Brain Gym practitioners are now located worldwide. The simple Brain Gym techniques increase oxygen to the brain, maintain cell-membrane polarity, increase ease of cross-lateral movement, stimulate the reticular activating system, activate balance to all parts of brain, and increase activation of neocortex. Their website is www.braingym.org. I was born with dyslexia; in my later years I have found Brain Gym to be a godsend.

23. Robert W. Hill, Ph.D., and Eduardo Castro, M.D., *Healing Young Brains: The Neurofeedback Solution* (Charlottesville, Va.: Hampton Roads, 2009).

24. Anat Baniel, *Kids Beyond Limits: Breakthrough Results for Children with Autism, Asperger's, Brain Damage, ADHD, and Undiagnosed Developmental Delays* (New York: Perigee, 2012).

25. Read Claudia Kalb, "When Does Autism Start?" *Newsweek,* February 28, 2005, pp. 45–53. Sue's story is in that article. Contact Jessica Kingsley Publishers for outstanding books about the autism spectrum and other brain/learning disorders. View their latest offerings on www.jkp.com. Another source, more controversial, is the work of William Stillman, who was born with Asperger's syndrome. His insights and teaching techniques are extraordinary. Contact him via his website, at www.williamstillman.com. He has written a number of books on the subject.

CHAPTER 11. A DIFFERENT PERSPECTIVE

1. Read Sally Patton, *Don't Fix Me, I'm Not Broken: Changing Our Minds about Ourselves and Our Children* (Blue Ridge Summit, Penn.: O Books/John Hunt Publishing, 2011).

2. Refer to Nassir Ghaemi, *A First Rate Madness: Uncovering the Links Between Leadership and Mental Illness* (New York: Penguin, 2011).

3. Lara Honos-Webb, Ph.D., *The Gift of ADHD: How to Transform Your Child's Problems into Strengths* (Oakland, Calif.; New Harbinger Publications, 2010). Also Lara Honos-Webb, Ph.D., *The Gift of ADHD Activity Book: 101 Ways to Turn Your Child's Problems into Strengths* (Oakland, Calif.: New Harbinger Publications, 2008).

4. The theory of the hunter gene/Edison gene mutation today known to cause ADHD is covered in depth in Thom Hartmann, *The Edison Gene: ADHD and the Gift of the Hunter Child* (Rochester, Vt.: Park Street Press, 2005).

5. Richard Pascale, Jerry Sternin, and Monique Sternin, "Bring the Outliers Inside," *Ode Magazine* (September 2010): 49–52. It is an excerpt from their book *The Power of Positive Deviance: How Unlikely Innovators Solve the World's Toughest Problems* (Boston: Harvard Business Press, 2010).

6. Thomas Armstrong, "Your Brain Is a Rain Forest," *Ode Magazine* (April/May 2010): 37–60. The article was an excerpt from Armstrong's book *Discovering the Extraordinary Gifts of Autism, ADHD, Dyslexia, and Other Brain Differences* (Washington, D.C.: DaCapo Lifelong/Perseus Books Group, 2010).

7. There is a book by this name: Eric H. Greenberg with Karl Weber, *Generation WE* (San Francisco, Calif.: Pachatusan Publishers, 2008).

8. Jane M. Healy, Ph.D., *Endangered Minds: Why Children Don't Think and What We Can Do about It* (New York: A Touchstone Book, 1990).

9. William Stillman, *The Soul of Autism* (Franklin Lakes, N.J.: New Page Books, 2008).

10. Lynne McTaggart, *The Bond: Connecting through the Space Between Us* (New York: Free Press/Simon & Schuster, 2011). She faces some serious criticism with this book, as the science she presents is faulty, based more on popular phrases that what has actually been established by physicists. Still, what she has to say is worth considering.

CHAPTER 12. GENERATIONAL FACTORS

1. From John Van Auken, "Soul Groups: Birds of a Feather Fly Together," *Ancient Mysteries Bulletin* (April 2006): 1–3. This bulletin is available through Edgar Cayce's A.R.E., are@edgarcayce.org. My thanks to John for giving me permission to quote. The 76 in the quote refers to 1776 and our nation's founding.

2. Neil Howe and William Strauss, *Generations: The History of America's Future, 1584 to 2069* (New York: William Morrow, 1991).

3. Refer to chapter five of *Beyond the Indigo Children* (Rochester, Vt.: Bear & Co., 2005).

4. Theresa H. McDevitt, *Why History Repeats: Mass Movements and the Generations, Past-Present-Future*, available through the American Federation of Astrologers (AFA), 6535 S. Rural Rd., Tempe, AZ 85283. This book is a real gem. What first caught my eye about Theresa's work was her article "A View into the Past, Present and Future," which appeared in the late summer 2011 issue of the *AFA Journal*, pp. 11–16, 31. I am a longtime member of the AFA, and wish to thank the organization and Theresa for allowing me to weave her work into mine and to quote her. You may reach Theresa directly at thevenuspress@aol.com.

5. See Rev. Alice Miller, "Uranus in Aries," *Journal of the American Federation of Astrologers* (Summer 2011): 9–14. A well-known astrologer, she wrote *Interceptions: Heralds of a New Age* and *Intercepted Planets: Possibilities for a New Age*. Both books are available from the AFA, 6535 S. Rural Rd., Tempe,

AZ 85283. I want to thank both Rev. Alice and the AFA for giving me permission to quote her. You may reach her at astrominister1@yahoo.com. Her website is www.lifeprintastrology.com.

6. Refer to my e-book *The Challenge of September 11*, available as a free download from my website, www.pmhatwater.com. I go in depth about my discoveries of what happened in the Inner Planes of Spirit when this tragedy occurred, and how that has affected mass mind and the "unfinished business" of the past several thousand years.

7. Janice Rhoshalle Littlejohn, "Frank 'Boondocks' Wit Hits Small Screen," *The Daily Progress Newspaper*, November 2, 2005, p. A11. For more information on Aaron McGruder's cartoons, go to www.cartoonnetwork.com.

CHAPTER 13. PUZZLED PARENTS

1. Adora started classroom teaching when her first book was published at age seven. She has campaigned for literacy and a love of learning around the world. She frequently speaks at educational conferences. To purchase her books and video and to find out more about her, access www.adorasvitak.com.

2. Meg Blackburn Losey, Ph.D., *Parenting the Children of Now: Practicing Health, Spirit, and Awareness to Transcend Generations* (San Francisco, Calif.: Red Wheel/Weiser, 2009).

3. Gordon Davidson, *Joyful Evolution: A Guide for Loving Co-creation with Your Conscious, Subconscious, and Superconscious Selves* (San Rafael, Calif.: Firebird Press, 2011). Gordon is part of The Center for Visionary Leadership, (415) 472-2540, www.joyfulevolution.net and www.visionarylead .org, cvidc@visionarylead.org. For decades this group has been on the leading edge of ethics in politics, communities that work, sustainability projects, international cooperation, and a healthy integration of spiritual truth. Whatever they do is done with exceptional integrity and common sense. I have known Gordon and his wife, Corinne McLaughlin, for many years and consider them both among the truly authentic voices speaking about enlightenment, higher consciousness, and the unlimited possibility within personal relationships.

4. Don Miguel Ruiz, *The Four Agreements: Toltec Wisdom Collection* (San Rafael, Calif.: Amber-Allen Publishers, 2001). Also Don Miguel Ruiz and Don Jose Ruiz with Janet Mills. *The Fifth Agreement: A Practical Guide to Self-Mastery* (San Rafael, Calif.: Amber-Allen Publishers, 2011).

5. Four great books on this topic are: Bobbi Conner, *Unplugged Play: No Batteries. No Plugs. Pure Fun* (New York: Workman Publishing, 2007). Richard Louv, *Last Child in the Woods: Saving Our Children from Nature-Deficit Disorder* (New York: Algonguin Books, 2008). Lenore Skenazy, *Free-Range Kids: How to Raise Safe, Self-Reliant Children (Without Going Nuts with Worry)* (Hoboken, N.J.: Jossey-Bass, 2010). Catriona MacGregor, *Partnering with Nature: The Wild Path to Reconnecting with the Earth* (Hillsboro, Ore.: Atria Books/Beyond Words, 2010).

6. I recommend two books in particular: William J. Bennett, ed., *The Children's Book of Virtues* (New York: Simon & Schuster, 1995). Anne McKay Garris, *Grandma Was Right: 39½ Slogans to Raise Children By* (Northridge, Calif.: Studio 4 Productions, 1995).

7. A provocative and surprising book that pursues this and other parenting issues: Po Bronson and Ashley Merryman, *NurtureShock: New Thinking about Children* (New York: Twelve/Hachette Book Group, 2011).

8. Gillison, M. L., "Human Papilloma Virus–Associated Head and Neck Cancer Is a Distinct Epidemiologic, Clinical, and Molecular Entity," *Seminars in Oncology* 31, no. 6 (Dec. 2004): 744–54.

9. Ken Jablonski, *A Letter of Love: A Gift for Your Loved Ones* (Tamarac, Fla.: Llumina Press, 2010). You can reach Ken at kenj@hanjinlogistics.com or through http://aletteroflove.com.

10. Tobin Hart, Ph.D., *The Secret Spiritual World of Children: The Breakthrough Discovery That Profoundly Alters Our Conventional View of Children's Mystical Experiences* (Makawao, Hawaii: Inner Ocean Publishing, 2003). Tobin Hart and his wife, Mary, created ChildSpirit Institute, which sponsors training and consultation, conferences, research and publications, programs for children and families, and a resource network. The nonprofit institute is dedicated to understanding and nurturing the spirituality of children and adults. Contact: ChildSpirit Institute, 1774 N. Hwy 113, Carrollton, GA 30117; (770) 714-9286; www.childspirit.org.

11. Lawrence R. Edwards, Ph.D., is the one you want to contact at Cincinnati Children's Hospital Medical Center: www.cincinnatichildrens.org/bio/e/lawrence-edwards.

12. Center for Spirituality and Psychology, West Roxbury, Mass.: www.mspp.edu/academics/academic-centers/psychotherapy-and-spirituality.

13. The guidebook for this is Joanne DiMaggio, *Soul Writing: Conversing with*

Your Higher Self, available from Olde Souls Press, LLC, P.O. Box 6475, Charlottesville, VA 22906; (434) 242-7348; info@oldesoulspress.com; www.oldesoulspress.com.

14. Laura and Kirkland Ross developed ways of using Solfeggio frequencies through the magic of digital network alignment. They call their company Omnipure and offer a selection of alignments (CDs) to aid in the healing, spiritual, and enlightenment process. My husband and I have the one called *DNA Music* and use it when overstressed or during long-distance driving. Contact: Omnipure, 1780 W. 9000 S., Suite III, West Jordan, UT 84088; www.omnipuremusic.com.

CHAPTER 14. EDUCATION ROCKS

1. The study conducted by Stanford University's Center for Research on Educational Outcomes was published in early summer 2010 and discussed in Evan Thomas and Pat Wingert, "Understanding Charter Schools," *Newsweek,* June 21, 2010.

2. The full account of what happened is covered in Michele Rhee, "What I've Learned," *Newsweek*, December 13, 2010, pp. 38–41. On her own, she has launched a "Students First" campaign (www.studentsfirst.org).

3. For the full report: Frosty Wooldrige, "Where Is the Outrage?" *News with Views,* February 27, 2006, www.newswithviews.com/Wooldridge/frosty131. htm.

4. Colin Powell and Alma Powell, "One in Three Kids," *USA Weekend,* February 26–28, 2010, pp. 6–7.

5. Terrence P. Jeffrey, "Two-Thirds of Wisconsin Public-School 8th Graders Can't Read Proficiently—Despite Highest Per Pupil Spending in the Midwest," CNSNews.com, February 22, 2011.

6. Mark Bauerlein, *The Dumbest Generation: How the Digital Age Stupefies Young Americans and Jeopardizes Our Future* (New York: Jeremy P. Tarcher, 2008).

7. Linda Kreger Silverman, Ph.D., *Upside-Down Brilliance: The Visual-Spatial Learner* (Denver: Deleon Publishing, 2002). Dr. Silverman and her colleague Betty Maxwell can be reached through Institute for the Study of Advanced Development, 1452 Marion Street, Denver, CO 80218; (303) 837-8378.

8. Howard Gardner, *Frames of Mind* (New York: Basic Books, 1983).

9. Soleira Green, "Quantum Intelligence, Beyond IQ, EQ and SQ: The Evolution of Intelligence," www.soleiragreen.com.

10. Marcia Jarmel and Ken Schneider, *Speaking in Tongues* (San Francisco: Patchwork Films, 2009). www.speakingintonguesfilm.info. Also refer to V. P. Collier and W. P. Thomas, *Educating English Learners for a Transformed World* (Albuquerque: Fuente Press, 2009). Other websites for more information: www.thomasandcollier.com and www.dlenm.org. Rosetta Stone Language Learning Systems, through live practice sessions with native speakers, features "more immersion as never before." Contact: (800) 306-1314; www.RosettaStone.com/ogs100.

11. John Hunter's World Peace Game for elementary schools is gaining a lot of attention worldwide. A documentary about this, *World Peace and Other 4th Grade Achievements,* is available from Rosalia Films, Inc., 1209 Hazel Street, Charlottesville, VA 22902; www.rosaliafilms.com.

12. Marietta McCarty, *Little Big Minds: Sharing Philosophy with Kids* (New York: Tarcher, 2006). For older kids, contact the University of Philosophical Research, 3910 Los Feliz Blvd., Los Angeles, CA 90027; (800) 545-4062; www.uprs.edu. Much of the courses and discussions they offer can be obtained online. McCarty is also the author of *How Philosophy Can Save Your Life: 10 Ideas That Matter Most* (New York: Tarcher/Penguin, 2009).

13. Some organizations working toward this end are: Center for Investigating Healthy Minds, Waisman Center, University of Wisconsin—Madison, (608) 263-2743, bthorne@wisc.edu, www.investigatinghealthyminds.org; HeartMath, which offers Heart Smarts, a new curriculum for helping students bridge academic and emotional learning, P. O. Box 1463, Boulder Creek, CA 95006, (831) 338-8500, info@heartmath.org, www.heartmath.org.

14. Contact Linda Redford directly to explore ways of using the Adawee Teachings in your school, or learning facility. These teachings are part of the Honor Series of Entertainment and Educational Tools. Contact: Linda Redford, Honor Kids International, 3231 Ocean Park Blvd., Suite 122, Santa Monica, CA 90405; honorkids7@aol.com; (310) 392-1200. Her motto is "A culture of peace requires a language of peace."

15. Joseph Campbell with Bill Moyers. *The Power of Myth* (New York: Anchor, 1991). Also available as a six-tape audio and video conducted by Bill Moyers.

I attended classes on this subject with Campbell back in Idaho in the 1970s. I count myself lucky for that initial training in mythology.

16. For more opportunities to learn how myths can be used in very real ways in our present culture and to improve our lives, explore the writings and teachings of Jean Houston. She also works directly with agencies within the United Nations to explore the "social artistry" possible when we are aware of our own creative genius. Her website: www.jeanhouston.com. I also recommend the Wisdom University for exploring ancient traditions and wisdom cultures and how that knowledge can be used in today's world to shape a better future for all of us. Access www.wisdomuniversity.org.

17. Malidoma Patrice Somé, *Ritual: Power, Healing and Community* (New York: Penguin Books, 1997).

18. To learn more about the insightful programs developed by David Oldfield and others, contact Midway Center for Creative Imagination, 2112 F Street N.W., #404, Washington D.C. 20037; (202) 296-2299, www.midwaycenter.com.

19. Try http://usa.autodesk.com to locate the CAD program Minecraft. It's free. SketchUp8 download (also free) is http://sketchup.google.com/download/gsu.html. Training tutorials can be located from that same address. The book is best: Aidan Chopra, *Google SketchUp 8 For Dummies* (Hoboken, N. J.: Wiley, John & Sons, 2010).

20. The report on changes in Perth, Australia, elementary schools was given by futurist and life coach Annimac on July 10, 2006. A telephone interview with her was conducted over a conference line by Alan Wilson of the Energy Alliance in the United Kingdom. I was privileged to be part of the audience who heard and interacted with her. The Energy Alliance highlights the value of family coaching, should parents have difficulties with their children. Soleira Green is part of this alliance. To reach Alan Wilson directly, contact alan@developyourchild.co.uk. To reach the Energy Alliance, contact www.developyourchild.co.uk.

21. Rachael Kessler, *The Soul of Education: Helping Students Find Connection, Compassion, and Character at School* (Alexandria, Va.: Association for Supervision and Curriculum Development, 2000). To reach ASCD directly, contact them at 1703 N. Beauregard Street, Alexandria, VA 22311-1714; (800) 933-2723.

22. The best place to access reasonable and healthy material about psychic/intuitive realities is the Association for Research and Enlightenment (A.R.E.). Although their materials are based on the psychic readings of the late Edgar

Cayce, the organization encompasses the entire field of the "extraordinary"—for both adults and children. Contact: Edgar Cayce's A.R.E., 215 67th Street, Virginia Beach, VA 23451-2061; (800) 333-4499; www.EdgarCayce.org; are@edgarcayce.org.

Another worldwide source of excellent material and personal instruction about mind training is the Monroe Institute. Contact: Monroe Institute, 62 Roberts Mtn. Road, Faber, VA 22938; (800) 541-2488; www.monroeinstitute .org; info@monroeinstitute.org.

An outstanding DVD on the subject is *Something Unknown Is Doing We Don't Know What*. Produced by Dutch filmmaker Renee Scheltema, it features on-site interviews with leaders in the field of parapsychology, along with actual test results as they occur. Handled as a spiritual journey into the science behind healing, it includes sessions of telepathy, precognition, tele-kinesis, and clairvoyance. Refer to www.somethingunknown.com.

Academy for Coaching Parents International (ACPI) is a parenting/coaching program specializing in the support of intuitives and fostering intui-tive gifts. They offer training for educators, teachers, counselors, and parents. Contact: Dr. Caron B. Goode, ACPI, 524 Cranbrook Drive, Fort Worth, TX 76131; (817) 847-8758; http://academyforcoachingparents.com; caron goode@mac.com.

An indispensable reference on the topic: Chris Carter, *Science and Psy-chic Phenomena: The Fall of the House of Skeptics* (Rochester, Vt.: Inner Tra-ditions, 2012).

Excellent how-to books by gifted professionals: Marcia Emery and Leland Kaiser, *PowerHunch: Living an Intuitive Life* (Hillsboro, Ore.: Atria Books/ Beyond Words, 2001). Penney Peirce, *The Intuitive Way: The Definitive Guide to Increasing Your Awareness* (Hillsboro, Ore.: Atria Books/ Beyond Words, 2009).

A research organization offering professional degrees: Institute of Transpersonal Psychology, 1069 East Meadow Circle, Palo Alto, CA 94303; (650) 493-4430, extension 216; itpinfo@itp.edu; www.itp.edu.

For kids, by kids: *Tiffany Howe and the Star Child Network,* a radio show and interactive blog for intuitive and spiritual children and young adults (www.heavenblessedlifecenter.com).

23. Bainbridge Graduate Institute, www.BGI.edu. Also, Presidio World College, www .presidioworldcollege.org. And, Brandeis University, www.brandeis.edu/global.

24. This actually happened in Charlottesville, Virginia, when Susan Oliver accepted her degree in business administration from Piedmont Virginia Community College—*after* receiving her diploma from William Monroe High School in Greene County. The full story was published in Brian McNeill, "Teen to Graduate both High School, Piedmont," *The Daily Progress Newspaper,* May 14, 2010.

25. Bill Strickland can be reached at Manchester Bidwell Corporation, 1815 Metropolitan Street, Pittsburgh, PA 15233; (412) 323-4005; wstricklandjr@mcg-btc.org; www.manchesterbidwell.org. *Make the Impossible Possible: One Man's Crusade to Inspire Others to Dream Bigger and Achieve the Extraordinary* is by Bill Strickland with Vince Rause (New York: Broadway Books, 2007).

26. Sustainability Workshop, Navy Yard Quarters A, 1413 Langley Avenue, Philadelphia, PA 19112, www.workshopschool.org. To reach Simon Hauger, email him at simon.hauger@workshopschool.org.

CHAPTER 15: FOOD/HEALTH AND THE ENVIRONMENT

1. For more information about the sugar ban in Lithonia, Georgia, access: www.educationworld.com and search for *sugar ban in schools.*

2. Aspartame (NutraSweet) Toxicity Info Center: www.holisticmed.com/aspartame.

3. On the issue of vitamin D in blacks, see www.NaturalNews.com/022039.html and Linda Villarosa, "Why Black People Need More Vitamin D," *The Root,* June 5, 2009, www.theroot.com (search for *vitamin D*).

4. Rob Dunn, *The Wild Life of Our Bodies: Predators, Parasites, and Partners That Shape Who We Are Today* (New York: Harper, 2011).

5. You might want to read Kaayla Daniel, Ph.D., CCN, "Plants Bite Back," The Weston A. Price Foundation, March 29, 2010, www.westonaprice.org/food-features/plants-bite-back.html.

6. Anton Kolesnikov, Vladimir G. Kutcherov, and Alexander F. Goncharov, "Methane-derived Hydrocarbons Produced under Upper-Mantle Conditions," *Nature Geoscience* (July 26, 2009): 566–70. Also available at www.nature.com; search for *Anton Kolesnikov.*

7. Ivette Soler, *The Edible Front Yard: The Mow-Less, Grow-More Plan for a Beautiful, Bountiful Garden* (Portland, Ore.: Timber Press, 2011).

8. Michael and Audrey Levatino, *Joy of Hobby Farming: Grow Food, Raise Ani-

mals, and Enjoy a Sustainable Life (New York: Skyhorse Publishing, 2011).

9. Lisa Taylor, *Your Farm in the City: An Urban Dweller's Guide to Growing Food and Raising Animals* (New York: Black Dog & Leventhal, 2011).

10. Norman Wirzba, ed., *The Essential Agrarian Reader: The Future of Culture, Community, and the Land* (Berkeley, Calif.: Counterpoint, 2004).

11. Sandy Moore and Deanna Moore, *The Green Intention: Living in Sustainable Joy* (Camarillo, Calif.: DeVorss & Co., 2011).

12. Carol Deppe, *The Resilient Gardener: Food Production and Self-Reliance in Uncertain Times* (White River Junction, Vt.: Chelsea Green, 2010).

13. Heather Rogers, *Green Gone Wrong: How Our Economy Is Undermining the Environmental Revolution* (New York: Scribner, 2010).

14. Carl von Essen, M.D., *Ecomysticism: The Profound Experience of Nature as a Spiritual Guide* (Rochester, Vt.: Bear & Co., 2010).

15. *Unacceptable energy* refers to free-energy sources such as zero-point vacuum energy, dirac sea, time derivative field, microelectrodynamic fluctuations, telluric current, Earth's core energy, and the G-strain energy of space-time. A leader in the field is Tom Bearden. Access to his work at www.cheniere.org/misc/oulist.htm and www.intalek.com/Papers/Handout3.pdf.

   A helpful book looking at the research being done in the field of alternative energy sources: Jeane Manning and Joel Garbon, *Breakthrough Power: How Quantum-Leap New Energy Inventions Can Transform Our World* (Salmon Arm, Canada: Amber Bridge Books, 2009).

   In October 2011, a major breakthrough with cold fusion was announced. The article, "Italian Cold Fusion Machine Passes Another Test" by Natalie Wolchover, was carried over MSNBC Television News. See www.msnbc.msn.com; search for *Italian cold fusion machine*, and look for Wolchover's name. This machine, with a small amount of input energy, was able to produce an outpouring of energy 10 times more than what was input. Check out the website of Hydro Fusion and the Leonardo Corporation: www.ecat.com.

16. This quote was taken from Shane Ellison, "Chemist Shows How Your Health Is Being Sabotaged," News with Views, March 5, 2011, www.newswithviews.com.

17. For more information about Dr. Stanislaw Burzynski, the effectiveness of his discovery, and the lawsuit that ensued against the Food and Drug Administration, go to www.mercola.com and search for *Burzynski the movie*.

18. For the full story of truck driver Brian Bennett and his discovery of a cream that successfully combats MRSA skin infections, access: http://news.bbc .co.uk/2/hi/health/3672983.stm.

19. Louisa L. Williams, M.S., D.C., N.D., *Radical Medicine: Cutting-Edge Natural Therapies That Treat the Root Causes of Disease* (Rochester, Vt.: Healing Arts Press, 2011). James F. Balch, M.D., and Mark Stengler, N.D., *Prescription for Natural Cures: A Self-Care Guide for Treating Health Problems with Natural Remedies Including Diet and Nutrition, Nutritional Supplements, Bodywork, and More* (Hoboken, N.J.; Wiley, 2011). Dr. Rajan SanKaran, *Homeopathy for Today's World: Discovering Your Animal, Mineral, or Plant Nature* (Rochester, Vt.: Healing Arts Press, 2011).

20. Robert O. Becker, M.D., and Gary Selden, *The Body Electric: Electromagnetism and the Foundation of Life* (New York: William Morrow and Co., Inc., 1985). This was a breakthrough book on the topic and has yet to be topped.

21. Caroline Myss, Ph.D., *Why People Don't Heal and How They Can* (New York: Three Rivers Press, 1998). C. Norman Shealy, M.D., Ph.D., *Energy Medicine: Practical Applications and Scientific Proof* (Virginia Beach, Va.: 4th Dimension Press, 2011). Donna Eden and David Feinstein, *Energy Medicine: Balancing Your Body's Energies for Optimal Heath, Joy, and Vitality (Updated and Expanded)* (New York: Tarcher, 2008). David Feinstein, Donna Eden, and Gary Craig, *The Promise of Energy Psychology: Revolutionary Tools for Dramatic Personal Change* (New York: Tarcher/Penguin, 2005). Dawson Church, Ph.D., *The Genies in Your Genes: Epigenetic Medicine and the New Biology of Intention* (Fulton, Calif.: Energy Psychology Press, 2007).

22. The boost music can make during surgery is remarkable, for the medical staff as well as the patient. Go to www.massgeneral.org and search for *Music in Medicine Research Group*. Also see M. M. Chiang, "Music for Healing: From Magic to Medicine," *Lancet* 376, no. 9757 (December 2010): 1980–81 and check out the Society for the Arts in Healthcare, www.thesah.org.

23. Refer to Dr. Damien G. Finniss, et. al., "Biological, Clinical, and Ethical Advances of Placebo Effects," *Lancet* 375 (9715) (February 20, 2010): 686–95.

Studies done about Seung-hui Cho, the student of Virginia Tech who massacred students and teachers alike in 2007, show that he was living on a cocktail of brainwashing drugs and violent video games. These put him over the top and contributed to the carnage. This same pattern has shown up in other school shootings and mass killings. Drugs like Prozac are now highly suspect in leading patients over the edge. Antidepressants as a whole are questionable as a long-term treatment option.

24. Refer to Jeneen Interlandi, "The New Oil," *Newsweek,* October 18, 2010, pp. 40–46.

25. "Monsanto Patents Asserted against American Farmers Rejected by Patent Office: PUBPAT Initiated Review Leads PTO to Find All Claims of All Four Patents Invalid," Public Patent Foundation, June 24, 2007, www .pubpat.org/monsanto-seed-patents.htm.

26. Jeffrey M. Smith, "Stop the Genetically Modified Madness," *ECHO* (July 2009).

27. Ronnie Cummins, Ben Lilliston, and Frances Moore Lappé, *Genetically Engineered Food: A Self-Defense Guide for Consumers* (Cambridge, Mass.: DaCapo Press, 2004).

28. Obtained from the website the Schwartz Report, August 25, 2011.

29. Recommended books: Andrew Kimbrell, *Your Right to Know: Genetic Engineering and the Secret Changes in Your Food* (San Rafael, Calif: Earth Aware Editions, 2007). Jeffrey M. Smith, *Genetic Roulette: The Documented Health Risks of Genetically Engineered Foods* (White River Junction, Vt.: Chelsea Green, 2007). Ronnie Cummins, Ben Lilliston, and Frances Moore Lappé, *Genetically Engineered Food: A Self-Defense Guide for Consumers* (Cambridge, Mass.: DaCapo Press, 2004).

CHAPTER 16. COMMUNITY

1. David Brooks, *The Social Animal: The Hidden Sources of Love, Character, and Achievement* (New York: Random House, 2011).

2. Paul Hawken, *Blessed Unrest: How the Largest Social Movement in History Is Restoring Grace, Justice, and Beauty to the World* (New York: Penguin, 2008).

3. Jay Walljasper, *All That We Share: A Field Guide to the Commons* (New York: The New Press, 2010). While you're at it, check out Ross Chapin, *Pocket Neighborhoods: Creating Small-Scale Community in a Large-Scale World* (Newtown, Conn.: Taunton Press, 2011).

4. Carolyn North, *Serious Fun: Ingenious Improvisations on Money, Food, Waste, Water, and Home* (Findhorn, Scotland: Findhorn Press, 2011).

5. To research Baubiologie, see http://hbelc.org. Also consult International

Institute for Bau-Biologie, 1401 A Cleveland Street, Clearwater, FL 33755; (727) 461-4371; http://buildingbiology.net/.

New Society Publishers carries a full line of books on every aspect of green remodeling and solar living, especially the *Real Goods Living Sourcebook* by John Schaeffer. Call (800) 567-6772 or explore their website at www.newsociety.com.

Don't forget *Natural Home Magazine* from Interweave Press, 201 E. Fourth Street, Loveland, CO 80537-5655; (970) 669-7692; www.naturalhomemagazine.com.

Be careful of artificial lighting—too big, too many could be a major risk factor for cancer. Even the new compact fluorescent bulbs have mercury in them. An excellent dowser for checking Earth energies, human-related energies, and electrical fields is Joey Korn. Contact him at 483 Sugar Creek Drive, Govetown, GA 30813; (877) 369-7464, joey@dowsers.com; www.dowsers.com. For more information about property and electrical dowsing, contact the American Society of Dowsers, P.O. Box 24, Danville, VT 05828; (802) 684-3417; www.dowsers.org.

6. John Michell, *The Dimensions of Paradise: Sacred Geometry, Ancient Science, and the Heavenly Order on Earth* (Rochester, Vt.: Inner Traditions, 2008), John Michell and Allan Brown, *How the World Is Made: The Story of Creation According to Sacred Geometry* (Rochester, Vt.: Inner Traditions, 2012). Scott Olsen, *The Golden Section: Nature's Greatest Secret* (New York: Walker Publishing Company, Inc., 2006). Scott Olsen, *Divine Proportion: The Mathematical Perfection of the Universe* (Somerset, U.K.: Alexian Limited, 2012). Stephen Skinner, *Sacred Geometry: Deciphering the Code* (New York: Sterling, 2006). Richard Heath, *Matrix of Creation: Sacred Geometry in the Realm of the Planets* (Rochester, Vt.: Inner Traditions, 2004). Richard Heath, *Sacred Number and the Origins of Civilization: The Unfolding of History through the Mystery of Number* (Rochester, Vt.: Inner Traditions, 2007).

7. Dr. David Lipert, *Muslim, Christian and Jew: Finding a Path to Peace Our Faiths Can Share* (Toronto: Faith of Life Publishing, 2010).

8. Rocco Errico, Th.D., Ph.D., "Did Jesus Die for Your Sins?" *Science of Mind Magazine* (August 1999): 104–5.

9. Jon Meacham, "The End of Christian America," *Newsweek,* April 13, 2009, p. 34.

10. Rev. Nancy Zala, *The Joy of Affirmative Prayer: A Guide for Parents* (Los Angeles: Filumthropix Inc., 2010).

11. Starhawk, *The Empowerment Manual: A Guide for Collaborative Groups* (Gabriola Island, B.C., Canada: New Society Publishers, 2011). Check out her website at www.starhawk.org. She is an activist with a long history of working with group dynamics, collective decision making, and dealing with difficult people.

12. Lauren Abramson, "The Real Fixers," *Newsweek*, September 19, 2011.

13. Deepak Chopra, Debbie Ford, and Marianne Williamson, *The Shadow Effect: Illuminating the Hidden Power of Your True Self* (New York: Harper One, 2011).

CHAPTER 17. THE NEW BUSINESS OF BUSINESS POLITICS

1. Mitch Horowitz, *Occult America: The Secret History of How Mysticism Shaped Our Nation* (New York: Bantam Books, 2010). And Robert R. Hieronimus, Ph.D., *Founding Fathers, Secret Societies* (Rochester, Vt.: Destiny Books, 2006).

2. There are many sources where one can investigate these radical movements. Chief among them is the Schwartz Report (www.schwartzreport .net). In an article dated August 25, 2011, the New Apostolic Reformation Movement is said to be one of the financial backers of the Tea Party. *Fresh Air,* a radio program aired on National Public Radio channels, covered what is beginning to look like "spiritual warfare from the religious right." Go to www.npr.org, and search for *spiritual warfare from the religious right.*

3. John Whitehead, "Is the Constitution on Life Support," *The Daily Progress*, September 25, 2011, pp. B1, B5. To reach John directly, e-mail johnw@ rutherford.org.

4. George Packer, "The Broken Contract," *New Yorker* (November/December 2011).

5. Allen D. Kanner, "Municipalities Take on Corporations," *ECHO Newspaper,* February 2011. To reach the Community Environmental Legal Defense Fund directly, visit www.celdf.org.

6. Michael J. Sandel, *What Money Can't Buy: The Moral Limits of Markets* (New York: Farrar, Strauss and Giroux, 2012).

7. This nugget of information came from Timothy Karr of FreePress.net. You may reach him via e-mail at info@freepress.net. This news item was also carried by all major news outlets on February 3, 2011.

8. What China is doing in Africa and South America has been the subject of much discussion on NPR, on television, and within the individual countries involved. Villainous dictators in Africa, for instance, are all too happy to have China on board. They pocket huge sums and benefit from the various projects, yet locals remain as poor as ever, sometimes on the verge of starvation (because the fruits of their labors are shipped back to China, or line the pockets of Chinese workers who live there).

9. Jeremy Rifkin, *The Third Industrial Revolution: How Lateral Power Is Transforming Energy, the Economy, and the World* (Hants, U.K.: Palgrave Macmillan, 2011).

10. Peter M. Senge, C. Otto Scharmer, Joseph Jaworski, and Betty Sue Flowers, *Presence: Human Purpose and the Field of the Future* (New York: Crown Business, 2008).

11. Refer to Bruce Lipton and Steve Bhaerman, *Spontaneous Evolution: Our Positive Future (and a Way to Get There from Here)* (Carlsbad, Calif.: Hay House, 2010).

12. Experiment with this wonderful book: Arupa Tesolin, *Ting: A Surprising Way to Listen to Intuition & Do Business Better* (New Delhi, India: Wisdom Tree Publishers, 2007).

13. Check out Rachel Botsman, *What's Mine Is Yours: The Rise of Collaborative Consumption* (New York: HarperBusiness, 2010).

14. Refer to Peter M. Senge, *The Fifth Discipline: The Art & Practice of the Learning Organization* (New York: Doubleday Business, 1994).

15. Vivian Scott, *Conflict Resolution at Work for Dummies* (New York: John Wiley & Sons, 2009).

16. Deepak Chopra, *The Soul of Leadership: Unlocking Your Potential for Greatness* (New York: Harmony, 2010).

17. Share your story about giving with fellow Thrillionaires at www.thrillionaires.org.

18. For information about *The Intelligent Optimist* magazine (formerly *Ode*), go to www.optimist.org/e/member/documents3.cfm

19. Clustered thinking is discussed in Howard Gardner, *Frames of Mind: The Theory of Multiple Intelligences* (New York: Basic Books, 2011).

20. You can reach Doug Krug through his company, e.l.solutions, 20436 E. Euclid Drive, Centennial, CO 80016; (303) 807-1903; dkrug@elsolutions.com. His book, *The Missing Piece in Leadership: How to Create the Future*

You Want (Centennial, Colo.: Mile High Press, 2011) is geared for organizations and businesses.

Also check out Julio Olalla and his Newfield Network. Considered by many to be the originator of the life-coaching movement, he has a long history of helping thousands of people to challenge traditional thinking. And he has a miraculous story of generosity and gratitude that has changed people's lives. Contact him through www.newfieldnetwork.com.

21. This book shows you how: Lisa Gansky, *The Mesh: Why the Future of Business Is Sharing* (New York: Portfolio Hardcover, 2010).

22. Specifics in Paul Hawken, Amory Lovins, L. Hunter Lovins, *Natural Capitalism: Creating the Next Industrial Revolution* (Oxford, England: Earthscan, 2008).

23. Louis Bohtlingk, *Dare to Care* (New York: Cosimo, 2012) is a revolutionary system of generating and handling money and finance. Bohtlingk's website is www.CareFirstWorld.com and his blog is www.CareFirstWorld.com/blog. To reach him, e-mail daretocare@carefirstworld.com.

24. Refer to Julia Baird, "Oil's Shame in Africa," *Newsweek*, July 26, 2010, p. 27.

25. Sylvia Clute, *Beyond Vengeance, Beyond Duality: A Call for Compassionate Revolution* (Charlottesville, Va.: Hampton Roads, 2010).

CHAPTER 18: THE FIFTH WORLD

1. See an example of one such boy in Ishmael Beah, *A Long Way Gone* (New York: Farrar, Straus and Giroux, 2008).

2. MedlinePlus, "Annual Report on U.S. Kids' Health a Mixed Bag," July 13, 2012, www.nlm.nih.gov/medlineplus/news/fullstory_127218.html.

3. William Strauss and Neil Howe, *Generations: The History of America's Future, 1584 to 2069* (New York: William Morrow & Co., 1991).

4. Stephanie Pappas, "Ancient Text Confirms Mayan Calendar End Date," June 28, 2012, www.livescience.com/21255-ancient-text-confirms-mayan-calendar-end.html.

5. Stephanie Pappas, "Nevermind the Apocalypse: Earliest Mayan Calendar Found," May 10, 2012, www.livescience.com/20218-apocalypse-oldest-mayan-calendar.html

6. This description of ether/aether that I was witness to during my third near-death experience can be found in my book *Future Memory* (Charlottesville, Va.: Hampton Roads, 1999), 156–59.

7. Reach Dr. Beichler at P.O. Box 624, Belpre, OH 45714; jebco1st@aol. com. I took this quote from a talk he gave at a conference of the Academy of Spirituality and Paranormal Studies (P.O. Box 614, Bloomfield, CT 06002-0614).

8. This spread of intelligence types was originated by Soleira Green, based on what has been verified and her own intuitive guidance. She can be reached via e-mail: soleira@SOULutions.co.uk.

9. Refer again to Peter M. Senge, *The Fifth Discipline: The Art & Practice of the Learning Organization* (New York: Doubleday Business, 1994). And Daniel H. Pink, *A Whole New Mind: Why Right-Brainers Will Rule the Future* (New York: Riverhead Trade, 2006).

   Also consider the work of Corinne McLaughlin and Gordon Davidson of The Center for Visionary Leadership, 6423 Hermsley Road, Charlotte, NC 28278. The center has a West Coast office at 369 3rd Street #563, San Rafael, CA 94901; (415) 472-2540; www.visionarylead.org; cvldc@ visionarylead.org.

10. Don Miguel Ruiz, *The Four Agreements* (San Rafael, Calif.: Amber-Allen, 2001) and Don Miguel Ruiz and Don Jose Ruiz with Janet Mills, *The Fifth Agreement* (San Rafael, Calif.: Amber-Allen, 2011).

CHAPTER 19. TIMELINES AND VARIATIONS

1. Itzhak Bentov, *Stalking the Wild Pendulum: On the Mechanics of Consciousness* (Rochester, Vt.: Destiny Books, 1958). Bentov's chart of objective/subjective/beyond I first used in my book *Future Memory* (pages 97–98), with the kind permission of his widow, Mirtala. It is of interest that while he was upstairs soaking in a tub, exploring the mechanics of consciousness, Mirtala was in the basement creating twenty-two sculptures—in essence displaying what he was discovering about the human journey and visions of heaven and Earth. Their work was simultaneous, without either one directing or influencing the other. Her website: http://home.earthlink.net/~mirtala/index.html. She has self-published two books through XLibris (www2 .xlibris.com), *Thoughtforms* and *Cosmic Visions;* both feature striking photos of her sculpture and also her poetry. She has created a line of jewelry and videos based on her sculptures. Contact her directly: mirtala@earthlink.net.

2. My book *Future Memory* (Charlottesville, Va.: Hampton Roads, 1999) goes

in depth about this phenomenon and what it implies, as well as creation itself and the part consciousness plays in creation.

3. This was revealed by David Childress (an authority on alternative histories and historical revisionism) at the A.R.E.'s Ancient Mysteries Conference, Virginia Beach, Va., October 7, 2007.

4. Barbara Hand Clow, *Catastrophobia: The Truth Behind Earth Changes* (Rochester, Vt.: Bear & Co., 2001).

5. Simon Winchester, *Krakatoa: The Day the World Exploded: August 27, 1883* (New York: Harper Perennial, 2005). There is also an audio book available through Harper Audio.

6. Refer to the following: Brad Steiger, *Worlds before Our Own* (San Antonio: Anomalist Books, 2007). Michael A. Cremo and Richard L. Thomspon, *Forbidden Archaeology: The Hidden History of the Human Race* (Los Angeles, Calif.: Bhaktivedanta Book Publishing, 1998). Christopher Dunn, *Lost Technologies of Ancient Egypt: Advanced Engineering in the Temples of the Pharaohs* (Rochester, Vt.: Bear & Co, 2010).

7. Maurice Chatelain, trans. by O. Berlings. *Our Ancestors Came from Outer Space* (West Sussex, U.K.: Little Hampton Book Services, Ltd., 1980). The quote appeared on page 411 of *The Source Field Investigations*—see the following note.

8. David Wilcock, *The Source Field Investigations: The Hidden Science and Lost Civilizations Behind the 2012 Prophecies* (New York: Dutton, 2011), 410–17.

CHAPTER 20. THE GREAT SHIFTING

1. Liz Goodwin, "Earth's Magnetic Pole Shifts, Screws Up Runway at Florida Airport," The Lookout News Blog, January 7, 2011.

2. My thanks to Dennis McCafferty, "The Good Side of Disasters," *USA Weekend,* February 20–22, 2009. I adapted his main points for this rendering.

3. Michael A. Cremo, *Human Devolution: A Vedic Alternative to Darwin's Theory* (Mayapur, India: Torchlight Publishing, 2003).

4. Claudia Kalb, "In Our Blood," *Newsweek*, February 6, 2006, pp. 47–55.

5. Refer to *Venture Inward Magazine*, published by the Association for Research and Enlightenment (A.R.E.), and John Van Auken's article "Ancient DNA & Cayce's Atlantis," (November/December 2009): 26.

6. BBC News, "'Hobbit' Joins Human Family Tree," October 27, 2004, http://news.bbc.co.uk/2/hi/science/nature/3948165.stm.

7. Refer to Sharon Begley, "Beyond Stones & Bones," *Newsweek,* March 19, 2007, pp. 53–58.

8. There are many books and articles about this. You might try Patrick Chouinard, *Forgotten Worlds: From Atlantis to the X-Woman of Siberia and the Hobbits of Flores* (Rochester, Vt.: Bear & Co., 2012). Also refer to Mark Amaru Pinkham, "Giants in the Earth: Are the Bible and Other Ancient Sources to be Believed?" *Atlantis Magazine*, no. 69 (May 2008): 38, 66–68. And Michael A. Cremo and Richard L. Thompson, *Forbidden Archaelogy: The Hidden History of the Human Race* (Los Angeles: Bhaktivedanta Book Publishing, 1998).

9. Robert Bauval and Thomas Brophy, Ph.D. *Black Genesis: The Prehistoric Origins of Ancient Egypt* (Rochester, Vt.: Bear & Co., 2011).

10. There are many sources for this, like the introductory article by Will Hart, "DNA Evidence for Atlantis: Beyond the Bering Strait—DNA Evidence Rocks the Boat" Genesis Race, May 21, 2006, www.genesisrace.com.

11. Charles C. Mann, *1493: Uncovering the New World Columbus Created* (New York: Alfred A. Knopf, 2011).

CHAPTER 21. A GRAND PLAN

1. Bruce H. Lipton, Ph.D. "The Rise of the Phoenix: An Evolving Global Humanity," *Mystic Pop Magazine* (Fall 2007). This article explains epigenetics. The magazine quit publication the following year, and was sold to another company. Bruce H. Lipton, Ph.D., is also author of *The Biology of Belief: Unleashing the Power of Consciousness, Matter & Miracles,* 13th ed. (Carlsbad, Calif.; Hay House, 2011).

2. Zecharia Sitchin, *The 12th Planet* (Rochester, Vt.; Bear & Co., 2011).

3. Paul Von Ward, *We've Never Been Alone: A History of Extraterrestrial Intervention* (Charlottesville, Va.: Hampton Roads, 2011). This book is a new, enhanced version of his former tome *God's, Genes & Consciousness*. Von Ward's websites are: www.vonward.com and www.reincarnationexperiment.org.

4. P. M. H. Atwater, L.H.D., *The New Children and Near-Death Experiences* (Rochester, Vt.: Bear & Co., 2003), 152–76.

5. Brad Steiger, *Worlds Before Our Own* (San Antonio: Anomalist Books, 2007).

6. Andrew Collins, *The Cygnes Mystery: Unlocking the Ancient Secret of Life's Origins in the Cosmos* (London: Watkins, 2010).

7. Joseph Robert Jochmans, "The Earth's Crystal Grid: Re-Discovering Gaia as a Living Evolving Energy Structure," *Atlantis Rising* 7 (1996). See also Jochmans, "Is Our Planet a Crystal?" *Atlantis Rising* 78 (November/December 2009): 39, 66–67.

8. Pierre Lecomte du Noüy, Ph.D., *Human Destiny* (New York: Longmans, Green and Co. 1947).

9. A wonderful book to help you find the "zone" of sacred silence is John Francis, Ph.D., *The Ragged Edge of Silence—Finding Peace in a Noisy World* (Washington, D.C.: National Geographic Society, 2011).

10. For an in-depth discussion of the biological imperative within transformational or threshold states—as if that was the *true* purpose of spiritual experiences—refer to chapter 22, pages 201–8 of my book *Near-Death Experiences: The Rest of The Story* (Charlottesville, Va.: Hampton Roads, 2011).

11. Rabbi Wayne Dosick, Ph.D., *The Real Name of God: Embracing the Full Essence of the Divine* (Rochester, Vt.; Inner Traditions, 2012).

12. For a more in-depth discussion of the Christhood model Jesus gave us, refer to chapter 24, pages 219–29 in my book *Near-Death Experiences: The Rest of The Story* (Charlottesville, Va.: Hampton Roads, 2011).

13. Check out Andrew Orlowski, "CERN 'Gags' Physicists in Cosmic Ray Climate Experiment. What Do These Results Mean? Not Allowed to Tell You," *Science* (July 18, 2011). Access it at www.theregister.co.uk/2011/07/18/cern_cosmic_ray_gag.

14. Todd C. Frankel, "The Butterfly People of Joplin," *St. Louis Post-Dispatch,* December 19, 2011.

Index

BOOKS OF RELATED INTEREST

Beyond the Indigo Children
The New Children and the Coming of the Fifth World
by P. M. H. Atwater, L.H.D.

The New Children and Near-Death Experiences
by P. M. H. Atwater, L.H.D.
Foreword by Joseph Chilton Pearce

The Immortal Mind
Science and the Continuity of Consciousness beyond the Brain
by Ervin Laszlo
with Anthony Peake

The Self-Actualizing Cosmos
The Akasha Revolution in Science and Human Consciousness
by Ervin Laszlo

Science and the Afterlife Experience
Evidence for the Immortality of Consciousness
by Chris Carter

Science and the Near-Death Experience
How Consciousness Survives Death
by Chris Carter

7 Reasons to Believe in the Afterlife
A Doctor Reviews the Case for Consciousness after Death
by Jean Jacques Charbonier, M.D.

ADHD and the Edison Gene
A Drug-Free Approach to Managing the Unique Qualities of Your Child
by Thom Hartmann

Inner Traditions • Bear & Company
P.O. Box 388
Rochester, VT 05767
1-800-246-8648
www.InnerTraditions.com

Or contact your local bookseller